Silencing the Witnesses

Also by Graeme Carlé and published by Emmaus Road Publishing

Eating Sacred Cows
A Closer Look at Tithing

Because of the Angels
Unveiling 1 Corinthians 11:2-16

The Red Heifer's Ashes
Mysteries of Ancient Israel

Born of the Spirit
A study guide for new believers

The Revelation series:
1. Dancing in the Dragon's Jaws
The Mystery of Israel's Survival

2. Slouching Towards Bethlehem
The Rise of the Antichrists

3. Gotta Serve Somebody
The Mystery of The Marks & 666

Silencing the Witnesses

Jerusalem & the Ascent of Secularism

Graeme Carlé

All proceeds from the sale of this book are used for the further publication of this and other similar work by Emmaus Road Publishing.

© 2017 Graeme Carlé
All rights reserved including the right of reproduction in whole or in part in any form. The moral rights of the author have been asserted.

First published 2017, revised 2020
Cover design by Olivia Carlé
Western Wall photo by Joe Sofair, IDF photo by Source Tactical Gear
Author photo by Samantha Ives
Book design and production by Peter Aranyi

ISBN 978-0-9941058-2-0

2020-23

Unless otherwise stated, all Scripture quoted is from the NEW AMERICAN STANDARD BIBLE®, Copyright ©1995 The Lockman Foundation. Used with permission.

Emmaus Road Publishing
PO Box 38 823 Howick, Auckland 2014 New Zealand
emmausroad.org.nz

Contents

Foreword	1
Introduction	8
1. 'A Measuring Rod' *To Comprehend*	13
2. "My Two Witnesses" *Literal or Metaphorical?*	26
3. Olive Trees and Lampstands *Endless Light*	47
4. Dead Men Speaking *Personified Texts*	65
5. Irresistible Testimony *Israel's Fate*	88
6. The Law and Christians *What's For Us?*	105
7. Obsolete and Disappearing? *Means of Atonement*	128
8. The Law's Curse *And Its Cause*	147
9. 20th Century Jewish Leaders *Suspending the Law*	166
10. In Sackcloth in Jerusalem *"O Jerusalem…"*	181
11. Conclusions *So Far…*	191
12. David's Legacy *More Than A Song*	198
13. Dead in the Street *Temporarily Silenced*	217
14. Gentiles Rejoicing *Secularism Triumphs*	238
15. Israel's Restoration *"Dem Dry Bones…"*	265
16. The Late Rain *Israel's Revival*	280
Conclusions	303
Epilogue	309

Appendix A – God's Covenants 312
Appendix B - Grown from 'Missionary Roots' 339

Bibliography.. 344
Index 355
Other books by Graeme Carlé 370

Illustrations
Figure 1 Timeline of Daniel's 70 Weeks 10
Figure 2 Map showing locality today 44
Figure 3 Arch of Titus, Rome 57
Figure 4 An Israelite lampstand 58
Figure 5 Israel's coat of arms 61

"You search the Scriptures because you think that in them you have eternal life; it is these that testify about Me; and you are unwilling to come to Me so that you may have life..."
— *Jesus of Nazareth (John 5:39-40)*

Dedication

2017 is the fiftieth anniversary of Israel regaining sovereignty of Jerusalem from the Jordanians. It is also the centenary of the ANZAC Mounted Division capturing Beersheba, opening the way for the liberation of Jerusalem from the Turkish Empire.

This book is dedicated to the memory of the 17,723 New Zealanders who served in this campaign – 1,146 were wounded and 640 were killed. Hundreds of these young New Zealanders today lie buried in Beersheba, Gaza, Haifa, Ramla, and Jericho, as well as in Jerusalem.

30 years later, in 1948 the British handed over the Palestinian Mandate to the United Nations and, after almost 2,000 years, Israel was born again as a sovereign nation. In the Six Day War of June 1967, Israel finally regained Jerusalem.

Thanks

Chris & Dianne Bryan, Chris & Melissa Hennessy, Dorothy Hayward, Jim Doak, Mike & Jill Meyer, Mohan & Amy Herath, Peter & Susan Ridley, Shane & Melissa Pope, Steve Varney, and Strahan Coleman for their constant love, encouragement, and financial support, and especially Arthur Amon, Chris Pan, Elizabeth Rowe, and Simone Varney for painstaking feedback as well. As for Olivia and Peter Aranyi, our publisher and friend, I love working with you because you are such amiable perfectionists.

Foreword

City of Peace?

Often referred to as the City of Peace, Jerusalem has seldom been peaceful.

Four thousand years ago, it was called Salem,[1] the city of Melchizedek, a Canaanite king who broke bread with Abraham (Gen 14:18-20). There on Mt Moriah,[2] Abraham was called to offer his beloved son, Isaac (Gen 22:2). However, by the time of Joshua's conquest in about 1400 BC, one of Melchizedek's successors, Adoni-Zedek, was fighting the Israelites (Josh 10:1). Accordingly:

> ...the sons of Judah fought against Jerusalem and captured it and struck it with the edge of the sword and set the city on fire (Judg 1:8)

The Canaanites rebuilt it, however, and in about 1350 BC, its king Abdi-Heba wrote at least six letters[3] from Uru-shalim[4] to Egypt's Pharaoh Akhenaten, asking for his help to fight off the Hebrews:

> May the king give thought to his land: the land of the king is lost... I am situated like a ship in the midst of the sea.[5]

Akhenaten responded and the city, now known as Jebus (Jud 10:10, 1 Chron 11:4-5), withstood the Israelites for the next three hundred years (Judg 1:21) until David captured its inner citadel, Zion, in about 1010 BC. David then bought what was

---

1 i.e. Peace.
2 Today's Temple Mount.
3 The Amarna Letters, EA285-290.
4 Sumerian *uru*, meaning city.
5 Amarna Letter EA288.

to become the Temple Mount from Ornan the Jebusite[6] for 600 shekels of gold (1 Chron 21:25)[7] and Jerusalem became the City of God.

In *Jerusalem Besieged,* Eric H. Cline[8] notes that Jerusalem is sacred to three major religions – Judaism, Christianity, and Islam – and thus hundreds of millions of people throughout the world. However:

> No other city has been more bitterly fought over throughout its history…There have been at least 118 separate conflicts in and for Jerusalem during the past four millennia – conflicts that ranged from local religious struggles to strategic military campaigns and that embraced everything in between. Jerusalem has been destroyed completely at least twice, besieged twenty-three times, attacked an additional fifty-two times, and captured and recaptured forty-four times. It has been the scene of twenty revolts and innumerable riots, has had at least five separate periods of violent terrorist attacks during the past century, and has only changed hands peacefully twice in the last four thousand years.[9]

He also notes:

> Today the struggle for Jerusalem and all of Israel continues without respite… Where once the ancient weapons were bronze swords, lances, and battle-axes, they are now stun grenades, helicopter gunships, remotely detonated car bombs, and suicidal young men and women armed with explosives. Although the individuals and their weapons may have changed, the underlying tensions and desires have not. And the end is not yet in sight.

---

6 One of ten Canaanite tribes described in Genesis 15:19.
7 It seems he first bought just Ornan's threshing floor and oxen for 50 shekels of silver (2 Sam 24:24) and later the whole plot of land.
8 Associate Professor of Classics and Anthropology, and Chair of the Dept. of Classical and Semitic Languages and Literatures, George Washington University, Washington, D.C.
9 Eric Cline, *Jerusalem Besieged: From Ancient Canaan to Modern Israel,* Anne Arbor, MI; University of Michigan Press, 2004, pp. 1-2.

Meron Benvenisti, the former deputy mayor of Jerusalem, has described the rival Jewish and Moslem claims to the Temple Mount as "a time bomb… of apocalyptic dimensions."[10]

'The Holy City'

Jerusalem is also the Holy City[11] because God set it apart for His own purposes:

> "Jerusalem, the city which I have chosen from all the tribes of Israel… the city where I have chosen for Myself to put My name." (1 Kin 11:32 & 36)

Jesus, therefore, referred to it as "the city of the great King" (Matt 5:35), quoting from Psalm 48:

> Great is the LORD, and greatly to be praised,
> In the city of our God, His holy mountain.
> Beautiful in elevation, the joy of the whole earth,
> Is Mount Zion in the far north,
> *The city of the great King.* (Psa 48:1-2, emphasis added)

God's choice sanctified Jerusalem, to sanctify meaning to make holy. Today, we easily confuse or conflate the terms 'holy' and 'righteous' but, Biblically, they are very different concepts: to be righteous is to be morally right, just, or innocent; to be holy is to be set apart for a particular purpose. Paul illustrates this to Timothy:

> 20. Now in a large house there are not only gold and silver vessels, but also vessels of wood and of earthenware, and some to honor and some to dishonor.
> 21. Therefore, if anyone cleanses himself from these things, he will be a vessel for honor, *sanctified*, useful to the Master, prepared for every good work. (2 Tim 2:20-21, emphasis added)

---

10 Ibid.
11 Isaiah 52:1; Nehemiah 11:1, 18; Daniel 9:24; Matthew 4:5, 27:53; Revelation 11:2.

The silver cutlery, crystal glasses and bowls that we keep for special occasions are Biblically 'holy', honoured and set apart from our everyday, household utensils and dishes.

Jerusalem's inhabitants, therefore, may be righteous or unrighteous and yet still be holy, set apart or sanctified by God for His purposes, whether for honour or dishonour, simply because they live there.

Clashing Claims: Jew vs. Muslim

Jewish passion for the city runs irrepressibly long and deep. The Hebrew Bible, our Old Testament, refers to Jerusalem 669 times and Zion 154 times, so 823 times in total, and their people were always to pray towards the Temple there (1 Kin 8:44). In the 6th Century BC, they lamented losing the city in words still famous in song today:

> 1. By the rivers of Babylon,
> There we sat down and wept,
> When we remembered Zion...
> 5. If I forget you, O Jerusalem,
> May my right hand forget her skill.
> 6. May my tongue cling to the roof of my mouth
> If I do not remember you,
> If I do not exalt Jerusalem
> Above my chief joy. (Psa 137:1-6)

Exiled again after the devastation of 70 AD, the Jews never forgot. For eight hundred years, the last words of the two most important days in the Jewish calendar, Pesach (Passover) and Yom Kippur (Day of Atonement) have been:

> *Le-shanah ha-ba'ah bi-Yerushalayim!* Next year in Jerusalem![12]

Having regained Jerusalem in 1967, their battle-cry is "Never

---

12 www.kolhamevaser.com/2014/04/the-meaning-of-next-year-in-jerusalem/, 31 Aug, 2015.

again!" – never again will they leave the land or the city. As Prime Minister Benjamin Netanyahu said on May 17, 2015:

> We will forever keep Jerusalem united under Israeli sovereignty... Jerusalem was only ever the capital of the Jewish people, not of any other people. Here our path as a nation began, this is our home and here we shall stay.[13]

As for Christians, Pope Urban II's ill-fated call to the Crusades led to an eighty-eight year occupation of Jerusalem between 1099 and 1187 AD which was disastrous for all concerned. The death toll of approximately 150,000[14] included most of the Crusaders and the thousands of women and children on the People's Crusade were easily captured and sold as slaves.

However, Christians have no Biblical claim at all on the city:

> For here we do not have a lasting city, but we are seeking the city which is to come. (Heb 13:14)

We are instead to seek 'the new Jerusalem, which comes down out of heaven from God' (Rev 3:12, 21:2).

The New Testament refers to 'old' Jerusalem 154 times and Zion, 7 times, so 161 times in total. Jesus, our Jewish Messiah, walked, taught, celebrated Jewish festivals, died, and was resurrected there. It was His nation's capital then and still is today, while we Gentiles have our own capital cities in every nation.

On the other hand, Muslims today claim the Temple Mount is their third holiest place after Mecca and Medina,

---

13 www.timesofisrael.com/netanyahu-jerusalem-only-ever-the-capital-of-the-jewish-people/, 31 Aug, 2015.
14 Contrary to popular belief that millions died. For details, see *Slouching Towards Bethlehem*, pp. 159-161. Edward H. Flannery estimated that Crusaders en route murdered 10,000 Jews in Europe in 1096, "probably one-fourth to one-third of the Jewish population of Germany and Northern France at that time." *The Anguish of the Jews: Twenty-Three Centuries of Antisemitism*, Paulist Press, 1985, p. 93.

despite all evidence to the contrary. As we saw in Book 2,[15] the Qur'an never refers to Jerusalem or Zion, and Muhammad never went there. Muslims were to turn their backs on Jerusalem as the place of the Jews and Christians, praying instead towards Mecca (Sura 2:142-145).

Why then claim Jerusalem? Because they believe Muhammad went to the Al-Aqsa Mosque (lit. the Farthest Mosque) on the Temple Mount on a 'night journey' on a winged steed called al-Buraq.[16] The Qur'an says he was taken by God from Mecca's 'Sacred Mosque to the farthest Mosque' (Sura 17:1). However, there was no mosque in Jerusalem until five years after he died in 632 AD – the Muslim armies did not capture Jerusalem until 637 AD and the Dome of the Rock was built fifty-five years later – so the Al-Aqsa Mosque is anachronistic.[17] In Muhammad's time, the farthest mosque from Mecca was in Medina, but nothing will dissuade Muslims from claiming Jerusalem anyway.

Now add to the mix the differing claims as to which son Abraham was called to offer on Mt Moriah: the Hebrew Bible says it was Isaac (Gen 22:2), father of Israel and the Jews, as does the New Testament (Heb 11:17-18); Muslims believe it was Ishmael,[18] forefather of Muhammad, and that the Jews corrupted the Biblical texts.

Professor Cline and Deputy Mayor Benvenisti's testimonies

---

15 *Slouching Towards Bethlehem*, hereafter referred to as *STB*, pp. 215-218.
16 Several hadiths, or traditional sayings, describe this as a white beast, bigger than a donkey but smaller than a mule, with two wings on its thighs. www.islamicparty.com/alaqsa/enter.htm, 6 Aug, 2011.
17 A number of hadiths refer to Jerusalem: www.islamicboard.com/general/134304952-jerusalem-talked-hadith.html, 11 Oct, 2016. Some teach that Jesus will return there, or Damascus, to help the Mahdi, kill Dajjāl (the Antichrist) and his 70,000 Jewish followers, and rebuke Christians for worshipping Him. www.discoveringislam.org/return_of_jesus.htm, 11 Oct, 2016. See also *STB*, pp. 171-172.
18 www.islamic-awareness.org/Quran/Contrad/MusTrad/sacrifice.html, 1 Sept, 2015.

seem undeniably true and frightening; the whole situation is like an apocalyptic time bomb.

Where better to look then than in the Apocalypse,[19] or Book of Revelation, to find out *God's plan* for it all?

---

19 Greek, *apokalupsis*, lit. an uncovering, i.e. a revelation.

Introduction

So Far...

In the first three books of this series, I used the meanings of a number of ancient Jewish metaphors to unlock some of the mysteries[20] of chapters 12, 13, and 14 of the Book of Revelation:

(i) In *Dancing in the Dragon's Jaws*,[21] I showed how Revelation 12's vision of the woman, the child, and the dragon explains what has been going on behind the scenes for Israel 'according to the flesh'[22] over the last 4,000 years; we saw why she has so often faced virulent anti-Semitism and genocidal attacks by vastly more powerful Gentile empires, yet miraculously survives today.

(ii) Identifying the woman as Israel rather than Mary or the church is essential to understanding three New Testament mysteries: Israel's partial hardening (Rom 11:25); the times of the Gentiles (Luke 21:24); the two returns of Elijah (Matt 17:11).

(iii) I showed how Daniel's mysterious time period, "a time, times and half a time" (Dan 7:25 and 12:7), is used by John (Rev 12:14), interchangeably with 'forty-two months' (Rev 11:2) and '1,260 days' (Rev 12:6), and is the second half of Daniel's 70th Week of years.

(iv) I showed Daniel's 70th Week to be Messiah's week and not, as popularly believed today, a future seven year

---

20 In ordinary use, a 'mystery' is a hidden or inexplicable matter but in Biblical usage, it is a revelation of profound truth.
21 Referred to hereafter as *DDJ*.
22 Paul uses this term to describe everyone born of Jewish parents (Rom 9:3), including Jesus (Rom 9:5).

period given over to the Antichrist.[23] The first half of the 70th Week was the three and half years of Jesus' ministry before He was crucified. This fulfilled Daniel 9:27 that "in the middle of the week, He [Messiah the Prince, not 'he' the Antichrist] will put a stop to sacrifice and grain offering" because He made them unnecessary.

(v) This leaves the second half of the 70th Week. Some teach it is yet to be fulfilled as a literal three and a half years but Daniel's prophecies in the 6th Century BC end with a mysterious period described as 'a time, times and half a time' to be understood only in 'the end time' (Dan 12:9) and also mentioned in Daniel 7:25. It is this period that features in three of John's visions, in Revelation 11, 12, and 13.

(vi) Given its mysterious nature, I searched for a metaphorical meaning and found it in Jesus' and James's reference to Elijah beginning and ending a drought of "three years and six months" (Luke 4:25, Jas 5:17). I showed this to be part of another mystery based on Elijah's two metaphorical returns (Matt 17:10-13) to start and end the metaphorical drought on Israel.

(vii) I showed how this period is also known as "the times of the Gentiles" because Elijah left the needs of Israel for "three years and six months" to help Gentiles. It is revealed in real time by the status of Jerusalem (Luke 21:24 cf. Rev 11:2).

(viii) In real time, it began with Jesus' crucifixion in 30 AD

---

23 Messiah's week of redemption was foreshadowed by Creation's week, Noah's week before the Flood, Jacob's working for a week of years to marry first Leah and then Rachel to found the nation of Israel, Joseph's saving the nation in a week of years of famine, the Hebrew marriage week, and Solomon's completing the Temple in a week of years. *DDJ*, pp. 102-6.

("in the middle of the week") and was to end when the Gentiles no longer rule over Jerusalem (Luke 21:24). Israel's recapturing Jerusalem in the Six Day War of 1967 reveals "a time, times and half a time" to be the last 2,000 years of Jewish history,[24] as illustrated here:

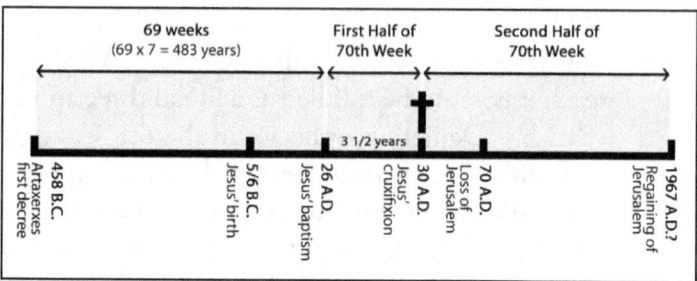

Figure 1 — Timeline of Daniel's 70 Weeks

(ix) In *Slouching Towards Bethlehem,* I used these key concepts to unlock Revelation 13, revealing what has been happening amongst 'all the nations' over the last 2,000 years as emperors became their gods. In the 20th Century alone, this led to the deaths of over 270 million men, women, and children.

(x) In *Gotta Serve Somebody*[25], I identified the Jewish metaphors and poetic devices of marks, measuring, numbers, and repetition, which explain the mark of the beast and its number 666, as well as the 144,000 of Revelation 14:1-15, and showed how the mark has also been around for last 2,000 years.

---

24 We cannot be dogmatic about this date because Israel immediately handed back the Temple Mount, the very heart of Jerusalem, to the Islamic waqf, or authority, which controls it today.
25 Referred to hereafter as *GSS*.

Revelation 11:1-13

We can now use these keys to unlock Revelation 11 because this vision also takes place over 'forty-two months' (Rev 11:2) and '1,260 days' (Rev 11:3), but with an additional 'three and half *days*' (Rev 11:9 and 11). I had to establish all of this beforehand because, as N.T. Wright points out:

> People find many books puzzling, but the Bible is often the most puzzling of all. People find many parts of the Bible puzzling, but Revelation is often seen as the most puzzling book of all. And people find Revelation puzzling, but the first half of chapter 11… is, for many, the most puzzling part of all. (There are some other strong contenders for this dubious distinction, but chapter 11 can hold its own).[26]

This is why, in negotiating the swamp of speculation and conjecture, I have been so careful to identify each of our stepping stones thus far. Revelation 11:1-13 still requires some meticulous stepping but will richly reward those arriving on the far side of the swamp by resolving other theological issues, such as the New Testament's most puzzling references to the role of the Law of Moses today, the fallen tabernacle of David, and the restored holiness of Jerusalem.

I will establish the identity of the two witnesses (Rev 11:3) and of 'the beast that comes up out of the abyss' which finally silences them (Rev 11:7). We will also see why the Gentiles rejoice at the death (Rev 11:9-10), and how the witnesses will be resurrected (Rev 11:11-12). I will also explain the extraordinary significance of the Melchizedek priesthood, to which every follower of Jesus belongs today, and the everlasting covenant God made with David.

---

26 *Revelation for Everyone*, London; SPCK Publishing, 2011, p. 97.

Text of Revelation 11:1-13

1. Then there was given me a measuring rod like a staff; and someone said, "Get up and measure the temple of God and the altar, and those who worship in it.
2. "Leave out the court which is outside the temple and do not measure it, for it has been given to the nations; and they will tread under foot the holy city for forty-two months.
3. "And I will grant authority to My two witnesses, and they will prophesy for twelve hundred and sixty days, clothed in sackcloth."
4. These are the two olive trees and the two lampstands that stand before the Lord of the earth.
5. And if anyone wants to harm them, fire flows out of their mouth and devours their enemies; so if anyone wants to harm them, he must be killed in this way.
6. These have the power to shut up the sky, so that rain will not fall during the days of their prophesying; and they have power over the waters to turn them into blood, and to strike the earth with every plague, as often as they desire.
7. When they have finished their testimony, the beast that comes up out of the abyss will make war with them, and overcome them and kill them.
8. And their dead bodies will lie in the street of the great city which mystically is called Sodom and Egypt, where also their Lord was crucified.
9. Those from the peoples and tribes and tongues and nations will look at their dead bodies for three and a half days, and will not permit their dead bodies to be laid in a tomb.
10. And those who dwell on the earth will rejoice over them and celebrate; and they will send gifts to one another, because these two prophets tormented those who dwell on the earth.
11. But after the three and a half days, the breath of life from God came into them, and they stood on their feet; and great fear fell upon those who were watching them.
12. And they heard a loud voice from heaven saying to them, "Come up here." Then they went up into heaven in the cloud, and their enemies watched them.
13. And in that hour there was a great earthquake, and a tenth of the city fell; seven thousand people were killed in the earthquake, and the rest were terrified and gave glory to the God of heaven.

1
'A Measuring Rod' To Comprehend

The vision begins with a command:

> 1. Then there was given me a measuring rod like a staff; and someone said, "Get up and measure the temple of God and the altar, and those who worship in it."

When I first read this passage, it raised several questions for me. I could understand John measuring a building but what was the point when he did not record any results? And why would God want him to 'measure… those who worship in it'? Not to count, but to measure with 'a measuring rod'. Does it matter if they were tall or short, or stout or thin? The expression has to be metaphorical but what does the metaphor mean?

As we established in Book 3,[27] 'calculating', 'marking off', 'weighing' and 'measuring' doubled as Hebrew metaphors for comprehending, understanding, and judging. For example, Job asked his friends:

> 7. "Can you discover the depths of God?
> Can you discover the limits of the Almighty?
> 8. "They are high as the heavens, what can you do?
> Deeper than Sheol, what can you know?
> 9. "Its measure is longer than the earth
> And broader than the sea". (Job 11:7-9)

Paul prayed for the Ephesians:

> 17. …that you, being rooted and grounded in love,
> 18. may be able to comprehend with all the saints what is the breadth and length and height and depth… (Eph 3:17-18)

---

27   *GSS*, pp. 132-133.

This is why, when Jesus taught on judging, He added measuring:

> "For in the way you judge, you will be judged; and by your standard of measure, it will be measured to you." (Matt 7:2)

Today we readily understand He means that if we judge carelessly or harshly, we will ourselves be judged carelessly or harshly; if we are discerning and merciful, we too will receive due care and mercy. God judges, having 'measured' properly, and He wants us to do likewise:

> "Do not judge according to appearance, but judge with righteous judgement." (John 7:24)

What then is the meaning of John's measuring? What was he to discern and understand about 'the temple of God and the altar, and those who worship in it'?

Happily, there is no need for guesswork because two Jewish prophets of old, Ezekiel and Zechariah, had earlier received similar visions. We need to understand these if we want to catch up with what would have been already understood by John's original 1st Century Jewish hearers, and Gentiles taught by them.

Ezekiel's Temple

In 573 BC (Ezek 40:1),[28] Ezekiel was in exile in Babylon when 'the hand of the Lord' took him back to Jerusalem where he saw a man 'with a line of flax and a measuring rod in his hand' (Ezek 40:3). The man then measured the temple and the altar, and the results are recorded in chapters 40-43.

While these can be read as literal measurements, there is also an implicit metaphorical meaning in Ezekiel's measuring

---

28 All the dates of Ezekiel are reckoned from the 597 BC exile. *The Zondervan Pictorial Encyclopedia of the Bible*, ed. Merrill C. Tenney, Grand Rapids; Zondervan, 1977, Vol 2, p. 455.

because he then prophesied God's judgement regarding *all those worshipping in it* – God would no longer allow to come near Him "the rebellious ones,...all the foreigners...[and] the Levites who went far from Me" (Ezek 44:6-14); only "the Levitical priests, the sons of Zadok... shall come near" (Ezek 44:15-16). The measuring of the temple and the altar was followed by God's judgement on all who wanted to worship there, whether to welcome or forbid them. John's measuring of 'the temple of God and the altar, and those who worship in it' therefore had a clear precedent in Ezekiel.

There is another similarity. Although separated by almost seven hundred years, both Ezekiel and John were taken in vision to Jerusalem when *there was no Temple or altar there to be measured.* Like John, Ezekiel knew that; he knew that thirteen years earlier, in 586 BC, the Babylonians had demolished Jerusalem and the First Temple (Ezek 33:21).

What then did Ezekiel actually see being measured? A future Temple.

His vision in 573 BC would have comforted the exiles, promising restoration and confirming Jeremiah's prophecy that they would return from Babylon (Jer 29:10). Thirty-seven years later, in 536 BC, the returnees began to rebuild the Temple on Solomon's foundations (Ezra 2:68), completing it in 516 BC (Ezra 6:15).[29] However, this was not Ezekiel's temple.[30] The Second Temple was so puny, 'the old men who had seen the first temple wept with a loud voice' (Ezra 3:12). It only became magnificent after Herod reconstructed it between 20 BC and 27 AD (Mark 13:1-2, John 2:20).

This Temple was razed to the ground by the Romans in 70 AD so by the time John saw the Temple Mount in 95-96 AD, the site was again lying desolate, following the fifth

---

29 *The Zondervan Pictorial Encyclopedia of the Bible*, Vol 2, p. 471.
30 The rabbis today are unanimous that this was not Ezekiel's Temple; they are expecting that to be the Third Temple, built either by Messiah or just before He comes.

'abomination of desolation'.[31]

What then did John measure? The Third Temple, a literal building, made of stone? Many Christians today believe so, based on their understanding of 2 Thessalonians 2:4 that the Antichrist will enthrone himself there before the Second Coming of Jesus. However, while this is possible, I believe there is a more satisfying answer to be found after we have looked at Zechariah.

Zechariah's Jerusalem

In 519 BC (Zech 1:7),[32] i.e. when the puny temple was almost finished, Zechariah had a vision but this was not about measuring the Temple but the city of Jerusalem:

> 1. Then I lifted up my eyes and looked, and behold, there was a man with a measuring line in his hand.
> 2. So I said, "Where are you going?" And he said to me, "To measure Jerusalem, to see how wide it is and how long it is."
> (Zech 2:1-2)

At that time, although the temple was almost finished, the city was still in ruins. It was not until 444 BC that Nehemiah's builders finished its walls (Neh 6:15).[33]

Zechariah's vision gave no results of the measuring – it was simply to confirm that Jerusalem would soon be rebuilt successfully.

In John's vision, however, he is specifically commanded to "not measure" the outer court, i.e. "the court of the Gentiles", or the city:

> 1. Then there was given me a measuring rod like a staff; and someone said, "Get up and measure the temple of God and the altar, and those who worship in it.
> 2. "Leave out the court which is outside the temple and do not

---

31 *STB*, pp. 275-278.
32 *The Zondervan Pictorial Encyclopedia of the Bible*, Vol 5, p. 1044.
33 Ibid., Vol 2, p. 471.

> measure it, for it has been given to the nations [i.e. Gentiles]; and *they will tread underfoot* the holy city for forty-two months." (Rev 11:1-2, emphasis added)

John was to measure the temple, the altar and the worshippers but not Jerusalem because the city would remain desolate, trodden underfoot by Gentiles, i.e. under Gentile domination, for "forty two months".

It is here we can apply the key we obtained in Book 1 when Jesus used the same expression:

> "…and they [Israel] will fall by the edge of the sword, and will be led captive into all the nations; and Jerusalem will be *trampled underfoot* by the Gentiles until the times of the Gentiles are fulfilled." (Luke 21:24, emphasis added)

From this parallel use of the trampling underfoot being for "forty-two months" and "the times of the Gentiles", I established that this time period of "a time, times and half a time" is not literal but metaphorical, its 'real' time being defined by the status of Jerusalem. From that, I concluded it seemed to end with Israel's regaining sovereignty over Jerusalem in the Six Day War of June, 1967.[34] I also established that it is the second half of Daniel's 70th Week, and the period between Elijah's two metaphorical comings.

John was therefore called to make a careful distinction: he was to measure the Temple, its altar and those who worship in it in the 1st Century; he was not to measure the city of Jerusalem because that would not be regained by Israel until the 20th Century.

---

34 I say 'seemed' because the victorious Israeli general, Moshe Dayan, handed back the heart of Jerusalem, the Temple Mount, to the Waqf, or Islamic Authority.

'A Spiritual House'

What then did John measure? What was he to discern and comprehend? He 'measured' the real Temple, the one that all the others only foreshadowed. As Peter wrote, also in the 1st Century, all who believe in Jesus are to come to Him…:

> 4. …as to a living stone which has been rejected by men, but is choice and precious in the sight of God,
> 5. you also, as living stones, are being built up as a spiritual house for a holy priesthood, to offer up spiritual sacrifices acceptable to God through Jesus Christ. (1 Pet 2:4-5)

So, if all of us who believe are 'living stones' being 'built up as a spiritual house', who is actually doing the building? Jesus as Messiah.

> 12. …"Thus says the LORD of hosts, 'Behold, a man whose name is Branch, for He will branch out from where He is; and He will build the temple of the LORD.
> 13. 'Yes, it is He who will build the temple of the LORD, and He who will bear the honor and sit and rule on His throne. Thus, He will be a priest on His throne, and the counsel of peace will be between the two offices.'" (Zech 6:12-13)

The *New American Standard Study Bible* comments:

> According to the Aramaic Targum (a paraphrase), the Jerusalem Talmud (a collection of religious instruction) and the Midrash (practical exposition), Jews early regarded this verse as Messianic… The coming Davidic King will also be a priest. [Since] such a combination was not normally possible in Israel [kings were to be descendants of David but priests only of Levi]…, the sect of Qumran expected two Messianic figures – a high priest Messiah and a Davidic one.[35]

This is why Jesus challenged the religious leaders of His day to think through the radical implications of Psalm 110:1 regarding

---

35 *NASB Study Bible* notes, pp. 1338-1339. Comment inserted.

Messiah,[36] or Christ:

> 41. Now while the Pharisees were gathered together, Jesus asked them a question:
> 42. "What do you think about the Christ, whose son is He?" They said to Him, "The son of David."
> 43. He said to them, "Then how does David in the Spirit call Him 'Lord', saying,
> 44. 'THE LORD SAID TO MY LORD, "SIT AT MY RIGHT HAND, UNTIL I PUT YOUR ENEMIES BENEATH YOUR FEET"'?
> 45. "If David then calls Him 'Lord', how is He his son?"
> (Matt 22:41-45)

David calls his son 'Lord' because the Messiah is greater than David, their greatest king and architect of the original Temple (1 Chron 28:11-19). David's inspired prophecy then makes a promise to Him:

> The LORD has sworn and will not change His mind,
> "You are a priest forever according to the order of Melchizedek."
> (Ps 110:4)

Psalm 110 is saying that the Messiah or Christ is forever both King and Priest in the new Jerusalem, just as Melchizedek was the King and Priest of old Jerusalem (Gen 14:18-20, Heb 7:1-28).

Zechariah's prophecy is therefore not only confirming Messiah's identity as 'a priest on His throne' (v. 13) but also revealing that He will build the Temple in which He will forever be priest (vv. 12 and 13).

And what Temple has Jesus been building for the last 2,000 years? The 'spiritual house', built of 'the living stones' of all the saints, all of us who trust in Him.

Accordingly, John was to use a new way and standard of measuring to comprehend the true, essential nature of

---

36 Anglicised form of Heb. *Mashiach*, lit. 'the Anointed One', from Israel's ancient practice of appointing priests, kings, and prophets by anointing them with oil; Christ anglicises Grk *Christos*, from the verb chrio, to anoint.

God's Temple. This is why John records no results of his measurements – there are none, other than a different perspective on what constitutes the Temple. We too should understand it in this way.

The Altar and the Worshippers?

What then is this temple's altar? Not one of stone or bronze but a spiritual altar on which we are to offer 'spiritual sacrifices', as Peter wrote:

> ...you also, as living stones, are being built up as a spiritual house for a holy priesthood, to *offer up spiritual sacrifices* acceptable to God through Jesus Christ.
> (1 Pet 2:5, emphasis added)

The writer of Hebrews explains further:

> 11. ...when Christ appeared as a high priest of the good things to come, He entered through the greater and more perfect tabernacle, not made with hands, that is to say, not of this creation;
> 12. and not through the blood of goats and calves, but through His own blood, He entered the holy place once for all, having obtained eternal redemption. (Heb 9:11-12)

This concept was easily understood by 1st Century Jewish believers, and refers to the Day of Atonement, when the high priest sprinkled the sacrificial goat's blood on the ark of the covenant inside the Holy of Holies (Lev 16:1ff.). For Jews, for one and a half thousand years before 30 AD, this annual event foreshadowed the resurrected Jesus sprinkling His own blood in 'the greater and more perfect tabernacle' when He ascended.

The body of the goat being burned outside the city (Lev 16:27) likewise foreshadowed Jesus' crucifixion outside the walls of Jerusalem. We see then His altar was the cross. Accordingly:

> 10. *We have an altar* from which those who serve the tabernacle [the Levitical priests] have no right to eat.
> 11. For the bodies of those animals whose blood is brought into the holy place by the high priest as an offering for sin, are burned outside the camp.
> 12. Therefore Jesus also, that He might sanctify the people through His own blood, suffered outside the gate…
> 15. Through Him then, let us continually offer up *a sacrifice of praise* to God, that is, the *fruit of lips that give thanks to His name*.
> 16. And do not neglect *doing good and sharing*, for with such sacrifices God is pleased. (Heb 13:10-16, emphasis added)

In other words, just as the two Temples[37] of stone foreshadowed God's 'spiritual house' of 'living stones', the Levitical priests' work foreshadowed our service – the rituals of the Mosaic Covenant provide us with amazing prophetic dramas and audio-visuals.

In verses 11-12 above, we see that just as on the annual Day of Atonement when the blood of a goat was sprinkled inside the Holy of Holies, in 30 AD Jesus' blood was applied inside the spiritual and eternal house of God. Since He has fulfilled that sacrifice 'once for all, having obtained eternal redemption' (Heb 9:12), we are to offer the spiritual equivalent of the continual grain offering by speaking or singing to 'continually offer up a sacrifice of praise' (Heb 13:15); instead of eating the shared meal of the peace offerings, we are to be 'doing good and sharing' our possessions (Heb 13:16).

Spiritual Sacrifices

This concept of the spiritual superseding the literal sacrifice is a familiar concept to Orthodox Jews today who have long believed that the service of the heart replaced the service of the hand. One of their most illustrious rabbis, Moses

---

[37] Solomon's was the First Temple; Ezra describes the Second Temple which Herod later beautified.

Maimonides,[38] was teaching the abolition of animal sacrifice in the 12th Century:

> As the sacrificial service is not the primary object, whilst supplications, prayers, and similar kinds of worship are nearer to the primary object, and indispensable for obtaining it, a great difference was made in the Law between these two kinds of service. The one kind, which consists in offering sacrifices… has not been made obligatory for us to the same extent as it had been before…

He argued that the Temple limited true worship:

> Only one temple has been appointed, "in the place which the Lord shall choose" (Deut xii, 26); in no other place is it allowed to sacrifice… and only the members of a particular family were allowed to officiate as priests. All these restrictions served to limit this kind of worship… But prayer and supplication can be offered everywhere and by every person.[39]

He taught that animal sacrifice was actually pagan in origin and God only allowed it in the Law to slowly wean Israel from idolatry into a purer, bloodless spirituality, that of prayer and thanksgiving.[40] What then of the atonement?

> In times when there is no Temple and we have no altar of atonement, there is only repentance. Repentance atones for all sins. Even one [who is] wicked his entire life and repents at the end, they (i.e., the Heavenly tribunal) do not recall his wickedness, as it is stated, 'And the wicked man will not stumble in his wickedness on the day of his repenting from his evil' (Ezekiel 33:12). The day of Yom Kippur (lit., 'the essence of Yom Kippur') atones for those

---

38 Known in rabbinical literature as Rambam, an acronym of Rabbi Moses Ben Maimon, he is referred to as the 'second Moses'. www.jewishencyclopedia.com/articles/11124-moses-ben-maimon, 3 Sept, 2015.
39 *The Guide for the Perplexed*, translated by Michael Friedlander, New York; Cosimo, Inc., 2007, p. 325.
40 www.ou.org/torah/parsha/rabbi-fox-on-parsha/parshat_vayikra_2/, 3 Sept, 2015.

who repent, as it is stated, 'For on this day he [the High Priest] will effect atonement for you…' (Lev 16:30).[41]

In other words, repentance plus the Day itself, without the sacrifice, will be enough. Accordingly:

> With the destruction of the Temple, the rabbis state that prayer and good deeds took the place of sacrifice.[42]

That is, this apparent change for the better was caused, and enforced, by the destruction of the Second Temple in 70 AD.

However, the New Testament gives a very different reason: when the Messiah came, the shadows became unnecessary (Col 2:17, Heb 8:5 and 10:1).

How then did John 'measure' this altar? Simply by understanding this.

What of the worshippers? How did John 'measure' them? By remembering Jesus' dialogue with a Samaritan woman some sixty years earlier:

> 19. The woman said to Him, "Sir, I perceive that You are a prophet.
> 20. "Our fathers worshiped in this mountain, and you people say that in Jerusalem is the place where men ought to worship."
> 21. Jesus said to her, "Woman, believe Me, an hour is coming when neither in this mountain nor in Jerusalem will you worship the Father.
> 22. "You worship what you do not know; we worship what we know, for salvation is from the Jews.
> 23. "But an hour is coming, and now is, when the true worshipers will worship the Father in spirit and truth; for such people the Father seeks to be His worshipers.
> 24. "God is spirit, and those who worship Him must worship in spirit and truth." (John 4:19-24)

Maimonides was almost right – 'prayer and supplication can be offered everywhere and by every person' – but he was tragically

---

41 www.torah.org/learning/mlife/LoRch1--3.html?print=1, 3 Sept, 2015.
42 www.jewishvirtuallibrary.org/jsource/Judaism/vegsacrifices.html, 4 Mar, 2013.

wrong to ignore the ever-present need for the atoning sacrifice that Jesus fulfilled.

So, if the Mosaic Covenant was no longer to apply to any Jew in the New Covenant, what was to happen to those who refused to enter the New? John hears the voice continuing to prophesy but before we go on, let us summarise what we have established so far.

Summary of Temple Measuring (Rev 11:1-2)

This vision of John's requires us to understand some Jewish history and Old Testament metaphors:

(i) At the time of John's vision (c. 95-96 AD), there was nothing left of the Second Temple for John to measure because the Romans had levelled every stone in 70 AD, just as Jesus had predicted (Matt 24:2) in 30 AD.

(ii) His measuring of the temple, the altar, and the worshippers echoes both Ezekiel's vision of 573 BC and Zechariah's vision of 519 BC, which followed the First Temple's destruction by the Babylonians in 586 BC.

(iii) Ezekiel's and Zechariah's visions were to reassure Israel that the Temple and the city of Jerusalem would soon be rebuilt. John's vision, however, differed. The command for him to measure the temple, the altar, and the worshippers was not to do so literally but metaphorically, i.e. using the common Jewish metaphor for comprehending or understanding. This is why he recorded no results.

(iv) He was to understand and prophesy, just as Peter had written thirty years earlier, that God was already building another Temple but this time, 'a spiritual house', comprised of 'living stones', for 'a royal priesthood' who offer 'spiritual sacrifices' (1 Pet 2:5 and 9) at a spiritual altar (Heb 13:10).

(v) This had been predicted some sixty years earlier by the Lord Himself to the Samaritan woman, that geographical location would no longer matter because God wants us to worship "in spirit and in truth" (John 4:21-24).

(vi) The city of Jerusalem was to remain under Gentile domination for 'forty-two months' (Rev 11:2), "until the times of the Gentiles are fulfilled" (Luke 21:24), i.e. the last 2,000 years.

2
"My Two Witnesses"
Literal or Metaphorical?

3. "And I will grant authority to My two witnesses, and they will prophesy for twelve hundred and sixty days, clothed in sackcloth."
4. These are the two olive trees and the two lampstands that stand before the Lord of the earth.
5. And if anyone wants to harm them, fire flows out of their mouth and devours their enemies; so if anyone wants to harm them, he must be killed in this way.
6. These have the power to shut up the sky, so that rain will not fall during the days of their prophesying; and they have power over the waters to turn them into blood, and to strike the earth with every plague, as often as they desire. (Rev 11:3-6)

Obviously, the description of the two witnesses as "olive trees" and "lampstands" is to be read metaphorically but what of the witnesses themselves? Are they literal or metaphorical?

Literal…

Some believe[43] the witnesses will be Enoch and Elijah, referring to some famous theologians of old such as Irenaeus (2nd Century), Tertullian (2nd Century), Hippolytus (3rd Century), Augustine (5th Century), Gregory the Great (6th Century), Bede (8th Century), and Thomas Aquinas (13th Century).

Their reasoning is usually based on Enoch and Elijah not having died. One argument is that Hebrews 9:27 is a doctrinal

---

43   e.g. www.dailycatholic.org/issue/10Mar/030407sm.htm, accessed 7 Sept, 2015. Or David R. Reagan www.lamblion.com/articles/articles_revelation11.php, 7 Sept, 2015.

statement – 'it is appointed for men to die once and after this comes judgement', i.e. everyone has to die at least once – so Enoch and Elijah are the only two who qualify[44] However, as Paul tells us, everyone who is alive at the return of the Lord also will not die (1 Cor 15:51-53), so Hebrews 9:27 cannot mean everyone has to die.

Tim LaHaye and Jerry Jenkins of the very popular *Left Behind* series[45] argue against one being Enoch:

> Two of the most colorful characters in all of Bible prophecy have to be the two supernatural prophets that burst on the scene during the first 1,260 days of the Tribulation… Some try to identify one of the witnesses with Enoch (because he never died, Genesis 5:24) and the other with either Elijah (who also never died, 2 Kings 2:11-12) or Moses. For three reasons, we are inclined to think they are Moses and Elijah…[46]

They then show how three identifying features point instead to Moses and Elijah.[47] Accordingly, in *Apollyon (The Destroyer is Unleashed)*, LaHaye and Jenkins imagine the witnesses' impact on Buck, one of their heroes:

> Some said they were Moses and Elijah incarnate, but if Buck had to guess, he would have said they were the two Old Testament characters themselves. They look and smelled centuries old, a smoky, dusty aroma following them.[48]

Merrill C. Tenney agrees:

> The two witnesses may be actual reappearances of [Moses

---

44 e.g. www.apocalypsesoon.org/xfile-11.html, 7 Sept, 2015.
45 These sixteen books, published between 1995 and 2007, have sold over 65 million copies and been adapted into feature films, a children's series, and graphic novels.
46 *Are We Living in the End-Times?* p. 292.
47 We will look at these soon, along with seven more.
48 The fifth novel of their series, *Apollyon (The Destroyer is Unleashed)*, p. 134.

and Elijah], these two great leaders of the past who championed God's cause against bitter opposition, or they may be symbolic of the law and the prophets. The former seems more likely in the light of Malachi 4:4-6, where Moses and Elijah are coupled together as mentors of a decadent age, and where the prediction of Elijah's return to earth is plainly taught.[49]

Or Metaphorical?

Some argue for a mixture of literal and metaphorical – 'two future prophets who minister in the power and character of Moses and Elijah'.[50] Michael Wilcock, however, chooses the wholly metaphorical interpretation:

> Interpreters have not been lacking who have expected a literal fulfillment of this section, as of the rest. At some unspecified date in the future will begin, presumably in Jerusalem, the three-and-a-half-year preaching career of these two remarkable people, God's witnesses. It will be followed by their martyrdom, and then (to the consternation of all) by their resurrection and rapture, and chaos in the city.
>
> If, however, the temple and city of verses 1 and 2 are symbolic, and the message of 10:11 is universal, it seems a great deal more likely that this passage also carries a non-literal meaning… and their title of 'lampstand' [ties in] with the symbolism of [Rev] 1:20… The witnesses… are the church in the world, God's people among the heathen nations.[51]

His reference to Revelation 1:20 is where John is told the seven lampstands he sees are the seven churches to which he is to

---

49 *Interpreting Revelation*, p. 191.
50 www.spiritandtruth.org/teaching/Book_of_Revelation/commentary/htm/03110301.htm, 19 Sep, 2016.
51 *The Message of Revelation*, p. 104.

write so Rev. Wilcock concludes the two witnesses symbolise 'the church in the world'.

N.T. Wright agrees:

> Now – this is the part which many find particularly difficult – it appears that the 'two witnesses' of verses 3-13 *are a symbol for the whole church in its prophetic witness, its faithful death, and its vindication by God.*[52]

Likewise Craig R. Koester:

> The two witnesses represent the community of faithful Christians.[53]

These symbolic or metaphorical interpreters see these two witnesses in Jerusalem as 'God's people among the heathen nations' in v. 8:

> And their dead bodies will lie in the street of the great city which mystically [Gk, *pneumatikos*, spiritually] is called Sodom and Egypt, where also their Lord was crucified. (Rev 11:8)

First, Michael Wilcock's explanation:

> The city where their corpses lie exposed to public gaze is no more literal than the rest. It cannot be one and the same time literally both Sodom and Egypt; and if those names are used metaphorically, why should not 'the city… where their Lord was crucified' be metaphorical also?[54]

N.T. Wright:

> John will make all this clear in the several chapters that follow… that the 'city' is Rome itself, or maybe in this case the public world of the entire Roman Empire.[55]

Craig R. Koester:

> Although John says that the witnesses are killed in "the

---

52 *Revelation for Everyone*, p. 99, emphasis in original.
53 *Revelation and the End of All Things*, p. 108.
54 *The Message of Revelation*, p. 106.
55 *Revelation for Everyone*, pp. 99-100.

great city" where Jesus was crucified (11:7-8), the passage cannot be limited to one place on earth…[but] can refer to the whole realm in which oppression takes place.[56]

Laurie Guy summarises this approach:

> The place of death of the two witnesses is ambiguous in the extreme. 'The great city' (11:8) would normally be Rome (as in 17:18). However, it is also described as 'Sodom' and 'Egypt', places which were bywords for evil and oppression. Then a fourth location is introduced – Jerusalem, 'where also their Lord was crucified.' All this indicates that the place of death is symbolic – simply a place of great evil – and that the witnesses are ideal rather than actual figures.[57]

However, it seems to me these metaphorical explanations create only more ambiguity and questions.

For example, 'if [Sodom and Egypt] are used metaphorically, why should not [Jerusalem]?' – perhaps it should not because we are actually *told* that Sodom and Egypt are *pneumatikos*, i.e. metaphorical, whereas the crucifixion of Jesus was in Jerusalem, a literal locality which is then given two metaphorical names?

And why can this passage 'not be limited to one place on earth' (Craig R. Koester) when it plainly seems to be? In how many other places on earth was Jesus crucified?

Hermeneutics

Before we go any further, we have to consider hermeneutics – how we are to understand Biblical texts. One of the major issues that divides the churches of God is a simple choice of whether a passage is to be read literally or metaphorically. Take, for example, Jesus' warning:

> "Truly, truly, I say to you, unless you eat the flesh of the Son of

---

56 *Revelation and the End of All Things*, pp. 109-110.
57 *Making Sense of Revelation*, p. 107.

Man and drink His blood, you have no life in yourselves. He who eats My flesh and drinks My blood has eternal life, and I will raise him up on the last day". (John 6:53-54)

Many of His disciples took this literally and stopped following Him (v. 66) because as Jews, they were forbidden to eat or drink blood (Lev 7:27). Today, the Roman Catholic and Eastern Orthodox Churches still read this literally. One result is the doctrine of trans-substantiation and the Mass, requiring a duly authorised priesthood to change bread and wine into the actual body and blood of Jesus to be consumed by authorised followers. The application is that those unauthorised, i.e. non-baptised Catholics, are excluded from the Mass.[58]

Protestants usually read this as metaphorical.[59] As a result, they seek further meaning, to unpack the metaphor as taught by Paul in 1 Corinthians 5:7 and Peter in 1 Peter 1:19, i.e. that Jesus was calling us all to partake of His imminent sacrificial death in the same way that every Jew was required to partake of the Passover lamb (Num 9:13). His death was also symbolised in another Jewish metaphor: blood is a symbol of life (Lev 17:11). His blood poured out therefore symbolises His life poured out, to be received by all of His disciples.

The application? If we have asked and received the Spirit of Jesus into the core of our beings, we have eternal life; if we have not asked and received Him, we do not have eternal life – we are simply not His (Rom 8:9). He explained further:

> "For My flesh is true food, and My blood is true drink... This is the bread which came down out of heaven; not as the fathers ate and died; he who eats this bread will live forever." (John 6:55 and 58)

---

[58] *The Seven Sacraments: The Foundation of Christian Living*, High School Edition, Sophia Institute for Teachers, 2014, p. 59.

[59] One notable exception was Martin Luther, leader of the German Reformation, who rejected trans-substantiation but taught sacramental union in which he still upheld the literal or Real Presence. He broke fellowship with Zwingli, leader of the Swiss Reformation, over this.

Our daily life-sustaining food and drink is, like the manna in the wilderness, transitory but His sacrifice will sustain us for eternity, if we will accept Him.

We see then that the literal reading leads to an odd outcome or dead-end while the metaphorical reading is a doorway to more profound teaching, provided the metaphor is correctly unpacked.[60]

Most of the Scriptures are not hard to read. Even children understand and love the stories, incidents and narratives. However, apocalyptic passages are by definition 'dark sayings' (Ps 78:2), allegories that have to be interpreted, and there is simply no other option than to consider at every step whether what we are reading is to be taken literally, metaphorically, or both.

And, as N. T. Wright points out, we must not...:

> ...dismiss apocalyptic language as 'merely metaphorical'. Metaphors have teeth... the complex metaphors available to first century Jews had particularly sharp ones...[61]

It is my conviction that we, the church of God, have failed to unpack some of these metaphors carefully enough.

Negotiating a Maze

As I see it, reading these passages is like entering a maze. Confronted by a wall, we have to decide whether to turn to the left or to the right, literal or metaphorical. While both ways are initially possible, if we turn left and walk on only to reach a dead-end, the only way forward is to actually retrace

---

60 This is also graphically illustrated by 1 Corinthians 11:2-16 where the Jewish metaphor of 'head' meaning both headship and autonomy has been so confused by a literal reading that some insist women must wear hats and veils while others redefine the passage as Paul's cultural baggage. Addressed in my book *Because of the Angels (Unveiling 1 Corinthians 11:2-16)*.

61 N.T. Wright, *Jesus and the Victory of God (Christian Origins and the Question of God*, Vol. 2), p. 321.

our steps and then turn right. Many, however, unwilling to admit their wrong turn, sit down and refuse to budge; others climb over the wall which takes them completely off the path into strange new doctrines.

Popularity is no help either. Consider the dead-ends and odd outcomes of the two most popular views of Revelation 12 where the woman giving birth to a son is being threatened by a seven-headed dragon.

Most Christians agree that the child is Jesus, but disagree about the identity of the woman. The Roman Catholics (1.2 billion adherents) officially choose the literal reading: the woman is Mary. Her crown of twelve stars, they believe, means she is Queen of the Angels.[62] Pope Pius XII (r. 1939-1958) added that she is the 'new Eve' who 'reigns over the entire world' and should be constantly invoked as 'the Mediatrix of peace'.[63] However, if we ask when she was given eagles' wings to fly into the wilderness to hide for three and a half years (Rev 12:6 and 14), there are no Biblical answers. This interpretation is a dead-end in the maze and created erroneous doctrines.

The second most popular view, held by most Protestants, chooses the metaphorical reading, ignores most of the woman's identifying features, and holds she is the faithful remnant of Israel who became the church. Some then choose a literal reading of the three and a half years and assume it was fulfilled in the 1st Century when the woman, now Christians, fled to a literal wilderness in Jordan, to 'a town in Perea called Pella',[64] on metaphorical wings; others believe that this escape

---

[62] This belief gave us in 1781 the name of one the most famous cities in the world, Los Angeles. Its Spanish name, *El Pueblo de Nuestra Senora la Reina de Los Angeles*, translates as The Town of Our Lady, the Queen of the Angels. See *DDJ*, pp. 8-11.

[63] http://w2.vatican.va/content/pius-xii/en/encyclicals/documents/hf_p-xii_enc_11101954_ad-caeli-reginam.html, accessed 27 Jan, 2017. Cf. 'For there is one God, and one mediator also between God and men, the man Christ Jesus' (1 Tim 2:5).

[64] Recorded by Eusebius in the 4th Century (Book III, 5:3).

by Christians on metaphorical wings is yet to happen at the Rapture, when she will escape from the literal Antichrist literally sitting in either a rebuilt literal temple in a literal Old Jerusalem or metaphorically sitting in a metaphorical temple in a metaphorical New Jerusalem, meaning the Church.

As I see it, it is far simpler and consistent to unpack the Jewish metaphors more carefully, as we did in Book 1, *Dancing in the Dragon's Jaws*. I established there that:

(i) The woman is metaphorical and all of her identifying features as foretold by Joseph's dream (Gen 37:9-11) reveal she is the nation of Israel 'according to the flesh' (Rom 9:3), called to give birth to Messiah 'according to the flesh' (Rom 9:5).

(ii) The dragon has seven heads because, throughout the woman's previous 2,000 year history, Satan was trying to prevent the birth of Messiah using six great Gentile empires, five of which had fallen,[65] the sixth, Rome, was still in power in John's day, and the seventh had 'not yet come' (Rev 17:10).

(iii) She successfully gave birth but, tragically, in 30 AD she rejected Jesus as Messiah so she was exiled to a metaphorical "wilderness of the peoples" (Ezek 20:35), echoing her original exile for disobedience in the Arabian wilderness in the 15th Century BC.

(iv) This exile's metaphorical time period, "the times of the Gentiles", was because she was literally "led captive into all the nations" (Luke 21:24). It was on metaphorical eagle's wings to reveal it was God in His sovereignty over the nations doing again what He did at the Exodus (Ex 19:4).

(v) He metaphorically 'nourished' her in the "wilderness

---

65 Egypt, Assyria, Babylon, Medo-Persia, and Greece.

of the peoples", hence her miraculous survival over the last 2,000 years, until it was time for her to be restored to her literal land again, the land of Israel. We see today the people of Israel 'according to the flesh' restored to the land of Israel.

Using Our Recovered Keys

This is where an interpretative key we found in Revelation 12 can help us unlock this mystery in Revelation 11. We will also see that the most satisfying explanation lies in navigating more carefully between the extremes of completely literal and completely metaphorical interpretations.

Beginning again in verse 3:

> 3. "And I will grant authority to My two witnesses, and they will prophesy for twelve hundred and sixty days, clothed in sackcloth."

We established in Book 1[66] from the mysteries of Elijah, the times of the Gentiles and the partial hardening of Israel that this mysterious time period of 'twelve hundred and sixty days' is not literal but a metaphor that refers to the last two thousand years.

This necessarily rules out the two witnesses being human beings, whether Enoch, Moses, Elijah or two future unnamed prophets 'who minister in the power and character of Moses and Elijah', since none of them has been alive and prophesying for the last two thousand years.

How then are we to understand these two as metaphorical witnesses? By doing what we did in the first three books in this series – by following their unique identifying features or characteristics back to their source in the Hebrew Bible, or what Christians call the Old Testament.

In what follows, I will often be referring to it as the Hebrew

---

[66] *DDJ*, pp. 94-126.

Bible rather than as the Old Testament because, firstly, the Jews not only collate the books into 24, rather than our 39,[67] but also into different order – their last book is Chronicles, instead of our Malachi. They call the whole collection the Tanakh, an acronym drawn from its three divisions: TaNaKh means the Torah (Law), Nevi'im (Prophets) and Ketuvim (Holy Writings). It will become apparent later why this matters.

Secondly, I want to emphasise that the text testifying to the Jewish people is their own Hebrew Bible, in whatever format they present it.

Identifying Features

The two witnesses have four similarities to Moses and Elijah and no other Old Testament figure, which I believe again rules out Enoch.

1. Fire devouring their enemies

> 5. And if anyone wants to harm them, fire flows out of their mouth and devours their enemies; so if anyone wants to harm them, he must be killed in this way. (Rev 11:5)

As we saw in Book 2,[68] fire like this can have very different meanings in the Scriptures. It can refer to the natural phenomenon of lightning, as in 'fire ran down to earth' in a thunderstorm (Ex 9:23-24), or to the Holy Spirit, appearing as tongues of fire on the Day of Pentecost (Acts 2:1-4). In Revelation 13, it refers to a counterfeit, demonic fire, where the spirit of antichrist confers an anointing that counterfeits the Holy Spirit.

Throughout ancient Israel's history, God communicated by

---

67 The twelve books of the Minor Prophets, for example, are in one called 'The Book of the Twelve'; the two books of Samuel are joined into one, as are the two books of Kings and of Chronicles, and Ezra is joined to Nehemiah.
68 *STB*, pp. 80-83.

fire to confirm His acceptance and blessing: when Moses and Aaron offered the Law's first offerings (Lev 9:23-24); Gideon saw it (Judg 6:21) as did David (1 Chron 21:26); when Solomon dedicated the Temple in Jerusalem (2 Chron 7:1-3). Daniel saw its source as the throne of the Ancient of Days: "a river of fire…flowing and coming out from before Him" (Dan 7:10). Elijah called down this fire to prove the LORD and not Baal was the true God, even pouring three lots of water over the wood of his burnt offering to show it was not natural fire (1 Kings 18:21-39).

Fire can also be God's judgment, as on Sodom and Gomorrah (Gen 19:24), and Jesus named James and John "Sons of Thunder" (Mark 3:17) because they wanted to call down fire on some opponents (Luke 9:54). Here in Revelation 11, the fire is God's judgement on those opposing the two witnesses.

It also helps us to identify them: only with Moses and Elijah did fire devour their opponents. God judged two hundred and fifty leaders for opposing Moses (Num 16:35) and two troops of soldiers for mocking Elijah (2 Kings 1:9-16). Moses and Elijah are therefore the only precedents for, and yet not a perfect match with, John's two witnesses because 'fire flows *out of their mouth* and devours their enemies' (Rev 11:5).

2. Calling for drought

> 6. These have the power to shut up the sky, so that rain will not fall during the days of their prophesying… (Rev 11:6)

This power, as we saw in Book 1,[69] is the very foundation of the mystery of Elijah and has occurred for the last 2,000 years. From John the Baptist until today, the spiritual rain has been withheld from the people of Israel until they turn to Jesus.

It was also one of the curses of the Law of Moses:

---

69 *DDJ*, pp. 118-131.

> 23. "The heaven which is over your head shall be bronze, and the earth which is under you, iron.
> 24. "The LORD will make the rain of your land powder and dust; from heaven it shall come down on you until you are destroyed." (Deut 28:23-24)

In all of Israel's history, only the Law of Moses and Elijah the prophet (1 Kin 17:1) could 'shut up the sky' (Rev 11:6).

3. Cursing[70]

> 6. ...and they have power over the waters to turn them into blood, and to strike the earth with every plague, as often as they desire (Rev 11:6)

This godly 'power over the waters to turn them into blood' was unique to Moses (Ex 7:17-21) but Pharaoh's ungodly magicians 'did the same with their secret arts' (Ex 7:22). In other words, as we saw in Books 1 and 2, the dragon and the beasts have supernatural power so these magicians could reproduce Moses' first two signs: turning water into blood, and the frogs.[71] Moses pressed on with the plagues until the Egyptian magicians ran out of power (Ex 8:18-19), finishing with the tenth, the death of Egypt's first-born.

Elijah did not turn water into blood or call for any curse other than drought and fire consuming his enemies. However, Elisha his successor was granted 'a double portion of (Elijah's) spirit' (2 Kin 2:9-10) and prophesied a miraculous provision of water that looked like blood in the red dawn light (2 Kin 3:16-24). He also cursed young men who mocked him (2 Kin 2:24), cursed his servant Gehazi with Naaman's leprosy (2 Kin 5:27), temporarily blinded an army (2 Kin 6:18-20), and prophesied a seven-year famine (2 Kin 8:1), the death of

---

70 Today 'cursing' usually means using offensive or blasphemous words but in Biblical days, it was invoking supernatural punishment.
71 We will see the significance of this in Book 5, *Kingdom Come*, when we come to the frog plague of Revelation 16:13.

Ahab and Jezebel (2 Kin 9:1-10), and of a royal official (2 Kin 7:19-20). No prophet of Israel cursed more.[72] All of this was done with a double portion of Elijah's spirit.

There is, however, a slight dissimilarity with the two witnesses because they 'strike the earth with every plague, as often as they desire'. (v. 6).

4. Their end

Another identifying characteristic of John's two witnesses is the mysterious end to their work:

> 7. When they have finished their testimony, the beast that comes up out of the abyss will make war with them, and overcome them and kill them…
> 11. But after the three and a half days, the breath of life from God came into them, and they stood on their feet; and great fear fell upon those who were watching them.
> 12. And they heard a loud voice from heaven saying to them, "Come up here." Then they went up into heaven in the cloud, and their enemies watched them. (Rev 11:7-12)

This is the only point at which Enoch is similar to these witnesses:

> Enoch walked with God; and he was not, for God took him. (Gen 5:24)

Moses and Elijah also finished their work in mysterious circumstances. Like these two witnesses, Elijah 'went up into heaven' but in a whirlwind and accompanied by horses and chariots of fire:

---

[72] Elisha also blessed more than anyone else. He miraculously purified the water of Jericho (2 Kin 2:19-22), multiplied oil for a widow (2 Kin 4:1-7), healed a barren woman, then raised her son from the dead (2 Kin 4:13-37), removed poison from food (2 Kin 4:38-44), healed the leprous Naaman the Syrian (2 Kin 5:10-14), miraculously raised a lost axe-head from a river (2 Kin 6:5-6), enabled his servant to see the armies of God (2 Kin 6:17) and predicted the end of a famine (2 Kin 7:1-19). Even his dead bones raised a man from the dead (2 Kin 13:20-21).

> 11. As they were going along and talking, behold, there appeared a chariot of fire and horses of fire which separated the two of them. And Elijah went up by a whirlwind to heaven. (2 Kin 2:11-12)

Moses was personally buried by the Angel of the Lord:

> And He buried him in the valley in the land of Moab, opposite Beth-peor; but no man knows his burial place to this day. Although Moses was one hundred and twenty years old when he died, his eye was not dim, nor his vigor abated. (Deut 34:6-7)

No other prophet or prophetess of ancient Israel received such treatment at the end of their service on earth and in John's vision, the two witnesses are also taken up by God (v. 12).

The conclusion? From these four identifying features, we are clearly supposed to identify the two witnesses not with Enoch, not with the church, but with Moses and Elijah and yet not quite. We need to keep digging.

Why Moses and Elijah Together?

These two remarkable men were separated in time by some seven hundred years, so why would they reappear together now? They are linked in six instances in Jewish history.

1. Both were named as essential to the future of Israel in the last prophecy of the Hebrew Bible[73]

God's final, authoritative prophecy as accepted by ancient Israel was given by Malachi in about 410 BC:

> 4. "Remember the law of Moses My servant, even the statutes and ordinances which I commanded him in Horeb for all Israel.
> 5. "Behold, I am going to send you Elijah the prophet before the coming of the great and terrible day of the LORD." (Mal 4:4-5)

"The great and terrible day of the LORD" is Judgement Day,

---

[73] The last book in the Tanakh is Chronicles but Malachi is the last recognised prophet.

when God will judge all the sins of all mankind of all time, and Elijah has a work to do beforehand, as we considered in Book 1.[74] Accordingly, all in Israel were to be faithful to Moses and to keep looking for Elijah.

This is why in New Testament times they were looking for the coming of Elijah as much as for the coming of Messiah, some thinking Jesus was Elijah (Mark 6:15). Others thought John the Baptist was, because he was dressed like him (2 Kin 1:8, Matt 3:4) and baptising in the Jordan where Elijah was last seen.

However, as we also saw in Book 1,[75] 'the great and terrible day of the LORD' has two fulfilments. The first was the crucifixion when Jesus was judged as if He had committed all the sins of all mankind throughout all time; the second will be Judgement Day for all those who do not accept His sacrificial death for them. John the Baptist fulfilled one metaphorical coming of Elijah but Jesus said that there was to be another (Matt 17:11-13).

2. Both had particularly miraculous ministries

Moses performed miracles before Israel's elders (Ex 4:1-9) and Egypt's Pharaoh (Ex 7:8-10), followed by ten plagues (Ex 7:17-11:10). He parted the sea (Ex 14:21-22), fed the people with meat and manna in the wilderness (Ex 16:11-15), healed Miriam's leprosy (Num 12:13-15), and produced water in the desert (Ex 17:6, Num 20:2-11).

Elijah confronted Ahab and Jezebel with a controlled three and a half year drought (1 Kin 17:1, Luke 4:25), parted the Jordan River (2 Kin 2:8), fed the widow and her son with undiminishing flour and oil (1 Kin 17:14), raised the child from the dead (1 Kin 17:21-22), and called down fire from heaven (1 Kin 18:36-38). Elisha did similarly spectacular

---

74 *DDJ*, pp. 136-147.
75 Ibid., pp. 128-129.

deeds, parting the Jordan (2 Kin 2:14), multiplying a widow's oil (2 Kin 4:3-6), raising the dead (2 Kin 4:32-37, 13:20-21), and healing Naaman's leprosy (2 Kin 5:14) but only because he received Elijah's mantle and a double-portion of his spirit (2 Kin 2:9-15).[76]

No other prophet came close to Moses and Elijah for miraculous powers until Jesus came.

3. Both ascended Mt Horeb on a forty-day fast

Moses was a shepherd in the Arabian desert when God called him at Mt Horeb (Ex 3:1), which is also known as Mt Sinai.[77] He then led Israel out of Egypt back to Horeb where he received the covenant (Ex 19:20) during two forty-day fasts (Ex 24:18, 34:28).

Elijah went to Mt Horeb on a forty-day fast (1 Kin 19:8) because Israel had forsaken the covenant (1 Kin 19:10, 19:14).

They therefore have a unique bond with Jesus in His forty-day fast (Matt 4:2).

4. Both were vindicated by heavenly fire

Moses and Elijah also have a unique typological bond with the Holy Spirit, foreshadowed by fire from heaven.

Moses received the Law on the Day of Pentecost (Ex 19:1,

---

76 For the typological significance, see *DDJ*, pp. 127-138.
77 The traditional location of Mt Sinai, as sanctified in about 325 AD by Helena, mother of the emperor Constantine, is very unlikely. Many scholars now agree with Charles A. Whittaker's conclusion in *The Biblical Significance of Jabal Al Lawz* that it is in Northern Arabia. Dr. Frank Moore Cross, Emeritus Professor of Hebrew at Harvard University, wrote: 'The archaic hymns of Israel are of one voice: Yahweh came from Teman, Mt Paran, Midian and Cushan (the song of Habakkuk); the song of Deborah sings of Yahweh going from Seir, marching forth from Edom; the Blessing of Moses states that Yahweh came from Sinai, beamed forth from Seir, shone from Mount Paran. These geographical designations cannot be moved west into the peninsula now called Sinai'. *From Epic to Canon: History and Literature in Ancient Israel*, Baltimore; John Hopkins University Press, 1998, p. 66.

19:11),[78] celebrated by the Jews as Hag Matan Torateinu (the Festival of the Giving of Our Torah) and also as Shavu'ot (the Festival of Weeks).[79] On that day, God appeared to all Israel, descending 'in fire' (Ex 19:18) and they trusted in Moses as His prophet (Ex 20:18-19). For Christians, this day is synonymous with the giving or descent of the Holy Spirit with 'tongues of fire' on the newly restored Twelve (Acts 1:21-26) and all who believed (Acts 2:1-4). Many thousands then trusted in Jesus as Messiah (Acts 2:41).

Elijah prayed for the fire to fall on an altar made of twelve stones (representing the tribes of the twelve sons of Jacob/Israel and foreshadowing the twelve apostles) and a sacrifice doused with twelve pitchers of water (1 Kin 18:31-38). This descent of fire caused Israel to trust again in the Lord as their God and Elijah as His prophet (1 Kin 18:39).

5. Both finished their earthly ministries supernaturally, across the Jordan from Jericho

In 2013, I stood on Mt Nebo, 'the top of Pisgah, which is opposite Jericho' (Deut 34:1) where Moses was given his last glimpse of the land, and I was struck by this remarkable convergence: Moses died and was buried east of the Jordan opposite Jericho (Deut 34:6); Elijah came from Jericho and crossed the Jordan to also disappear from there (2 Kin 2:4-15).

Five hundred years later, Jesus came there too. John was baptising in the Jordan near Jerusalem when Jesus came to be baptised (Matt 3:5-6, 13; John 1:28), to begin His work where Moses and Elijah had left off.

---

78 Pentecost is from the Greek for 50, the festival being the day after seven weeks are measured from the Day of First Fruits, the day after Passover (Lev 23:15-16). Accordingly, it is also known as the Festival of Weeks.

79 www.jewfaq.org/holidayc.htm, 8 Sept, 2015. Also Ian Robinson, *If Anyone Thirsts: Biblical Spirituality from the Desert*, Eugene, OR; Wipf and Stock Publishers, 2016, pp. 107-108.

Figure 2 — Map showing locality today

6. Both met with Jesus on the earth.

Moses finally reached the Promised Land, and Elijah came back over the Jordan:

> 1. Six days later Jesus took with Him Peter and James and John his brother, and led them up on a high mountain by themselves.
> 2. And He was transfigured before them; and His face shone like the sun, and His garments became as white as light.
> 3. And behold, Moses and Elijah appeared to them, talking with Him. (Matt 17:1-3)

It was not Abraham, Melchizedek, Deborah, Isaiah, Jeremiah, Ezekiel or Daniel. It was not even Elisha, who did twice the miracles of Elijah.

Luke adds that:

> ...Moses and Elijah, who, appearing in glory, were speaking of His departure [Gk, *exodos*] which He was about to accomplish at Jerusalem. (Luke 9:30-31)

After one and a half thousand years, Moses is alive and 'appearing in glory', along with Elijah who is likewise reappearing after five hundred years, to talk with Jesus who is being revealed in His glory as Messiah. And what were they discussing? The end of His work and 'His departure' or exodus from the earth.

They have a unique bond with Jesus and His work.

However, while Moses and Elijah have so many similarities to John's two witnesses, they are not exactly like them. We have more to do to understand the allusions.

Summary of the Witnesses (Rev 11:3, 5-6)

This vision can only be understood if we use the key recovered in Book 1:

(i) The two witnesses testify for 1,260 days which we established is a metaphor for "the times of the Gentiles", i.e. the last 2,000 years. This rules out the witnesses being mortal men; they must be metaphorical or symbolic of something else.

(ii) The witnesses' four identifying features are miracles unique to Moses (15th Century BC) and Elijah (9th Century BC) but with minor differences: whereas Moses and Elijah were vindicated in their day by fire from heaven, in John's vision, the fire comes from their mouth; the two witnesses can also strike more frequently, with "every plague, as often as they desire" (Rev 11:6).

(iii) Moses and Elijah also have a unique bond in Israel's history in six ways: they were both named as essential to Israel's future in the last prophecy of the Hebrew Bible; they both had particularly miraculous powers; they both went to Mt Sinai/Horeb on a forty day fast; they were both instrumental in God's manifesting as fire to Israel, prefiguring the coming of the Holy Spirit; they both finished their earthly ministries supernaturally, even at the same place – across the Jordan from Jericho; they were both present when Jesus was transfigured on the mount.

(iv) John's two witnesses are very similar to but not exactly like Moses and Elijah, i.e. they plainly allude to them, but, as we will see, there is yet more unpacking of the metaphor.

3
Olive Trees and Lampstands
Endless Light

John describes the two witnesses as:

> ...the two olive trees and the two lampstands that stand before the Lord of the earth. (Rev 11:4)

These two metaphors may seem odd to us today but were very familiar to John's 1st Century Jewish listeners because both images were used by Zechariah:

> 1. Then the angel who was speaking with me returned and roused me, as a man who is awakened from his sleep.
> 2. He said to me, "What do you see?" And I said, "I see, and behold, *a lampstand* all of gold with its bowl on the top of it, and its seven lamps on it with seven spouts belonging to each of the lamps which are on the top of it;
> 3. also *two olive trees* by it, one on the right side of the bowl and the other on its left side."
> 4. Then I said to the angel who was speaking with me saying, "What are these, my lord?"
> 5. So the angel who was speaking with me answered and said to me, "Do you not know what these are?" And I said, "No, my lord." (Zech 4:1-5, emphasis added)

Zechariah sees a single lampstand and two olive trees and asks what they are (v. 4). However, instead of answering his question, in vv. 6-10 the angel tells him about a stone with seven eyes that he has just been shown (Zech 3:9, which we will look at next). Zechariah, however, twice more asks about the olive trees:

> 11. Then I said to him, "What are these two olive trees on the right of the lampstand and on its left?"
> 12. And I answered the second time and said to him, "What are

> the two olive branches which are beside the two golden pipes, which empty the golden oil from themselves?" (Zech 4:11-12)

Why are these trees so interesting to Zechariah that he ignores what the angel is trying to tell him? Because they are miraculous, supplying the lampstand with olive oil without any human effort. Ancient Israel's only light source after nightfall was the oil lamp and Zechariah would have seen many before but fuelling them was a long and drawn out process. Oil had to first be extracted from the fruit, which required tending, harvesting, pressing, purifying and storing, and then lamps had to be continually replenished. These wonderful olive trees are doing it all and in endless supply.

He is so focussed on the trees that he ignores the lampstand and the stone.

Finally, after his third time of asking, the angel questions him:

> 13. So he answered me, saying, "Do you not know what these are?" And I said, "No, my lord." (Zech 4:13)

The angel has been avoiding Zechariah's question but now at last he answers it:

> 14. Then he said, "These are the two anointed ones who are standing by the Lord of the whole earth." (Zech 4:14)

"Anointed ones" (literally, 'sons of oil') was a generic term for those confirmed in their role as priests (Ex 40:13-15), kings (1 Sam 10:1, 2 Kin 9:3) or prophets (1 Kin 19:16) by having oil poured over their heads. Psalm 133 describes how this was done.

This raises at least three more questions to me: the olive trees symbolise two men but who? Why was the angel so reluctant to answer Zechariah? And how does this vision relate to John's two lampstands and two olive trees?

For answers, we have to read Zechariah 3, setting aside Revelation 11 for the rest of this chapter to understand

Zechariah's olive trees and lampstand and, in particular, how they relate to the stone with seven eyes.

"Behold, the Stone"

Zechariah's vision of the lampstand and the olive trees is the fifth in a series of eight which are worth every effort to understand because they provide the basis for a number of images in the Book of Revelation as well as for events in Jesus' life and for His second coming.[80] For our purposes here, we will look only at the fourth and fifth (Zechariah 3 and 4) as well as the prophetic coronation in Zechariah 6:9-15.[81]

The two men featured are Joshua the high priest and Zerubbabel the governor[82] who were, in 520 BC, jointly leading the community of those who had returned from the Babylonian exile. Some therefore presume they must be the two olive trees[83] but, as we will see, it is not that easy.

Immediately prior to seeing the lampstand and the olive trees, Zechariah sees Joshua being re-consecrated as high priest (Zech 3:1-7) and is then commanded:

> 9. "For *behold, the stone* that I have set before Joshua; on one stone are *seven eyes*. Behold, I will engrave an inscription on it," declares the LORD of hosts, "and I will remove the iniquity of that land in one day." (Zech 3:9, emphasis added)

---

80 These were all received in 519 BC (Zech 1:7). Mark J. Boda, *The Book of Zechariah: The New International Commentary of the Old Testament*, Grand Rapids, Michigan/Cambridge, U.K; William B. Eerdmans Publishing, 2016, pp. 107-108.
81 The eight night visions (Zech 1:7-6:8) include images later repeated in John's Revelation including a scroll, a woman worshipped in Babylon and four chariots with different coloured horses. Zechariah also received a series of spectacular prophecies for both comings of Messiah (Zech 9:1-14:21).
82 A descendant of David, he and Joshua had been called by Haggai to rebuild the Temple (Hag 1:1-8). Zechariah is confirming this call.
83 For example, *The New Oxford Annotated Bible*, p. 1360 Hebrew Bible.

Surprisingly, Zechariah does not behold the stone with seven eyes,[84] focussing instead on the olive trees. The angel, however, ignores his questions about the trees and prophesies about the stone because it is to complete the Temple:

> 6. Then he said to me, "This is the word of the LORD to Zerubbabel saying, 'Not by might nor by power, but by My Spirit,' says the LORD of hosts.
> 7. 'What are you, O great mountain? Before Zerubbabel you will become a plain; and he will bring forth *the top stone* with shouts of "Grace, grace to it!"'" (Zech 4:6-7, emphasis added)

Zechariah was to listen to "the word of the LORD to Zerubbabel" (v. 6) and to tell Zerubbabel: this "top stone" set before Joshua as priest signifies that Zerubbabel as governor will succeed in rebuilding the Temple. Their joint leadership is confirmed, and God is pleased with their work:

> 8. Also the word of the LORD came to me, saying,
> 9. "The hands of Zerubbabel have laid the foundation of this house, and his hands will finish it. Then you will know that the LORD of hosts has sent me to you.
> 10. "For who has despised the day of small things? But *these seven* will be glad when they see the plumb line in the hand of Zerubbabel – these are the *eyes of the LORD* which range to and fro throughout the earth." (Zech 4:8-10, emphasis added)

Why did the angel ignore Zechariah's questions? Because the stone is vastly more important than the two olive trees. This is a seeing, living stone. Its 'seven eyes' (Zech 3:9) are 'glad' even in 'the day of small things' because 'these are the eyes of the LORD' (Zech 4:10).

They are the same seven eyes that John saw on the Lamb with seven horns:

---

[84] *The New Oxford Annotated Bible* (*NRSV*) translates this phrase as 'a single stone with seven facets' (which the *NIV* offers in its margin as an alternative), commenting this was 'perhaps an element in the priestly garb', p. 1360, Hebrew Bible. This is very unlikely, as will become evident.

> And I saw… a Lamb standing, as if slain, having seven horns and seven eyes… (Rev 5:6)

We will look soon at the meaning of the seven horns and seven eyes. For now, let us be clear that the stone is unmistakably predicting Messiah and that God will 'remove the iniquity of that land in one day' (Zech 3:9).

The Stone and the Branch

Closely connected to the metaphor of the Stone is another Messianic metaphor, the Branch:

> 8. "Now listen, Joshua the high priest, you and your friends who are sitting in front of you – indeed they are men who are a symbol, for *behold*, I am going to bring in *My servant the Branch*.
> 9. "For *behold, the stone* that I have set before Joshua; on one stone are *seven eyes*. Behold, I will engrave an inscription on it," declares the LORD of hosts, "and I will remove the iniquity of that land in one day." (Zech 3:8-9, emphasis added)

"My servant the Branch" (v. 8) being Messiah was not a new idea in Jewish history. Several hundred years earlier, Isaiah had prophesied in similar terms of Messiah coming after the exile:

> 1. Then a shoot will spring from the stem of Jesse [i.e. David's dynasty]
> And *a branch* from his roots will bear fruit.
> 2. The Spirit of the LORD will rest on Him… (Isa 11:1-4, emphasis added)

Likewise Jeremiah:

> 5. "Behold, the days are coming," declares the LORD,
> "When I will raise up for David *a righteous Branch*;
> And He will reign as king and act wisely
> And do justice and righteousness in the land…" (Jer 23:5, emphasis added)
>
> 14. "Behold, days are coming," declares the LORD, "when I will fulfill the good word which I have spoken concerning the

house of Israel and the house of Judah.
15. "In those days and at that time I will cause *a righteous Branch of David* to spring forth; and He shall execute justice and righteousness on the earth." (Jer 33:14-15, emphasis added)

Zechariah well knew that Jeremiah's prediction of seventy years in exile was being completed (Zech 1:12, 7:5) so he should have been expecting "My servant the Branch" (Zech 3:8). He also should have been alert to the Messianic nature of the seven-eyed stone he had just been commanded to "behold" (Zech 3:9) but he was initially distracted by the two miraculous olive trees.

Almost six hundred years later, Peter knew the true value of the stone:

And coming to Him [Jesus] as to a *living stone* which has been rejected by men, but is choice and precious in the sight of God... (1 Pet 2:4, emphasis added)

Easy for him to see in hindsight but Peter had made the same mistake as Zechariah – he had been so over-awed by Moses and Elijah appearing on the mountain that he had not seen how vastly more significant Jesus is as the Son of God (Matt 17:2-5).

Zechariah should also have known[85] Isaiah's prophecy, given and treasured amongst the Jews almost two hundred years earlier, which spoke of Messiah as a stone, the cornerstone in the foundation that determines the placing of every other stone:

16. Therefore thus says the Lord GOD,
"Behold, I am laying in Zion a stone, a tested stone,
A costly cornerstone for the foundation, firmly placed.
He who believes in it will not be disturbed.
17. "I will make justice the measuring line
And righteousness the level..." (Isa 28:16-17)

Likewise, Psalm 118:[86]

---

85 He was a priest and called to teach (Mal 2:7).
86 It is unknown when this psalm was written but at the very latest, if

> 22. The stone which the builders rejected has become the chief corner stone.
> 23. This is the LORD's doing; it is marvellous in our eyes.
> (Psa 118:22-23)

Jesus taught He was fulfilling Psalm 118 (Matt 21:42, Mark 12:10-11, Luke 20:17); Peter quoted both Isaiah 28 and Psalm 118 (1 Pet 2:6-7, Acts 4:11), as did Paul (Rom 9:33, Eph 2:20-21).

What then was Zechariah supposed to understand in 519 BC?

The issue being addressed in this vision was that the exiles, Zechariah included, had been despising the day of small things, weeping over the puniness of the Temple they were rebuilding. The angel therefore was explaining to Zechariah that the seven-eyed stone is 'the top stone' (Zech 4:7) of the Temple, its crowning glory, and prefigures Messiah's coming.

"Not by Might, Nor by Power…"

How then was Zechariah's Temple prophecy fulfilled and how is it relevant to the two olive trees?

Zechariah was to encourage Zerubbabel to complete the rebuilding:

> "The hands of Zerubbabel have laid the foundation of this house, and his hands will finish it. Then you will know that the LORD of hosts has sent me to you." (Zech 4:9)

He had "laid the foundation of this house" in 537 BC[87] but in 530 BC, all work had ceased due to fierce opposition. Now in 519 BC,[88] Zerubbabel was being encouraged to finish it:

---

post-exilic, it would have been written in Zechariah's time.
87 Ezra 3:8-11, 5:16. F. Charles Fensham, *The Books of Ezra and Nehemiah: The New International Commentary of the Old Testament*, Grand Rapids; William B Eerdmans Publishing, 1982, p. 61.
88 Zechariah 1:7. Mark J. Boda, *The Book of Zechariah: The New International Commentary of the Old Testament*, Grand Rapids, MI/ Cambridge, U.K; William B. Eerdmans Publishing, 2016, p. 64.

> 6. Then he said to me, "This is the word of the LORD to Zerubbabel saying, 'Not by might nor by power, but by My Spirit,' says the LORD of hosts.
> 7. 'What are you, O great mountain? Before Zerubbabel you will become a plain; and he will bring forth *the top stone* with shouts of "Grace, grace to it!"'" (Zech 4:6-7, emphasis added)

To the depleted returnees from Babylon, these difficulties must have seemed insurmountable, as immovable as mountains, but God can do the impossible. Job argues that God "removes the mountains" (Job 9:5) and Jesus assures us similarly:

> "... truly I say to you, if you have faith the size of a mustard seed, you will say to this mountain, 'Move from here to there,' and it will move; and nothing will be impossible to you". (Matt 17:20)

The returnees' "great mountain" would "become a plain". Although Zerubbabel had none of the resources of David and Solomon's royal 'might and power' in building the First Temple, God was assuring him he had the Spirit of God (Zech 4:6) so he would succeed, which he did in 516 BC.[89]

What then was the point of the lampstand and the two olive trees?

We will consider the lampstand soon but the two olive trees symbolised the endless supply of oil, the Spirit of God, which God would give Zerubbabel to overcome all obstacles, no matter how large. He was also to know that God was pleased with him, that the 'seven eyes' of Messiah were 'glad' when they saw him picking up the tools of rebuilding (Zech 4:10). Who then were the olive trees?

Joshua and Zerubbabel?

Zechariah was then commanded to act on the visions regarding Joshua and Zerubbabel by making a crown for Joshua to demonstrate how Joshua in his priesthood and Zerubbabel

---

[89] Ezra 6:14-16. F. Charles Fensham, 1982, p. 92.

as the governor of the rebuilding are together foreshadowing Messiah:

> 11. "Take silver and gold, make an ornate crown and set it on the head of Joshua the son of Jehozadak, the high priest.
> 12. "Then say to him, 'Thus says the LORD of hosts, "Behold, a man whose name is Branch, for He will branch out from where He is; and He will build the temple of the LORD.
> 13. "Yes, it is He who will build the temple of the LORD, and He who will bear the honor and sit and rule on His throne. Thus, He will be a priest on His throne, and the counsel of peace will be between the two offices."'" (Zech 6:11-13)

"The two offices" (v. 13) are king and priest. Joshua and Zerubbabel would be successful in building and ministering in this temple but together they symbolise the Branch who will build another, future temple (vv. 12-13).

Five hundred and fifty years later, Jesus explained that what validated Him as Messiah was His ability to rise from the dead to build this temple. He had been challenged after He had cleansed the Second Temple:

> 18. The Jews then said to Him, "What sign do You show us as your authority for doing these things?"
> 19. Jesus answered them, "Destroy this temple, and in three days I will raise it up."
> 20. The Jews then said, "It took forty-six years to build this temple, and will You raise it up in three days?"
> 21. But He was speaking of the temple of His body.
> 22. So when He was raised from the dead, His disciples remembered that He said this; and they believed the Scripture and the word which Jesus had spoken. (John 2:18-22)

Rising from the dead would not only vindicate Him as Messiah but also begin His building of 'a spiritual house' made of 'living stones' (1 Pet 2:4-8). This then brings us back to John's vision of a new temple, altar, and worshippers in Revelation 11.

So were Joshua and Zerubbabel the two olive trees, as some teach? For example, in the New Oxford Annotated Bible:

> The *two olive trees* likely represent Joshua and Zerubbabel. The idea of shared leadership between a priest and royal figure [is] fundamental to Haggai and Zechariah…[90]
>
> Haggai hoped that Zerubbabel would fulfill hopes for a restored Davidic messiah… Though the Temple was rebuilt and became the foundation of the Judean restoration, Zerubbabel disappears from the scene; his fate is unknown.[91]

However, although Zerubbabel was a grandson of the last anointed king of Judah, Jeconiah (1 Chron 3:16-17, Ezra 3:2), he was never anointed as king, being appointed only as governor.[92] Zechariah's crown was not placed on Zerubbabel but on Joshua the high priest. He also did not quite 'disappear from the scene' – he reappears in Matthew 1:12-13, in the genealogy of Joseph, Jesus' stepfather.

As we can see above, their two roles were not as the trees but instead to foreshadow the Stone with the seven eyes, the Messiah who is both High Priest and Temple Builder.

Haggai and Zechariah?

Others teach that the two olive trees must be Haggai and Zechariah. They base this on Ezra's summary of Israel's restoration from Babylon:

> And the elders of the Jews were successful in building through the *prophesying of Haggai the prophet and Zechariah* the son of Iddo. And they finished building according to the command of the God of Israel and the decree of Cyrus, Darius, and Artaxerxes king of Persia. (Ezra 6:14, emphasis added)

---

90 *The New Oxford Annotated Bible*, p. 1360 Hebrew Bible.
91 Ibid., p. 1356.
92 The Jews created a role, the Exilarch, to denote David's exiled descendants as kings-in-waiting but none were recognised Biblically. Geoffrey Herman, *A Prince Without a Kingdom: The Exilarch in the Sassanian Era*, Tubingen; Moir Sieback, 2012, p. 1.

These two are more likely as Ezra specifically identifies the empowerment for the task as coming 'through the prophesying [i.e. the words of the Holy Spirit] of Haggai and Zechariah'. It was the Holy Spirit who was continually fuelling the lampstand but, in order to understand who He used to do so, we need to understand Zechariah's lampstand.

The Lampstand

There is some debate over its exact shape. The lampstand in Moses' tabernacle was the famous seven-branched menorah; it is described in detail in Exodus 25:31-40. The Second Temple also had a menorah (1 Maccabees 1:21), and its shape was preserved for posterity on the Arch of Titus by the victorious Romans celebrating their loot from the sacking of Jerusalem in 70 AD, as in Figure 3.

Figure 3 — Arch of Titus, Rome. Photo by Philip Church

It is therefore possible that Zechariah's looked the same, some reading his description as meaning the seven lamps were being fuelled via seven pipes from a central bowl. However, the bowl itself is a complication:

> "I see, and behold, a lampstand all of gold *with its bowl on the top of it*, and its seven lamps on it with seven spouts belonging to each of the lamps which are on the top of it..."
> (Zech 4:2, emphasis added)

This seems to describe the seven lamps as on the rim of a central bowl, with each lamp having seven spouts, i.e. making a total of forty-nine spouts.

Figure 4 — An Israelite lampstand from c. 800 BC

John Mark Hicks is Professor of Theology at Lipscomb University in Nashville, Tennessee, and he argues that this was also the shape of the ten lampstands in Solomon's Temple, i.e. the First Temple. As evidence, he offers Figure 4 with the comment:

> Interestingly, such bowls have been found at archeological sites and always at religious sites (cf. R. North, *Biblica* 51 [1978] 183-205).[93]

---

93 http://johnmarkhicks.com/2012/02/09/zechariah-41-14-two-olive-trees-and-the-oil-of-god/, 7 Mar, 2013.

However, the menorah in Solomon's Temple were made 'in the way prescribed for them' (2 Chron 4:7) and the only prior prescription was the Tabernacle's lampstand (Ex 25:31-40).

Either way, we can be sure that Zechariah's golden lampstand, whether it was seven lamps or seven times seven spouts on seven lamps, was clearly designed to shed much light. What actually matters is the number seven because, as we established in Book 3, the repetition is to accentuate that number and seven signifies completeness or perfection.[94]

What then does all this mean?

A Lampstand Represents A Church

Zechariah did not ask about the significance of the lampstand he saw, which implies he knew, so it was not until John saw seven golden lampstands in his Revelation that we are given a definitive interpretation:

> 20. "As for the mystery of… the seven golden lampstands, …the seven lampstands are the seven churches." (Rev 1:12 & 20)

John's message was to be sent to "the seven churches that are in Asia" (Rev 1:4).[95] Today 'churches' often means buildings but the Greek word translated as 'church' is *ekklesia*:

> From a compound of *ek* [out, from] and a derivative of *kaleo* [to call]; a calling out, that is, (concretely) a popular meeting, especially a religious congregation (Jewish synagogue, or Christian community of members on earth or saints in heaven or both): – assembly, church.[96]

Accordingly, John was writing to those assembling or gathering in those seven cities to hear his message being read out (Rev 1:3). This helps us better understand Jesus' teaching:

---

94 *Gotta Serve Somebody*, pp. 146-149.
95 Ephesus, Smyrna, Pergamum, Thyatira, Sardis, Philadelphia, and Laodicea.
96 *Strong's Hebrew and Greek Dictionaries*, G1577, p. 1646.

> "Now no one after lighting a lamp covers it over with a container, or puts it under a bed; but he puts it on a lampstand, so that those who come in may see the light." (Luke 8:16. See also Matt 5:15, Mar 4:21, and Luke 11:33).

We are not given light for ourselves alone but for everyone in our assemblies or churches as well.

This also means that the lampstand Zechariah saw was the Old Testament church, the congregation or assembly of the nation of Israel. There was only one rather than seven because the remnant who had returned from Babylon had all come together to rebuild the Temple and the walls of Jerusalem.

See too Isaiah's famous prophecy regarding Israel after the Babylonian exile:

> 1. "Arise, shine; for your light has come,
> And the glory of the LORD has risen upon you.
> 2. "For behold, darkness will cover the earth
> And deep darkness the peoples;
> But the LORD will rise upon you
> And His glory will appear upon you.
> 3. "Nations will come to your light,
> And kings to the brightness of your rising." (Isa 60:1-3)

"Nations will come to your light" means that Israel was to enlighten all the Gentiles. However, the lampstand produced no light of itself but instead held up the lamps on which the oil flamed. In the same way, the nation of Israel was to live in all the ways of God so that His light, His glory, would appear upon them.

This was beautifully foreshadowed in the Tabernacle of Moses. Although the priests were to maintain and trim the lamps, Moses was told:

> "You shall charge the sons of Israel, that they bring you clear oil of beaten olives for the light, to make a lamp burn continually." (Ex 27:20)

In other words, the oil was to come from all the people of God. Accordingly, Paul taught that when Christians gather, we should all come prepared to share whatever inspiration God has given us:

> What is the outcome then, brethren? When you assemble, each one has a psalm, has a teaching, has a revelation, has a tongue, has an interpretation. Let all things be done for edification. (1 Cor 14:26)

After the destruction of Jerusalem and the Second Temple in 70 AD, the menorah was increasingly used by the exiled Jews as a symbol of the nation of Israel:

> Depictions of the menorah are found on clay oil lamps, on gold glass, on seals, on coins, on amulets and on synagogue lintels, mosaics and chancel screens. The menorah was incised on sarcophagi and was painted, carved and drawn on tomb walls. Indeed, it became the most popular symbol of Judaism in the post-Destruction period.[97]

Figure 5 — Israel's coat of arms

It is still used as such today on Israel's coat of arms where it is flanked by two olive branches, as in Figure 5.

Accordingly, in Zechariah's vision the lampstand symbolised the congregation of the nation of Israel.

---

97 Center for Online Judaic Studies article, http://cojs.org/was-there-a-seven-branched-lampstand-in-solomons-temple/, 27 Jan, 2017.

'The Seven Spirits of God'

John also gives us the interpretation of the seven lamps:

> And there were seven lamps of fire burning before the throne, which are the seven Spirits of God (Rev 4:5)

He had earlier written:

> John to the seven churches that are in Asia: grace to you and peace, from Him who is and who was and who is to come, and *from the seven Spirits* who are before His throne, and from Jesus Christ, the faithful witness, the firstborn of the dead, and the ruler of the kings of the earth. (Rev 1:4-5, emphasis added)[98]

In this Trinitarian greeting, John refers to the Holy Spirit as seven-fold. Some try to establish this as a literal number, based on the Messianic Branch prophecy of Isaiah 11:2:

> 1. Then a shoot will spring from the stem of Jesse,
> And a branch from his roots will bear fruit.
> 2. The Spirit of the LORD will rest on Him,
> The spirit of wisdom and understanding,
> The spirit of counsel and strength,
> The spirit of knowledge and the fear of the LORD.

Personally, I read 'the seven spirits of God' as metaphorical. In Book 3, we established that seven, being the number of the Sabbath, can also mean complete, finished or perfect, i.e. nothing wrong or lacking.[99] The meaning of the seven lamps, therefore, is perfect light – nothing is dark or hidden from Him:

> For to us God revealed them through the Spirit; for the Spirit searches all things, even the depths of God. (1 Cor 2:10)

Zechariah's seven lamps each having seven spouts echoes the Holy Spirit's festival, Pentecost or Weeks, which was measured out by seven weeks or Sabbaths (Lev 23:15-16).

---

98 The seven Spirits of God are also referred to in Revelation 3:1 and 5:6.
99 *GSS*, pp. 146-149.

This is why Zechariah sees not only the seven lamps but also the Stone with the seven eyes; seven eyes signify perfect vision. He then hears what the eyes are looking for:

> 10. "For who has despised the day of small things? But these seven will be glad when they see the plumb line in the hand of Zerubbabel – these are *the eyes of the LORD which range to and fro throughout the earth.*" (Zech 4:10, emphasis added)

Some five hundred years earlier, Hanani the prophet had explained this expression:

> "For the eyes of the LORD *move to and fro throughout the earth* that He may strongly support those whose heart is completely His." (2 Chron 16:9, emphasis added)

Accordingly, the angel using this expression in the 5th Century BC was to assure Zerubbabel and Joshua that God was always watching them, strongly supporting them as they rebuilt the Temple.

John's vision confirms this understanding of the seven eyes and the seven Spirits of God:

> And I saw... a Lamb standing, as if slain, having seven horns and *seven eyes*, which are the *seven Spirits of God, sent out into all the earth.* (Rev 5:6, emphasis added)

This vision adds seven horns which in ancient Jewish thinking symbolise power and strength (1 Sam 2:10) so seven horns signify perfect power and strength: Messiah died as a Lamb but He lives and reigns as the all-seeing, all-powerful One.

Returning to the two olive trees, we can see they are not Zerubbabel and Joshua but are helping Zerubbabel and Joshua. Does this make Haggai and Zechariah the two olive trees? No, and Haggai is not even mentioned in Zechariah. Even though their prophesying gave much light to the nation of Israel at that time, there were two other men whose anointing had given Israel much more light – as we will see in the next chapter, the two olive trees allude to Moses and Elijah.

We have yet to find why they are also lampstands in Revelation 11:4 but let us summarise what we have established so far about the olive trees.

Summary of Revelation 11:4

John's vision of the two olive trees and two lampstands in the 1st Century AD echoes Zechariah's from the 6th Century BC:

(i) Zechariah saw two olive trees but only one lampstand (Zech 4:2-3).

(ii) Immediately beforehand, he had seen Joshua being re-consecrated as high priest, and then seated before a stone with seven eyes (Zech 3:3-9).

(iii) Although told to "behold the stone", Zechariah was so intrigued by the olive trees that he kept asking about them, only to be ignored until the angel had finished giving the interpretation of the stone.

(iv) The message of the stone was that Zerubbabel would finish building the Second Temple, and also predicted the coming of Messiah who would build the real Temple of God, made with living stones.

(v) Zerubbabel, as governor, and Joshua, as the high priest, were also signs, prefiguring Messiah having both roles.

(vi) The lampstand Zechariah saw symbolised the people of the nation of Israel who were to hold up for all the nations the light of the oil from the two olive trees.

(vii) The olive trees were not Joshua and Zerubbabel, nor Haggai and Zechariah. We will now establish how they allude to Moses and Elijah.

4
Dead Men Speaking
Personified Texts

Why were Zechariah and John not told directly that the two olive trees symbolise Moses and Elijah? Why were they left as shadowy figures and allusions?

Firstly, because Moses had died and Elijah had ascended to heaven hundreds of years earlier and any contact with the dead was strictly forbidden:

> 10. "There shall not be found among you anyone who…
> 11. …casts a spell, or *a medium,* or *a spiritist,* or *one who calls up the dead.*
> 12. "For whoever does these things is detestable to the LORD; and because of these detestable things the LORD your God will drive them out before you. (Deut 18:10-12, emphasis added)

The testimony of the two olive trees was therefore not direct communication, as it was from the living prophets, Haggai and Zechariah. In Jewish thinking, however, there was a way the dead could still speak. For example, Abel:

> By faith Abel offered to God a better sacrifice than Cain, through which he obtained the testimony that he was righteous, God testifying about his gifts, and through faith, *though he is dead, he still speaks.* (Heb 11:4, emphasis added)

'Though he is dead, he still speaks', i.e. his righteous lifestyle continues to be a testimony to this day. The metaphor is also used, and often misunderstood today, in Hebrews 12:1:

> Therefore, since we have so great a cloud of witnesses surrounding us, let us also lay aside every encumbrance and the sin which so easily entangles us, and let us run with endurance the race that is set before us…

Many of these witnesses had just been named throughout the previous chapter, the well-known 'faith chapter', Hebrews 11, as Enoch, Noah, Abraham, Sarah, Joseph, Moses, Rahab, and so on, but they are all dead. Some, like Abel, had been killed for their faith:

> They were stoned, they were sawn in two …they were put to death with the sword… (Heb 11:37)

In what way then are they 'witnesses'?
The Living Bible translates this as:

> Since we have such a huge crowd of men of faith watching us from the grandstands, let us…

This is not at all what was meant. These witnesses are not watching us, cheering in the grandstand – they are instead testifying to us in that many of them died for their faith (Heb 11:35-37). Our English word 'martyr', meaning one who dies for their faith, comes from the Greek noun, *martus*, which is literally 'witness', one who testifies.

'A Witness'

In considering the two witnesses of Revelation 11, we have to remember that in Biblical days, objects were often called 'witnesses'. Abraham gave Abimelech seven ewe lambs as 'a witness' of his agreement with Abimelech regarding a disputed well (Gen 21:30). Jacob and Laban set up a heap of stones and a pillar, saying:

> "This heap is a witness, and the pillar is a witness, that I will not pass by this heap to you for harm, and you will not pass by this heap and this pillar to me, for harm." (Gen 31:52)

Two of the tribes of Israel built and named an altar 'Witness' to affirm their commitment to God and the other tribes (Josh 22:34). When all the tribes recommitted themselves to the Mosaic Covenant, Joshua set up a stone, saying:

> "Behold, this stone shall be for a witness against us, for it has heard all the words of the LORD which He spoke to us; thus it shall be for a witness against you, so that you do not deny your God." (Josh 24:27)

More importantly for our purpose, however, they also saw covenants as witnesses. Laban and Jacob settled their dispute, saying:

> "So now come, let us make a covenant, you and I, and let it be *a witness* between you and me." (Gen 31:44, emphasis added)

It was to remember the covenant that they set up the heap of stones and pillar, as above.

With this in mind, consider the words of Moses:

> 24. It came about, when Moses finished writing the words of this law in a book until they were complete,
> 25. that Moses commanded the Levites who carried the ark of the covenant of the LORD, saying,
> 26. "Take this book of the law and place it beside the ark of the covenant of the LORD your God, that it may remain there as *a witness* against you." (Deut 31:24-26, emphasis added)

Moses called the completed "book of the law", the Scriptures, "a witness" (v. 26) which would testify against Israel whenever they sinned or broke the covenant. The Law would always provide them with a testimony, or testimonies, as to His will and where they had gone wrong:

> All the paths of the LORD are lovingkindness and truth
> To those who keep His covenant and His *testimonies*. (Psa 25:10, emphasis added)

'The Testimony'

From the very beginning, Moses had been commanded:

> "You shall put into the ark *the testimony* which I shall give you."
> (Ex 25:16, emphasis added)

The testimony was initially the two tablets of stone containing the ten commandments (Ex 31:18, Deut 10:4) so the ark of the covenant was also known as "the ark of the testimony" (Ex 25:22) and was housed in "the tabernacle of the testimony" (Ex 38:21). However, the ten commandments were only the beginning of the written law (Deut 4:13-14)[100] and Moses did not finish writing until forty years after the Exodus (Deut 31:24).

To the five books of the Law were slowly added the sacred writings of the Prophets and inspired Wisdom such as Job's and Solomon's, headed by the Book of Psalms (Luke 24:44). All of these Scriptures were to enable Israel to check everything they heard:

> To the law and to the testimony! If they do not speak according to this word, it is because they have no dawn. (Isa 8:20. Also 2 Tim 3:14-17)

All of the inspired writers are still testifying, speaking through their words recorded in the Scriptures. For example, on the Day of Pentecost, Peter says King David is speaking of Jesus:

> "God raised Him up again, putting an end to the agony of death, since it was impossible for Him to be held in its power. For *David says* of Him, 'I SAW THE LORD...'"
> (Acts 2:24-25, emphasis added)

In quoting Psalm 16 here, Peter is adding David's testimony for us to make an informed judgement from the evidence of two or three witnesses. Paul does likewise when he quotes Psalm 69:22:

---

100 The rabbis today count the Law's written commandments as 613.

And *David says*, "LET THEIR TABLE..." (Rom 11:9)

All of these deceased believers are speaking to us from the pages of our Bibles. Each text is personified as if the dead are speaking to us, not literally but metaphorically. And, similarly, I have been doing this when I have quoted Peter and Paul as still speaking to us.

Personifying the Scriptures

Like Moses above (Deut 31:26), Paul personified Scripture when he wrote to the Galatians:

> The Scripture, *foreseeing* that God would justify the Gentiles by faith, *preached* the gospel beforehand to Abraham, *saying*, "ALL THE NATIONS..." (Gal 3:8, emphasis added)

As literal papyrus or parchment, of course, 'the Scripture' neither foresaw nor preached anything; instead, it is the written record or testimony of God's foresight. We also see this personification in Paul's letter to the Romans:

> Now we know that whatever the Law says, *it speaks* to those who are under the Law... (Rom 3:19, emphasis added)

He went on to describe the Scriptures, the Law and the Prophets, as witnesses:

> But now apart from the Law the righteousness of God has been manifested, *being witnessed by* the Law and the Prophets... (Rom 3:21, emphasis added)

This expression 'being witnessed by' is ambiguous here in the *NASB* – but it does not mean being watched by. The Greek verb, *martureo,* means to testify, to bear witness. Accordingly, the *NIV* has 'to which the Law and the Prophets testify'; the *ESV*, that they 'bear witness to it'; the *ISV*, 'is attested by the Law and the Prophets'.

Jesus likewise personified the Scriptures as witnesses. In

John 5, He tries to help His opponents to judge Him properly by listening not just to Him (John 5:31) but also to other witnesses such as the Scriptures:

> 39. "You search the Scriptures because you think that in them you have eternal life; it is *these that testify* about Me..." (John 5:39, emphasis added)

'As the Scripture says' or 'said' is a common New Testament expression.[101] Jesus then goes a step further:

> 45. "Do not think that I will accuse you before the Father; *the one who accuses you is Moses*, in whom you have set your hope.
> 46. "For if you believed Moses, you would believe Me, for he wrote about Me.
> 47. "But if you do not believe *his writings*, how will you believe My words?" (John 5:45-47, emphasis added)

Notice, the Lord has gone from personifying the Scriptures, to "his writings", to Moses himself being their present accuser.

This way of speaking was readily understood in New Testament times. Consider James's words to the assembly in Jerusalem:

> 21. "For Moses from ancient generations has in every city those who preach him, since he is read in the synagogues every Sabbath." (Acts 15:21)

Or Paul, writing to the Romans:

> 19. But I say, surely Israel did not know, did they? First Moses says, "I WILL MAKE YOU JEALOUS BY THAT WHICH IS NOT A NATION..." (Rom 10:19)

When we read this verse today, we easily accept 'Moses says' as a figure of speech; we accept that in Deuteronomy 32:21, Moses is still saying today what God Himself is still saying today. Moses is being a faithful witness.

---

101 e.g. John 7:38, 7:42, 19:37; Romans 4:3, Galatians 4:30.

'Moses and the Prophets'

Moses is not alone in speaking or testifying from the Scriptures. All the recorded prophets still testify to us:

> 27. Then beginning with Moses and with *all the prophets*, He [Jesus] explained to them the things concerning Himself in all the Scriptures...
> 44. Now He said to them, "These are My words which I spoke to you while I was still with you, that all things which are written about Me in *the Law of Moses and the Prophets and the Psalms* must be fulfilled."
> 45. Then He opened their minds to understand the Scriptures. (Luke 24:27, 44-45, emphasis added)

As mentioned earlier, this division into three of the Hebrew Bible (v. 44) is the source of its Jewish name, the Tanakh: TaNaKh is an acronym of Torah (Law), Nevi'im (Prophets) and Ketuvim (Holy Writings), Psalms being the major book in the Writings. The most common division, however, is into two, the Law and the Prophets:

> Philip found Nathanael and said to him, "We have found Him of whom *Moses in the Law* and also *the Prophet*s wrote – Jesus of Nazareth, the son of Joseph" (John 1:45)

> "So, having obtained help from God, I stand to this day testifying both to small and great, stating nothing but what *the Prophets and Moses* said was going to take place" (Acts 26:22)

> ...he was trying to persuade them concerning Jesus, from both the *Law of Moses* and from *the Prophets*, from morning until evening. (Acts 28:23)

However, one of the prophets has another and unique role – Elijah.

Moses and Elijah

We can readily see that Moses has a unique role in Israel – as the mediator of the national covenant, he was the founder and definer of the nation. In Egypt, Abraham's family through Isaac and Jacob had grown into numbers feared by Pharaoh (Ex 1:5-10) but it was not until they followed Moses in the Exodus that they became a nation (Ex 19:5-6). Paul therefore wrote:

> …all were baptized into Moses in the cloud and in the sea…
> (1 Cor 10:2)

But what of Elijah? Why would he have a unique role among the Prophets? Elijah was the supreme enforcer and restorer of Israel's national identity.

We need to understand that the primary role of all of the prophets was to enforce the Law, as Gordon Fee and Douglas Stuart explain:

> More individual books of the Bible come under this heading [the Prophets] than under any other….[and] contain a vast array of messages from God.[102]
>
> *The Prophets were covenant enforcement mediators…*
> [The Mosaic Covenant] contains not only rules to keep, but describes the sorts of punishments that God will necessarily apply to His people if they do not keep the Law, as well as the sorts of benefits He will impart to them if they do. The punishments are often called "curses" of the covenant, and the benefits "blessings"…God does not merely give His law, but He enforces it. Positive enforcement is blessing; negative enforcement is curse. This is where the prophets come in…[103]
>
> Moses was the mediator for God's law… The prophets… are God's mediators, or spokespersons, for the covenant…

---

102 Gordon D. Fee and Douglas Stuart, *How to Read the Bible for all it's Worth*, Grand Rapids; Zondervan, 2002, p. 149.
103 Ibid., p. 151, emphasis in original.

> Therefore, one must always bear in mind that the prophets did not invent the blessings or curses they announced… Through them God announced His intention to enforce the covenant… but always on the basis of and in accordance with… Leviticus 26, Deuteronomy 4 and Deuteronomy 28-32.[104]

While Elijah has no book named after him, he stands out as the enforcer. He began his ministry when Israel was in an appalling state:

> 30. Ahab the son of Omri *did evil* in the sight of the LORD *more than all who were before him.*
> 31. It came about, as though it had been a trivial thing for him to walk in the sins of Jeroboam the son of Nebat, that he married Jezebel the daughter of Ethbaal king of the Sidonians, and went to serve Baal and worshiped him.
> 32. So he erected an altar for Baal in the house of Baal which he built in Samaria.
> 33. Ahab also made the Asherah. Thus Ahab *did more* to provoke the LORD God of Israel *than all the kings of Israel* who were before him. (1 Kin 16:30-33, emphasis added)

Elijah confronted Ahab and prophesied a drought that only he could end (1 Kin 17:1), the three and a half year drought that we identified as foreshadowing the metaphorical "time, times and half a time" in Books 1, 2 and 3. Before ending the drought, he confronted Ahab again:

> 19. "Now then send and gather to me all Israel at Mount Carmel, together with 450 prophets of Baal and 400 prophets of the Asherah, who eat at Jezebel's table."
> 20. So Ahab sent a message among all the sons of Israel and brought the prophets together at Mount Carmel.
> 21. Elijah came near to all the people and said, "How long will you hesitate between two opinions? If the LORD is God, follow Him; but if Baal, follow him". But the people did not answer him a word. (1 Kin 18:19-21)

---

104 Ibid, p. 151-152.

Thus began the famous confrontation where Elijah called down fire from heaven which, as we saw in Book 2, foreshadows the Day of Pentecost in 30 AD when the Holy Spirit fell on the believers, and which is counterfeited by the 'strange fire' of the antichrists.[105]

This creates a unique bond with Moses. Jews rightly celebrate the Day of Pentecost in 1446 BC[106] as the day the Law was given to Moses (Ex 19:1, 10-11) while Christians rightly celebrate the day in 30 AD when the Holy Spirit was poured out on all who believed in Jesus (Acts 2:17-18). The ministries of Moses and Elijah are therefore uniquely entwined with Jesus in His giving of the Holy Spirit.

Elijah, Enforcer and Restorer

After the fire fell from heaven, the people of Israel were restored to God and dealt with the false prophets:[107]

> 39. When all the people saw it, they fell on their faces; and they said, "The LORD, He is God; the LORD, He is God."
> 40. Then Elijah said to them, "Seize the prophets of Baal; do not let one of them escape." So they seized them; and Elijah brought them down to the brook Kishon, and slew them there. (1 Kin 18:39-40)

Elijah then prayed for the drought to end (1 Kin 18:41-45) and pronounced God's judgement on Ahab and Jezebel (1 Kin 21:17-26).

Then came more fire from heaven. When Elijah pronounced God's judgement on Ahab's son Ahaziah (2 Kin 1:3-4), Ahaziah sent a squad of fifty soldiers to arrest Elijah. In response to

---

105 *STB*, p. 80-91.
106 According to 1 Kings 6:1, the Exodus took place 480 years before 'the fourth year of Solomon's reign', i.e. 966 BC. See too David Rohl, *Exodus: Myth or History?* St Louis Park, MN; Thinking Man Media, 2015, p. 162.
107 As I established in *GSS*, they were thereby accepting again the sixth mark of God's ownership.

their haughty disrespect, Elijah again called down fire from heaven but this time on the soldiers and God judged them. The second squad of fifty were no better and were similarly dispatched. The third squad were respectful so God sent Elijah with them to repeat His judgement on Ahaziah (2 Kin 1:9-17).

No other prophet in Jewish history enforced God's covenantal judgement by starting and ending a drought in Israel and by calling down fire from heaven against opponents.

His role in restoring Israel and the rain is emphasised by Jesus:

> "Elijah is coming and will restore all things" (Matt 17:11)

This is why the last words of the Old Testament[108] are:

> "Remember *the law of Moses* My servant, even the statutes and ordinances which I commanded him in Horeb for all Israel.
> "Behold, I am going to send you *Elijah the prophet* before the coming of the great and terrible day of the LORD".
> (Mal 4:4-5, emphasis added)

More than anyone else ever could, these two men embody the Law and the Prophets.

'The Two Olive Trees'

> These are the two olive trees and the two lampstands *that stand before the Lord of the earth*. (Rev 11:4, emphasis added)

When Elijah came to the end of his public ministry, he still had one last miracle to display. Like Moses parting the Red Sea, Elijah parted the waters of the Jordan to 'cross over on dry ground' (2 Kin 2:7-8). As noted earlier, in doing so, he

---

108 Christians arrange it as 39 books, ending with Malachi, whereas the Jewish Bible is arranged as 24 books, ending with Chronicles. However, all agree that Malachi's words are the last chronologically. *The Hebrew Study Bible*, Oxford & New York; Oxford University Press, 2003, p. 1268.

went to the same side of the Jordan as Moses, outside the land of Israel opposite Jericho, where Moses was last seen (Deut 34:1-6, 2 Kin 2:5-8) and where Jesus was baptised.

The next time Elijah is seen, he is back in the Promised Land with Jesus and Moses:

> 1. Six days later Jesus took with Him Peter and James and John his brother, and led them up on a high mountain by themselves.
> 2. And He was transfigured before them; and His face shone like the sun, and His garments became as white as light.
> 3. And behold, Moses and Elijah appeared to them, talking with Him. (Matt 17:1-5)

Remember now what the angel said to Zechariah about the two olive trees?

> "These are the two anointed ones who are standing by the Lord of the whole earth". (Zech 4:14)

Jesus now has "all authority in heaven and on earth" (Matt 28:18) so it is no coincidence that John uses the same expression:

> These are the two olive trees and the two lampstands *that stand before the Lord of the earth*. (Rev 11:4, emphasis added)

The two olive trees are Moses and Elijah, but in a very particular way: they are not as individuals returning to Jerusalem from the dead but, being dead, they are still speaking through the Law and Prophets, i.e. the Hebrew Bible. This will be confirmed as we go on.

'The Two Lampstands'

I established earlier that a lampstand symbolises a group of people. What then should we make of these two olive trees also being lampstands?

To answer this, we need to consider three issues.

1. When does a group become a lampstand?

Israel as a nation began to reveal the light of God when they entered His covenant:

> 5. 'Now then, *if you will indeed obey My voice and keep My covenant*, then you shall be My own possession among all the peoples, for all the earth is Mine
> 6. and you shall be to Me a kingdom of priests and a holy nation'. (Ex 19:5-6, emphasis added)

Israel were only a lampstand to 'all the peoples' when they were obedient and kept His covenant; when they disobeyed, they offered no light to anyone.

In John's day, those gathering in the seven cities in Asia Minor churches were only lampstands when they too obeyed His voice and kept His covenant:

> "Therefore remember from where you have fallen, and repent and do the deeds you did at first; or else I am coming to you and will *remove your lampstand* out of its place – unless you repent". (Rev 2:5, emphasis added)

This was simply common sense rather than a harsh threat: if they again shone the light of God, their gathering would truly be a lampstand but if not, He would scatter them.

So, a group is only a lampstand when they are obeying and revealing God.

2. What is the source of light on a lampstand?

Light comes from its burning lamps – the stand without them enlightens no-one. These symbolise the Holy Spirit, as seen earlier in John's interpretation:

> And there were seven lamps of fire burning before the throne, which are the seven Spirits of God... (Rev 4:5)

The light from the lampstands seen by Zechariah and John comes from the fire of the Holy Spirit.

However, lamps can also be a metaphor for the word of God:

> Your word is a lamp to my feet
> And a light to my path. (Ps 119:105)

From this we see these lampstands, whether Israel or the churches, only give light when inhabited by the Spirit of God and when holding up the word of God.

3. How did the lampstands get their burning lamps?

The seven churches received them in about 56 AD from Paul and his companions ministering the Spirit of God and the word of God to Asia Minor (Acts 18:19ff).

The nation of Israel received them in 1446 BC from Moses, when he brought them the Spirit of God and the word of God at Mt Sinai. By 858 BC,[109] however, the nation of Israel was no longer a lampstand. Ahab and Jezebel had led them into such idolatry that Elijah was sent to judge Ahab, Jezebel, and the false prophets, and to restore the nation to the Spirit of God and the word of God.

Moses, therefore, was the lampstand who established Israel as a lampstand and Elijah was the lampstand who re-established Israel as a lampstand.

Why then would John see these two lampstands at the end of the 1st Century? Because the nation of Israel, having rejected Jesus as Messiah, is again no longer a lampstand – their lampstand has been removed "out of its place" and the people scattered to all the nations. However, their Scriptures, the Hebrew Bible, still shine in the darkness:

> So we have the prophetic word [i.e. the Scriptures] made more sure, to which you do well to pay attention as to *a lamp shining in a dark place*, until the day dawns and the morning star arises in your hearts. But know this first of all, that no prophecy of Scripture is a matter of one's own interpretation… (2 Pet 1:19-20, emphasis added)

---

109 Iain Provan, V. Phillips Long, Tremper Longman III, *A Biblical History of Israel*, Louisville, KY; Westminster John Knox Press, 2003, p. 264.

This means that Moses and Elijah are still testifying, providing oil and light to Israel.

Luke 16

There is a very common and longstanding misconception in Christendom that ever since Jesus gave us the New Covenant, the Old Testament has nothing to say. Jesus, however, explicitly taught the opposite in Luke 16. He began by warning the Pharisees of the dangers of being rich and religious:

> 14. Now the Pharisees, who were lovers of money, were listening to all these things and were scoffing at Him.
> 15. And He said to them, "You are those who justify yourselves in the sight of men, but God knows your hearts; for that which is highly esteemed among men is detestable in the sight of God". (Luke 16:14-15)

He explained that the only way into the kingdom is by our being forgiven:

> 16. "The Law and the Prophets were proclaimed until John; since that time the gospel of the kingdom of God has been preached, and everyone is forcing his way into it." (Luke 16:16)

John had baptised everyone, 'tax collectors and prostitutes' included (Matt 21:31-32), who came repentant and wanting forgiveness for their sins (Luke 3:3). However, Jesus explained, this was not because He was lowering standards – the Law would still apply to every Jew who rejected Him:

> 17. ""But it is easier for heaven and earth to pass away than for one stroke of a letter of the Law to fail." (Luke 16:17)

To illustrate this, He told them about Lazarus and the rich man.

Lazarus and the Rich Man

Assuming that the reader will already know the story (Luke 16:19-31), I will go straight to Jesus' conclusion. The rich man had asked Abraham to send Lazarus to warn his five brothers of what would happen to them after death:

> 29. "But Abraham said, 'They have Moses and the Prophets; let them hear them.'
> 30. "But he said, 'No, father Abraham, but if someone goes to them from the dead, they will repent!'
> 31. "But he said to him, 'If they do not listen to Moses and the Prophets, they will not be persuaded even if someone rises from the dead.'" (Luke 16:29-31)

What is Abraham's response? That since they are Jewish, they should all be listening to "Moses and the Prophets" (v. 29). Abraham does not mean literally – after all, Moses and all the prophets are there with him in Paradise, waiting for the Messiah; he means figuratively or metaphorically – though dead, they are all still speaking through the Scriptures.

The rich man objects that the Scriptures are not enough to persuade them but "if someone goes to them from the dead", i.e. is resurrected, they will listen and repent (v. 30). Abraham's sad response is that if they cannot hear the truth from the Scriptures, not even a resurrection will persuade them (v. 31). He was right – since 30 AD, most of Abraham's children have ignored Jesus. What then is Abraham's counsel to them?

> "They have Moses and the Prophets; let them hear them."

They have the Hebrew Bible, i.e. they still have Moses and Elijah testifying to them, and have for the last two thousand years.

Let there be no doubt. The Hebrew Bible is unequivocal in its testimony. The primary Jewish problem is not a lack of external evidence for faith in Jesus but their reluctance to put their faith in Him, as enjoined by their own sacred text:

> 39. "You search the Scriptures because you think that in them you have eternal life; it is these that testify about Me;
> 40. and you are unwilling to come to Me so that you may have life." (John 5:39-40)

This does not require a great intellect or education. Jesus prayed:

> 25. ..."I praise You, Father, Lord of heaven and earth, that You have hidden these things from the wise and intelligent and have revealed them to infants.
> 26. "Yes, Father, for this way was well-pleasing in Your sight." (Matt 11:25-26)

What we all need, Jews and Gentiles, is revelation, i.e. the Father revealing everything to us as we trust Him with child-like humility and faith. Jesus therefore invites us to learn from Him:

> 28. "Come to Me, all who are weary and heavy-laden, and I will give you rest.
> 29. "Take My yoke upon you and learn from Me, for I am gentle and humble in heart, and YOU WILL FIND REST FOR YOUR SOULS.
> 30. "For My yoke is easy and My burden is light." (Matt 11:28-30)

To this day, He has much to teach us about Himself, Moses, and the Prophets.

Resurrection Day Bible Studies?

Jesus' attitude towards the testimony of the Hebrew Bible can be seen in two extraordinary but often overlooked events on the day of His resurrection. Consider His highest priority on that day – He led His disciples on a study of Moses and the Prophets, not once but twice.

1. On the Road to Emmaus

As recorded in Luke 24, Jesus joined two unheralded disciples, one named Cleopas and the other unnamed, as they were walking home to Emmaus, a little village about seven miles or ten kilometres from Jerusalem (v. 13), a two hour walk. They were devastated that He had just been crucified (vv. 19-21) and bewildered by reports of His resurrection (vv. 22-24).

He could have simply revealed Himself to them and enjoyed their stunned excitement but instead, 'their eyes were prevented from recognising Him' (v. 16) and He reproved them:

> "O foolish men and slow of heart to believe in all that the prophets have spoken! Was it not necessary for the Christ to suffer these things and to enter into His glory?" (Luke 24:25-26)

He then led them on one of the most amazing Bible studies of all time:

> Then beginning with *Moses* and with *all the prophets*, He explained to them the things concerning Himself in *all the Scriptures*. (Luke 24:27, emphasis added)

Their hearts began to burn within them (v. 32) as He showed them that the Messiah had to die and be raised from the dead to fulfil all the predictions of Moses and all the Prophets. Only after He had finished this very long and thorough study did He reveal Himself to them (v. 31).

What are we to make of this? That Jesus did not want anything, even His own presence, to distract them from this study; He considered it more important that they understood the testimony of the Law and the Prophets than that they saw Him physically resurrected from the dead.

2. In Jerusalem

The two disciples immediately returned to Jerusalem (v. 33), arriving just in time to join Jesus' second Bible study, this time with all the disciples there. He began by reminding them:

> 44. ... "These are My words which I spoke to you while I was still with you, that all things which are written about Me in the Law

of Moses and the Prophets and the Psalms must be fulfilled."
45. Then *He opened their minds* to understand the Scriptures. (Luke 24:44-45, emphasis added)

As we saw earlier, "the Law and the Prophets and the Psalms" describe all three parts of the Hebrew Scriptures, i.e. the Tanakh, so this was a very thorough study. This time, however, He added more details of what should be seen in those Scriptures:

> 46. and He said to them, "Thus it is written, that the Christ would suffer and rise again from the dead the third day,
> 47. and that repentance for forgiveness of sins would be proclaimed in His name to all the nations, beginning from Jerusalem." (Luke 24:46-47)

To the necessity of the Christ or Messiah dying and rising from the dead, Jesus added that His resurrection had to be on the third day (v. 46) and that His message was for everyone everywhere (v. 47).

Given these details, we too are supposed to find and marvel at these Messianic prophecies. A few are well-known, e.g. Jesus as the Passover lamb, the suffering servant of Isaiah 53, and the crucifixion in Psalm 22. However, many others are to be found scattered throughout Israel's history, from Abraham's offering up Isaac in about 2050 BC to other prophetic dramas in the festivals and sacrificial rituals of the Law from 1446 BC, to David's 11th Century BC psalms, to unusual events such as Jonah's resurrection in the 8th Century BC.[110]

Anyone willing to look can find them – in my own searching of the Hebrew Bible, I have found twenty-one of these extraordinary predictions of Jesus' death, resurrection, and the gospel going to all the nations. I explain six of these elsewhere, the most spectacular of which is Israel's ritual for

---

[110] It is often assumed that Jonah survived for three days but he describes himself as going to Sheol, the place of the dead (Jon 2:3-7), which would mean he died and was resurrected. See *DDJ*, pp. 37-38.

cleansing from the defilement of death, the red heifer's ashes.[III]

Why was this Jesus' top priority on that day? Because He was soon to leave them, to physically ascend, but He knew the testimony of the Scriptures would remain with them, and us, until heaven and earth pass away.

Paul offered these studies as evidence when he went to the synagogues:

> 2. And according to Paul's custom, he went to them, and for three Sabbaths reasoned with them from the Scriptures,
> 3. explaining and giving evidence that the Christ had to suffer and rise again from the dead, and saying, "This Jesus whom I am proclaiming to you is the Christ." (Acts 17:2-3)

Apollos did too, being 'mighty in the Scriptures' (Acts 18:24):

> ...for he powerfully refuted the Jews in public, demonstrating by the Scriptures that Jesus was the Christ. (Acts 18:28)

Summary of Revelation 11:1-6

(i) Many believe the two witnesses are literal, being two of the three Old Testament figures who had a mysterious end: Enoch, Moses, and Elijah. They also believe the period of their testifying, 1,260 days (Rev 11:3), is literal so the two must be yet to appear in the middle of a future seven-year long Great Tribulation.

(ii) All four of the witnesses' identifying features — destroying enemies with supernatural fire, creating droughts and plagues, turning water into blood, and God taking them at the end of their ministries — point uniquely to Moses and Elijah, thus ruling out Enoch.

(iii) Others believe the two witnesses are metaphorical and signify the church. They base this on the seven

---

III *The Red Heifer's Ashes: Mysteries of Ancient Israel*, Emmaus Road Publishing, 2001.

lampstands symbolising seven churches in Revelation 1:20 and believe there are only two here because Jesus sent out His apostles and evangelists two-by-two.

(iv) The two witnesses are indeed metaphorical but none of their identifying features point to the church, only to Moses and Elijah. We need to better understand the metaphor.

(v) Moses and Elijah are uniquely linked in six ways: both were named as essential to Israel's future in the last prophecy of the Hebrew Bible; both had particularly miraculous powers; both went to Mt Sinai/Horeb on a forty day fast; both were instrumental in God's manifesting as fire to Israel, prefiguring the coming of the Holy Spirit; both finished their earthly ministries supernaturally, even at the same place – across the Jordan from Jericho, where Jesus was baptised; both were there when Jesus was transfigured on the mount.

(vi) Moses mediated the covenant and thus symbolises the Law while Elijah was the supreme enforcer of the covenant so he embodies the role of the Prophets. Together they signify the Law and the Prophets – the two witnesses of Revelation 11 are therefore the Law and the Prophets.

(vii) This is a well-established Biblical concept: Moses designated the Law to be "a witness" (Deut 31:26), testifying whenever anyone in Israel sinned; it was called 'the testimony', being carried in the 'ark of the testimony', and dwelling in the 'tent/tabernacle of the testimony'; Jesus frequently described the Law as Moses 'speaking' or 'testifying'.

(viii) Paul specifically wrote of the Law and the Prophets being witnesses (Rom 3:21) and he, Peter and James wrote of them preaching, speaking, testifying, foreseeing, and predicting.

(ix) John describes the two witnesses as two olive trees *and* two lampstands, referring us to Zechariah's earlier vision of one lampstand being continuously fueled by two olive trees. Zechariah's lampstand signified the nation of Israel, the only congregation of God's people in his time; his two olive trees symbolise Moses and Elijah, not as individuals but as symbols of the Law and the Prophets which fueled Israel as a lampstand.

(x) In John's vision, however, his two olive trees also symbolise Moses and Elijah but his two lampstands do not symbolise the nation of Israel because their lampstand had been removed in 70 AD when the Jews were scattered. Instead, John's lampstands also refer us to Moses and Elijah who brought the light to Israel, Moses as the mediator of the covenant and the Scriptures, and Elijah as the supreme enforcer of the covenant.

(xi) In Jesus' teaching about Lazarus and the rich man in Hades, Abraham tells the rich man that his brothers should be listening to "Moses and the Prophets" (Luke 16:29 & 31), i.e. the Scriptures. This would help them identify Jesus as Messiah because the Scriptures testify of Him.

(xii) Jesus held the testimony of the Law and the Prophets to be so important that on the day He was resurrected, His first priority was to take the two disciples on the road to Emmaus through 'all the Scriptures… beginning with Moses and with all the prophets'

(Luke 24:27). He then led the apostles and all who had gathered in Jerusalem through 'the Law of Moses and the Prophets and the Psalms' until they too had found Him there (Luke 24:44-45).

(xiii) Paul and Apollos did likewise.

5
Irresistible Testimony
Israel's Fate

Israel has been powerless to resist the testimony of the two witnesses throughout the 'twelve hundred and sixty days' (Rev 11:3), the last 2,000 years:

> 5. And if anyone wants to harm them, fire flows out of their mouth and devours their enemies; so if anyone wants to harm them, he must be killed in this way.
> 6. These have the power to shut up the sky, so that rain will not fall during the days of their prophesying; and they have power over the waters to turn them into blood, and to strike the earth with every plague, as often as they desire (Rev 11:5-6)

As established earlier, the fire flowing 'out of their mouth' is God's vindication of the voice of the Law and the Prophets, not literally but spiritually destroying their unbelieving Jewish opponents over the last 2,000 years.

When Moses and Elijah walked the earth, their strongest opponents were often their own countrymen. In Moses' case, those rejecting the revelation restricting the incense to Aaron and his sons were…:

> …two hundred and fifty leaders of the congregation, chosen in the assembly, men of renown… Fire… came forth from the LORD and consumed the two hundred and fifty men who were offering the incense. (Num 16:2 & 35)[112]

This fire from the Lord did not consume Amalekite or Canaanite enemies but 'leaders of the congregation, chosen… men of renown' in Israel. Even after God had publicly judged these men, they remained popular in Israel:

---

112 The main leaders, Korah, Dathan, and Abiram, and their followers were swallowed up by the earth (Num 16:24-33).

> 41. But on the next day *all the congregation* of the sons of Israel grumbled against Moses and Aaron, saying, "You are the ones who have caused the death of the LORD's people."
> 42. It came about, however, when the congregation had assembled against Moses and Aaron...
> (Num 16:41-42, emphasis added)

This opposition was not in private – 'all the congregation' openly 'assembled against' the two men who had spoken the word of God to them and led them out of Egypt. Accordingly, the Lord began to judge the assembly and they were only saved by Moses and Aaron's high priestly intercession:

> 47. Then Aaron took [the censer] as Moses had spoken, and ran into the midst of the assembly, for behold, the plague had begun among the people. So he put on the incense and made atonement for the people.
> 48. He took his stand between the dead and the living, so that the plague was checked.
> 49. But those who died by the plague were 14,700, besides those who died on account of Korah. (Num 16:47-49)

The fire and the plague, then, were signs and wonders, God's vindication of Moses' words as His own.

In Elijah's case, consider his repeated complaint to God regarding Israel's state:

> "I have been very zealous for the LORD, the God of hosts; for the sons of Israel have forsaken Your covenant, torn down Your altars and killed Your prophets with the sword. And I alone am left; and they seek my life, to take it away". (1 Kin 19:10 and 14)

The Lord responded that Elijah was not alone because 7,000 have not been worshipping Baal (v. 18). However, this also confirms that the vast majority of the sons of Israel were covenant-breakers.

Elijah was then sent to pronounce God's judgement on the new king of Israel, Ahaziah, for worshipping Baal (2 Kings 1:2-4, 16-17). Ahaziah responded, not by repenting but by sending squads of soldiers to arrest him (vv. 9-13) so, in response to Elijah's prayer, fire fell and consumed the first two squads.

Again, the fire was to vindicate Elijah as truly speaking the word of God. The third squad sent to arrest Elijah behaved very differently, having seen what had happened to the first two so they were unharmed.

"Vengeance for the Covenant"

There was a covenant-penalty for those who "act with hostility against" God and His covenant-enforcers, the prophets:

> 14. "But if you do not obey Me and do not carry out all these commandments,
> 15. if, instead, you reject My statutes, and if your soul abhors My ordinances so as not to carry out all My commandments, and so break My covenant…
> 23. "… but act with hostility against Me,
> 24. then I will act with hostility against you; and I, even I, will strike you seven times for your sins.
> 25. "I will also bring upon you *a sword which will execute vengeance for the covenant…*" (Lev 26:14-15, 23-25, emphasis added)

There will be consequences if we ignore God. In Israel's case, it was usually the loss of God's presence and protection, leading to loss of prosperity, health, life,[113] or land as Gentile empires invaded them and exiled them:

> 32. "I will make the land desolate so that your enemies who settle in it will be appalled over it.
> 33. "You, however, I will scatter among the nations and will draw out *a sword after you*, as your land becomes desolate and your cities become waste…" (Lev 26:32-33, emphasis added)

While exile from the land was the ultimate penalty for Israel to make amends, it was never to be permanent:

---

[113] Details given in *DDJ*, pp. 150-155.

> 43. "For the land will be abandoned by them, and will make up for its sabbaths while it is made desolate without them. They, meanwhile, will be *making amends for their iniquity*, because they rejected My ordinances and their soul abhorred My statutes". (Lev 26:43, emphasis added)

It is very important here that we do not confuse vengeance with vindictiveness, unforgiveness, or bitterness. God is never vindictive, unforgiving, or bitter. Vengeance is simply the administration of justice, in many cases to vindicate by establishing the innocence of victims and/or the veracity of witnesses.

In Revelation 11, the issue is the veracity of God's two witnesses. The sword executing vengeance for the covenant on Israel, in exile among the nations, has been coming from the mouth of the Law and the Prophets throughout the last two thousand years.

Remembering Covenants

The covenant being enforced in Leviticus 26:25 is the Mosaic. However, in Leviticus 26:40-46, the Lord reminds Moses of His covenant made over four hundred years earlier with Abraham, Isaac, and Jacob, that He would always help their descendants, even in exile:

> 40. "If they confess their iniquity and the iniquity of their forefathers, in their unfaithfulness which they committed against Me, and also in their acting with hostility against Me -
> 41. I also was acting with hostility against them, to bring them into the land of their enemies – or if their uncircumcised heart becomes humbled so that they then make amends for their iniquity,
> 42. then *I will remember My covenant* with Jacob, and *I will remember also My covenant* with Isaac, *and My covenant* with Abraham as well, *and I will remember the land*. (Lev 26:40-42, emphasis added)

Many believe this means God will only help them if they repent. However, He is telling them what they must do before they can legitimately expect Him to act; it does not rule out His acting graciously.[114] Even if they do not repent, His "vengeance for the covenant" will never mean the end of Israel as a nation:

> 44. "Yet in spite of this, when they are in the land of their enemies, *I will not reject them, nor will I so abhor them as to destroy them, breaking My covenant with them*; for I am the LORD their God.
> 45. "But *I will remember* for them *the covenant* with their ancestors, whom I brought out of the land of Egypt in the sight of the nations, that I might be their God. I am the LORD."
> 46. These are the statutes and ordinances and laws which the LORD established between Himself and the sons of Israel through Moses at Mount Sinai. (Lev 26:44-46, emphasis added)

In other words, although the Lord knew that Israel would break the Mosaic Covenant many times and be exiled twice, firstly to Assyria and Babylon and then by the Romans to "all the nations", He would not break it. He remembers all His covenants.

This is why Paul was so confident:

> 1. I say then, God has not rejected His people, has He? May it never be! ...
> 2. God has not rejected His people whom He foreknew. ...
> 11. I say then, they did not stumble so as to fall, did they? May it never be! (Rom 11:1-2, 11)

His expression 'May it never be!' means 'Absolutely not!'[115] God will never reject Israel as a nation – as individuals who

---

114 We will consider this in detail in Chapter 14, in regard to Ezekiel's predictions.
115 Grk, *me genoito*. Paul uses this, the strongest negative Greek expression, 14 times in his letters, always after rhetorical questions, to pronounce the thought absurd, outrageous, abhorrent.

reject Him, yes (Matt 7:21-23, 2 Tim 2:12-13), but as a nation, impossible.

Let us consider the historical record.

Israel's Last 2,000 Years

In Book 1, we saw how Revelation 12 described all 4,000 years of Jewish history.

For the first 2,000 years after Abraham, the woman who is 'Israel according to the flesh' was being prepared to give birth to the promised Seed or Child, the Messiah:

> But when the fullness of the time came, God sent forth His Son, born of a woman, born under the Law… (Gal 4:4)

Throughout those first 2,000 years, the dragon tried to prevent His birth using six great Gentile empires, five of which had fallen[116] while the sixth, Rome, was still in power in John's day.

Tragically, when the time finally came and Jesus appeared, the woman rejected her own Son!

As punishment, she was exiled for the last 2,000 years – from the land into the wilderness (Ezekiel's 'wilderness of the peoples') for 'a time, times and half a time', i.e. 'the times of the Gentiles'. She regained sovereignty over her land in 1948, and in 1967, she finally regained sovereignty over Jerusalem.

All this time, the dragon's hatred for her continued unabated, manifesting in repeated attempts by Gentile nations to destroy her but, true to the promise of Leviticus 26, God nourished the woman in the wilderness (Rev 12:6 & 14) and promised her restoration at Elijah's second return (Matt 17:11). Revelation 12 therefore revealed the consequences to Israel, focussing on Satan's attacks with Gentile complicity and collaboration.

In Books 2 and 3, we saw in Revelation 13 the last 2,000 years of Gentile history. We Gentiles who reject Jesus as God

---

116 Egypt, Assyria, Babylon, Medo-Persia, and Greece.

in the flesh have instead frequently accepted our emperors as gods in the flesh, from the Romans in John's day to Stalin, Hirohito, Mussolini, Hitler, Mao Zedong, Pol Pot, et al, in ours.

In this, the fourth book in the series, we see again the last 2,000 years of Jewish history in Revelation 11 but from the perspective of Israel's culpability. They have been facing the "sword of vengeance for the covenant" of Moses, and Elijah's enforcement.

We also see what Jesus meant when He tried to warn Israel regarding the Hebrew Bible:

> 45. "Do not think that I will accuse you before the Father; the one who accuses you is Moses, in whom you have set your hope.
> 46. "For if you believed Moses, you would believe Me, for he wrote about Me.
> 47. "But if you do not believe *his writings*, how will you believe My words?" (John 5:45-47, emphasis added)

"Days of Vengeance"

The first major "vengeance for the covenant" after the Crucifixion was in 70 AD. Jesus was very specific when He warned in 30 AD:

> 20. "But when you see Jerusalem surrounded by armies, then recognize that her desolation is near.
> 21. "Then those who are in Judea must flee to the mountains, and those who are in the midst of the city must leave, and those who are in the country must not enter the city;
> 22. because *these are days of vengeance,* so that *all things which are written will be fulfilled."*
> (Luke 21:20-22, emphasis added)

Forty years[117] later, just as the Lord had warned, these "days

---

117 The number forty is itself significant because it symbolises a time of testing (e.g. 40 day fasts by Moses, Elijah, and Jesus; Israel's 40 years in the wilderness; Goliath's 40 days taunting of Israel). Israel were

of vengeance" came for the nation of Israel and the city of Jerusalem. It is easy to read this expression as a generic term but He relates it to "all things which are written" being "fulfilled" (v. 22). The timing of this judgement was specifically predicted by Daniel (Dan 9:26-27) but who first wrote that there would be "vengeance for the covenant"? Moses did, in Leviticus 26:25.

Some Study Bible cross-references from Luke 21:22[118] take us instead to Isaiah, Jeremiah and Hosea:

> "For the day of vengeance was in My heart,
> And My year of redemption has come" (Isa 63:4)
>
> "Shall I not punish these people?" declares the LORD,
> "On a nation such as this shall I not avenge Myself?" (Jer 5:29)
>
> The days of punishment have come,
> The days of retribution have come;
> Let Israel know this! (Hos 9:7)

In overlooking Leviticus 26:25, these commentators seem to have missed the promised vengeance of the Law referred to by these prophets: Jeremiah 5:29 is quite specific to 'these people' and 'a nation such as this' – these people and this nation, Israel, were those in His covenant. Likewise, Hosea 9:7, 'Let Israel know this!'

As for the timing, look again at Daniel. In 539 BC[119], he recorded Gabriel's prophecy:

> 26. "Then after the sixty-two weeks the Messiah will be cut off and have nothing, and the people of the prince who is to come will destroy the city and the sanctuary.
> And its end will come with a flood; even to the end there will be war; *desolations are determined.*
> 27." ... a complete destruction, *one that is decreed...*"
> (Dan 9:26-27, emphasis added)

---

granted forty years to change their minds regarding Jesus.
118 e.g. *Zondervan NASB Study Bible*, p. 1503; *The New Oxford Annotated Bible*, p. 138 New Testament.
119 Joyce C. Baldwin, *Daniel (Tyndale Old Testament Commentaries)*, Leicester; InterVarsity Press, 1978, p. 164.

This remarkable prophecy of the 70th Week was very specific.[120] Following Messiah's being "cut off", i.e. executed in 30 AD, the Romans destroyed "the city and the sanctuary", i.e. Jerusalem and the Second Temple, in 70 AD. "The prince who is to come" was Titus, the Roman general whose "people" broke into Jerusalem and who soon after became Emperor.[121]

And what did Gabriel mean when he said "desolations are (already) determined"? Those predicted by Moses in Leviticus 26, as we saw above:

> 31. "I will lay waste your cities as well and will make *your sanctuaries desolate*, and I will not smell your soothing aromas.
> 32. "I will make *the land desolate* so that your enemies who settle in it will be appalled over it.
> 33. "You, however, I will scatter among the nations and will draw out a sword after you, as *your land becomes desolate* and your cities become waste.
> 34. "Then the land will enjoy its Sabbaths all *the days of the desolation*, while you are in your enemies' land; then the land will rest and enjoy its Sabbaths.
> 35. "All *the days of its desolation* it will observe the rest which it did not observe on your Sabbaths, while you were living on it".
> (Lev 26:31-35, emphasis added)

Daniel clearly understood that this desolation of Jerusalem in

---

120 See also *DDJ*, pp. 93-113.

121 It is ironic that some commentators deny Daniel's historicity and supernatural inspiration, deciding instead that his accuracy must be due to back-dating by much later authors pretending to be him: "the history recorded in these visions suggest that they were composed sometime before 164 BC" (*The New Oxford Annotated Bible*, Augmented 3rd Edition, New York; Oxford University Press, 2001, p. 1267, Hebrew Bible). To make this theory fit, they have to ignore Daniel's fourth empire being Rome, despite Jesus saying He was inaugurating the kingdom of stone predicted in Daniel 2 (Matt 21:43-44) as the Son of Man predicted in Daniel 7 (Matt 26:54). They also ignore Daniel 9:26 being explicitly fulfilled in 70 AD, just as Jesus predicted in 30 AD (Luke 21:22-24). Lastly, they ignore Jesus' validation when He called him "Daniel the prophet" (Matt 24:15, Mark 13:14) and quoted his words, as above.

586 BC was due to Leviticus 26 because, immediately preceding Gabriel's prophecy, he had been praying:

> 11. "Indeed all Israel has transgressed Your law and turned aside, not obeying Your voice; so *the curse has been poured out on us, along with the oath which is written in the law of Moses* the servant of God, for we have sinned against Him.
> 12. "Thus He has confirmed His words which He had spoken against us and against our rulers who ruled us, to bring on us great calamity; for under the whole heaven there has not been done anything like what was done *to Jerusalem*.
> 13. "As *it is written in the law of Moses*, all this calamity has come on us; yet we have not sought the favor of the LORD our God by turning from our iniquity and giving attention to Your truth". (Dan 9:11-13, emphasis added)

The "days of vengeance" poured out on Israel in 586 BC and in 70 AD were fulfilments of the Mosaic Covenant.

Vengeance is Covenant-Keeping

While the days of vengeance necessarily end, the covenant does not. Jesus was explicit:

> 17. "Do not think that I came to abolish the Law or the Prophets; I did not come to abolish but to fulfill.
> 18. "For truly I say to you, *until heaven and earth pass away*, not the smallest letter or stroke shall pass from the Law until all is accomplished." (Matt 5:17-18, emphasis added)

Fulfilling is not abolishing or nullifying. On the contrary, the Law will not pass away from those still under it until "heaven and earth pass away", i.e. on the Last Day, the Day of Judgement, when at last all will have been accomplished. Paul confirms its role on that Day:

> 11. For there is no partiality with God.
> 12. For all who have sinned without the Law will also perish without the Law, and *all who have sinned under the Law will be judged by the Law*. (Rom 2:11-12, emphasis added)

Some might assume, as I once did, that this only refers to those who died before 30 AD but some twenty years after that, Paul was writing to the Galatians:

> For as many as are of the works of the Law are under a curse; for it is written, "CURSED IS EVERYONE WHO DOES NOT ABIDE BY ALL THINGS WRITTEN IN THE BOOK OF THE LAW, TO PERFORM THEM." (Gal 3:10)

In other words, the penalty of the Law was still applying to those still under it. So too do the obligations:

> And I testify again to every man who receives circumcision, that he is under obligation to keep the whole Law. (Gal 5:4)

James, the Lord's brother, confirms this too:

> For whoever keeps the whole law and yet stumbles in one point, he has become guilty of all. (Jas 2:10)

Present-Day Relevance

Why then do many commentators today not make this connection between Leviticus 26 and the events of 70 AD? Because they usually believe the Law became irrelevant after the New Covenant was inaugurated in 30 AD but Paul certainly did not:

> Do we then nullify the Law through faith? May it never be! On the contrary, we establish [Grk, *histemi*, to make stand, uphold] the Law... (Rom 3:31)

He is not saying the Law was nullified or irrelevant – he is saying it is still being upheld or vindicated. The only question is, for whom?

For years, I assumed that since all who trust in Jesus are no longer 'under Law but under grace' (Rom 6:14) that the Law is no longer over anyone. I assumed wrongly. All Jews not trusting in Him are still 'under the Law'. Paul wrote in about 55 AD, twenty-five years after the New Covenant was inaugurated:

> To the Jews I became as a Jew, so that I might win Jews; to those who are under the Law, as under the Law though not being myself under the Law, so that I might win those who are under the Law... (1 Cor 9:20)

He does not say, 'those who think they are under the Law but they are not, because that is now defunct'; he says they are still 'under the Law'.

In Romans 7, he spells out why: because without Jesus, the only way a Jew can be free from the Mosaic Covenant is by death:

> 1. Or do you not know, brethren (for I am speaking to those who know the Law), that the Law has jurisdiction over a person as long as he lives?

He compares their situation to marriage:[122]

> 2. For the married woman is bound by law to her husband while he is living; but if her husband dies, she is released from the law concerning the husband.
> 3. So then, if while her husband is living she is joined to another man, she shall be called an adulteress; but if her husband dies, she is free from the law, so that she is not an adulteress though she is joined to another man.

His analogy is that all Jewish believers in Jesus used to be married to the Law and only became free to marry Jesus because they died:

> 4. Therefore, my brethren, *you also were made to die to the Law* through the body of Christ, so that you might be joined to another, to Him who was raised from the dead, in order that we might bear fruit for God. (Rom 7:1-4, emphasis added)

---

122   He also wrote about divorce and remarriage in 1 Corinthians 7:15, as did Jesus in Matthew 5:31-32 and 19:9, but his point here is God's original intention of marriage as being "till death do us part".

Obviously, this is not by physical death but by being born again, as Jesus told Nicodemus. We all need a new spiritual beginning; this necessarily means we have to die to the old life. For Gentiles, this is to our sinful life; for Jews, this is to their sinful life and to the Mosaic Covenant.

We see this again when Paul wrote to the Galatians:

> For through the Law I died to the Law, so that I might live to God (Gal 2:18)

He knew that the only way out from under the Law was to die to it. However, he is also acknowledging that the Law rightly put him to death for his sinfulness.

This is still the situation for every Jew today who does not yet believe in Jesus.

Dual Covenant Theology?

This is not an argument for Dual or Two Covenant Theology, i.e. the belief that Jews or Jewish proselytes are still to trust in the Mosaic Covenant for salvation and that it is only Gentiles that are saved through trusting in the New Covenant.[123] American preacher John Hagee, for example, believes:

> In fact trying to convert Jews is a waste of time ... Jews already have a covenant with God that has never been replaced by Christianity.[124]

It is said that Pope John Paul II was likewise arguing for this when he addressed the West German Jewish community on 17 November, 1980, describing them as:

> ...the people of God of the Old Covenant, never revoked by God. [cf. Rom. 11:29][125]

---

123   Nahum N. Glatzer, *Franz Rosenzweig: His Life and Thought*, New York; Schocken Books, 1961, p. 341.
124   *Houston Chronicle*, April 30, 1988, section 6, p. 1.
125   www.ccjr.us/dialogika-resources/documents-and-statements/roman-catholic/pope-john-paul-ii/297-jp2-80nov17, 18 Jun, 2015. The

Twenty years later, on 12 March, 2000, when John Paul was at Yad Vashem,[126] the Holocaust Museum in Jerusalem, he made a long-overdue apology to Israel on behalf of the Roman Catholic Church, adding:

> We are deeply saddened by the behavior of those who in the course of history have caused these children of yours to suffer, and asking your forgiveness we wish to commit ourselves to genuine brotherhood with the people of the Covenant.[127]

He therefore may have believed in Dual or Two Covenant Theology. However, it seems more likely he was simply acknowledging that both Old and New Covenants are still in force: the unrevoked Old Covenant for Jews and Gentile converts to Judaism; the New Covenant for followers of Jesus, Jew or Gentile.

It is here we find the insurmountable problem faced by everyone under the Old or Mosaic Covenant – it can only provide forgiveness of sins through its animal sacrifices:

> "For the life of the flesh is in the blood, and I have given it to you on the altar to make atonement for your souls; for it is the blood by reason of the life that makes atonement". (Lev 17:11)

> And according to the Law, one may almost say, all things are cleansed with blood, and without shedding of blood there is no forgiveness. (Heb 9:22)

---

inserted reference to Rom 11:29 reads 'the gifts and the calling of God are irrevocable'.

126 Heb. 'a place and a name', from Isaiah 56:5: "Even unto them will I give in My house and within My walls a place and a name better than of sons and of daughters: I will give them an everlasting name that shall not be cut off". The promise is to eunuchs who are childless (Isa 56:4); Yad Vashem seeks to honour every victim of the Holocaust, especially the 1.5 million children, too young to have their own. www.yadvashem.org/yv/en/remembrance/childrens_memorial.asp, 20 Aug, 2016.

127 www.pbs.org/newshour/bb/religion-jan-june00-apology_3-13/, 18 Jun, 2015.

Without animal sacrifices, the Law cannot provide forgiveness.

As for the sacrifices, none in themselves ever could take away sins. They were only ever to foreshadow what was to come:

> 1. For the Law, since it has *only a shadow of the good things to come* and not the very form of things, can never, by the same sacrifices which they offer continually year by year, make perfect those who draw near.
> 2. Otherwise, would they not have ceased to be offered, because the worshipers, having once been cleansed, would no longer have had consciousness of sins?
> 3. But in those sacrifices there is a reminder of sins year by year.
> 4. For it is impossible for the blood of bulls and goats to take away sins. (Heb 10:1-4, emphasis added)

The Law was, and still is, to reveal to the Jews their sinfulness and their need for faith in innocent sacrifices, which all foreshadowed Jesus of Nazareth as Christ or Messiah. They, and we Gentiles, can only ever be saved from sin by faith in Him.

All who are under the Law who refuse to accept Jesus remain under the Law. This is why James the Lord's brother changed his mind regarding Gentiles becoming Jews:

> 19. "Therefore it is my judgement that we do not trouble those who are turning to God from among the Gentiles [by circumcising them],
> 20. but that we write to them that they abstain from things contaminated by idols and from fornication and from what is strangled and from blood.
> 21. "For Moses from ancient generations has in every city those who preach him, since he is read in the synagogues every Sabbath." (Acts 15:19-21)

I used to wonder why, if Moses had been rendered obsolete, James thought it was good that Moses was still being preached so we will look at this in Chapter 7 – Obsolete and Disappearing? In the meantime, we see James concluding there was no point in the church preaching Moses when the synagogues in every city were already doing that – the church needed to preach Jesus.

Summary of Revelation 11:5-6

In these verses, we see that:

(i) No one can resist the testimony of the two witnesses because 'fire flows out of their mouth and devours their enemies' (v. 5) and they can 'strike the earth with every plague, as often as they desire' (v. 6).

(ii) When Moses and Elijah walked the earth, their words were vindicated by heavenly fire destroying their Jewish opponents. Over the last 2,000 years, the words of the Law and the Prophets have out-lasted and spiritually destroyed 'anyone who wants to harm them' (v. 5).

(iii) The plagues are 'vengeance for the covenant' (Lev 26:25) and included the loss of God's presence and protection, leading to Israel losing their prosperity, health, life, or land as Gentile empires invaded and exiled them. The exiles were never to be permanent but only until they had made 'amends for their iniquity' (Lev 26:43).

(iv) God's vengeance is not vindictive or unforgiving but, faithful to His covenant, administering justice, vindicating the innocence of victims, and the veracity of witnesses.

(v) Throughout Israel's 4,000 year history, God has remembered His covenants with Abraham, Isaac, and Jacob, as well as with their descendants under the Law and the Prophets, which is why there were "days of vengeance" and restorations.

(vi) Jesus taught the everlasting nature of the Law to Jews, and Paul taught it to Gentile Christians in Rome, Corinth, and Galatia.

(vii) Dual Covenant Theology is ruled out because the Mosaic Covenant now has no sacrifices for sin so atonement is only possible through Jesus.

6
The Law and Christians
What's For Us?

There is much confusion in our churches today over the significance of the Law so in the next two chapters, I aim to dispel that. We must be very clear that the Law of Moses:

(i) Still applies to every Jew and every Gentile proselyte[128] who does not yet believe in Jesus as Messiah (Num 15:15-16). They will one day be judged according to the Law (Rom 2:12).

(ii) It does not apply to anyone who believes in Jesus, whether Jew or Gentile, 'for you are not under law but under grace' (Rom 6:14).

(iii) It has never applied to Gentiles. They will be judged 'without the Law' (Rom 2:12) but according to the law 'written in their hearts' (Rom 2:14-16).

If we are trusting in Jesus, the guilt of our sin is gone because, through grace, He paid the penalty on the cross. We are, however, to overcome the power of sin in our 'flesh', i.e. our sinful nature, by living in the Spirit. The Law could never achieve that:

> 3. For what the Law could not do, weak as it was through the flesh, God did: sending His own Son in the likeness of sinful flesh and as an offering for sin, He condemned sin in the flesh, 4. so that the requirement of the Law might be fulfilled in us, who do not walk according to the flesh but according to the Spirit. (Rom 8:3-4)

---

128 i.e. Gentiles who have converted to Judaism (Acts 13:43).

"According to the Spirit"

When God gave us the New Covenant, He was not, as some think, changing one rule book for another (Jer 31:31-34). He was offering us a personal relationship in which His Spirit enters our bodies to dwell, creating a new heart, with His values and motivations:

> 26. "Moreover, I will give you *a new heart* and put *a new spirit* within you; and I will remove the heart of stone from your flesh and give you a heart of flesh.
> 27. "I will put *My Spirit* within you and *cause you* to walk in My statutes, and you will be careful to observe My ordinances." (Ezek 36:26-27, emphasis added)

Jesus explained further:

> "...the Helper, the Holy Spirit, whom the Father will send in My name, He will *teach* you all things, and bring to your remembrance all that I said to you... He will *guide* you into all the truth". (John 16:13 , 14:26, emphasis added)

It can therefore take a while for us to learn His new covenant 'statutes' and 'ordinances'.

To illustrate this, let me describe my own experience, which may also show why I will never be casting the first stone at anyone.

Before I was converted in August 1973, I was an atheistic evolutionist and promiscuous liberal-thinker, advocating for the legalisation of marijuana, abortion, and gay rights. I found God in a moment of prayer while listening to some lesbian friends arguing over a cheating partner. It was several days before I could tell them what had just happened to me and when one asked me privately how I now saw sexual morality, I had no real answer for her other than that I now felt able to do whatever He wanted of me. I later discovered the New Testament teaching of Romans 1:22-27 so I showed it to my friend and she was delighted and relieved. She explained that she had always felt inwardly torn between the part of her that wanted to be a lesbian and the part of her that hated it, and she now knew which part of herself to side with.

Personally, I desperately wanted to be free from my smoking forty cigarettes a day, and I was within a week, but my attitude towards marijuana and hashish only slowly changed as I realised those highs were insignificant compared to the joys of God's presence and revelations. I also came to see that any intoxication dulls our spiritual senses (Eph 5:18).

During that first week, I received a revelation of Creation but it took me several years to revisit all of my beliefs and arguments for evolution. It was months before God showed me, through Isaiah 1:15-18, my culpability in pressuring my ex-fiancée to have an abortion and, over the next year, I slowly put things right with my parents and others.

Peter describes this spiritual process or progression after our rebirth:

> 4. ...He has granted to us His precious and magnificent promises, so that by them you may become partakers of the divine nature, having escaped the corruption that is in the world by lust.
> 5. Now for this very reason also, applying all diligence, *in your faith supply* moral excellence, and in your moral excellence, knowledge... (2 Pet 1:4-5, emphasis added)

Having myself become a 'partaker of the divine nature' simply by believing 'His precious and magnificent promises' (v. 4), I soon saw my need for 'moral excellence' (v. 5) and I needed to know what that meant (v. 5). Peter continues:

> 6. and in your knowledge, self-control, and in your self-control, perseverance, and in your perseverance, godliness,
> 7. and in your godliness, brotherly kindness, and in your brotherly kindness, love. (2 Pet 1:6-7)

I knew that although it was going to take a while to apply everything, I also knew I would keep changing inwardly, both in understanding and in motivation, and that my ultimate goal was to become more loving.

What Then of the Law?

Many of the Jewish leaders of the Early Church (Acts 15:1-5), including Peter, Barnabas, and James the Lord's brother, were initially confused over whether new Gentile believers were still to keep the Law (Gal 2:11-13) but not Paul. It took fifteen years before the issue was finally resolved, when the Council in Jerusalem reached unanimous agreement (Acts 15:25) with Paul's revelation:

> 3. And I testify again to every man who receives circumcision, that he is under obligation to keep the whole Law.
> 4. You have been severed from Christ, you who are seeking to be justified by law; you have fallen from grace. (Gal 5:3-4)

Circumcision was essential under the Law (Josh 5:2-7) but is not in Christ. It is allowable for hygiene or medical reasons but, always optional; it must never be done 'to be justified by law' (v. 4).[129]

Christians today happily accept this regarding circumcision but there is still quite some confusion in our churches today regarding food, alcohol, pilgrimages, festivals, Sabbaths, giving, and sexual morality. For example, the Seventh Day Adventists believe all Christians should keep the Sabbath as the Law requires, from Friday sundown until Saturday sundown, and abstain from the Law's unacceptable foods and alcohol:

> The fourth commandment of God's unchangeable law [i.e. the Ten Commandments] requires the observance of this seventh-day Sabbath... Along with adequate exercise and rest, we are to adopt the most healthful diet possible and

---

[129] After the doctrine had been settled, Paul had Timothy circumcised but only to be culturally sensitive to their Jewish brethren (Acts 16:3). Similarly, he took part in Nazirite vows (Acts 18:18, 21:26).

abstain from the unclean foods identified in the Scriptures. Since alcoholic beverages, tobacco, and the irresponsible use of drugs and narcotics are harmful to our bodies, we are to abstain from them as well.[130]

While we should indeed eat and drink sensibly, it is not because we are under the Law:

> 16. Therefore no one is to act as your judge in regard to food or drink or in respect to a festival or a new moon or a Sabbath day -
> 17. things which are *a mere shadow* of what is to come; but the substance belongs to Christ. (Col 2:16-17, emphasis added)

The *NIV* translates v. 17 as 'a shadow of the things that were to come; the reality, however, is found in Christ.' In other words, the Law foreshadowed a real person, Jesus, and real issues which can only be properly addressed in His new covenant.

Shadow or Reality?

This confusion about the Law and Christians can be seen in most denominations today in any failure to let go the Law's shadows of priests, garments, altars, sacrifices, buildings, pilgrimages, and festivals and to accept the New Covenant's realities.

For example, the Law required particular people (Aaron and the Levites) dressed in particular garments (priestly robes) to offer particular animal and grain sacrifices on literal altars in particular buildings made of literal stones to which all the men of Israel were to gather on particular days and festivals. These foreshadowed Jesus and what He has done, is doing, and will do for us. Some also foreshadowed how every Christian

---

130   Articles 20 and 22 of their *28 Fundamental Beliefs*, www.adventist.org/fileadmin/adventist.org/files/articles/official-statements/28Beliefs-Web.pdf, 3 Aug, 2016. See also the Restored Church of God, https://rcg.org/articles/acfftoc.html, 3 Aug, 2016.

should respond to Him in our 'royal priesthood' (1 Pet 2:9),[131] as Peter wrote:

> you also, as living stones, are being built up as a spiritual house for a holy priesthood, to offer up spiritual sacrifices acceptable to God through Jesus Christ. (1 Pet 2:5)

Accordingly, to the degree that any of our denominations retains particular priests,[132] wearing particular garments, offering anything to God as a sacrifice for sin, in particular buildings, on particular days and festivals, to that degree we have not yet understood or outworked the New Covenant's realities (Heb 9:8-12).

Let us consider seven of these issues more carefully.

1. Food

The Law's prescribing of 'clean' and 'unclean' foods was not based on healthy or unhealthy foods but to keep Israel distinct as a people until Jesus came.[133] This is why Jesus declared that all food would become clean under the New Covenant (Mark 7:19) and why God commanded Peter to eat what he thought was still unclean:

> 13. A voice came to him, "Get up, Peter, kill and eat!"
> 14. But Peter said, "By no means, Lord, for I have never eaten anything unholy and unclean."
> 15. Again a voice came to him a second time, "What God has cleansed, no longer consider unholy."
> 16. This happened three times... (Acts 10:13-16)

If the food laws were for health and hygiene, why would God

---

131 We will look at this priestly order of Melchizedek in Chapter 12 – David's Legacy.
132 I refer here only to the role of priests and not to those set apart to preach, teach, prophesy, administer, etc.
133 'Clean' and 'unclean' does not refer to states of dirtiness but only to what God would accept. Accordingly, we Gentiles who were 'unclean' because we had no atonement for our sinfulness are now 'clean' through faith in Jesus.

command Peter to eat unhealthy and unhygienic food?[134] Peter realised this actually meant he was no longer to avoid associating and eating with Gentiles (Acts 10:28, 15:7-11), although he temporarily abandoned this revelation in Antioch (Gal 2:12) before later standing firm (Acts 15:7-11). Paul therefore warned us to watch out for those who...:

> 3. ...advocate abstaining from foods which God has created to be gratefully shared in by those who believe and know the truth.
> 4. For everything created by God is good, and nothing is to be rejected if it is received with gratitude;
> 5. for it is sanctified by means of the word of God and prayer.
> (1 Tim 4:3-5)

Dietary restrictions are allowable for health or medical reasons but not to please God – they are optional. Tobacco is not mentioned in the Scriptures, coming from the Americas, but, as I see it, having lost friends to emphysema and lung cancer, should be avoided for healthy living.

This freedom to eat any food means Messianic Jews, i.e. Jews trusting in Jesus as Messiah, can choose whether to eat kosher food or not at any time, whether for personal preference or cultural connection, as Paul did (1 Cor 9:20-21).

2. Alcohol

Intoxication is plainly forbidden under the New Covenant:

> And do not get drunk with wine, for that is excess, but be filled with the Spirit... (Eph 5:18)

Obviously, getting drunk is not from wine alone but from any 'strong drink' (Deut 14:26) or today's 'recreational' drugs and narcotics – any kind of intoxication is crossing God's line

---

134 Some argue that pigs and shellfish, for example, are still to be avoided because of what they eat. Using that logic, we should also avoid eating fruit and vegetables because of what they eat, especially strawberries and mushrooms which thrive on manure!

(Prov 20:1).

Under the Law, three key leaders of Israel were life-long abstainers, keeping the Nazirite vow[135] (Num 6:1-21): Samson (Judg 13:3-5), Samuel (1 Sam 1:11), and John the Baptist (Luke 1:13-15). Their mothers kept this vow temporarily, during their pregnancies (Judg 13:4, 1 Sam 1:11-15, Luke 1:15). Even as a Christian, Paul kept a temporary Nazirite vow (Acts 18:18) and paid the Temple expenses of four other Jewish Christians who did too (Acts 21:23-26), to keep credibility with the Jews he was trying to reach:

> To the Jews I became as a Jew, so that I might win Jews; to those who are under the Law, as under the Law though not being myself under the Law, so that I might win those who are under the Law... (1 Cor 9:20)

The Law also commanded priests to temporarily abstain while on duty (Lev 10:9), likewise rulers (Prov 31:4), lest they be forgetful or lose discernment (Prov 31:5). However, as Jesus pointed out, both partaking and abstaining can be misconstrued:

> 16. "But to what shall I compare this generation? It is like children sitting in the market places, who call out to the other children,
> 17. and say, 'We played the flute for you, and you did not dance; we sang a dirge, and you did not mourn.'
> 18. "For John came neither eating nor drinking, and they say, 'He has a demon!'
> 19. "The Son of Man came eating and drinking, and they say, 'Behold, a gluttonous man and a drunkard, a friend of tax collectors and sinners!' Yet wisdom is vindicated by her deeds."
> (Matt 11:16-19)

Jesus and John the Baptist were both righteous before God, yet Jesus' moderate drinking was condemned as that of a

---

[135] To understand this vow and its typological meaning, see the author's *Because of the Angels*, pp. 25-29.

drunkard (v. 19) and John's abstaining was ascribed to demonic madness (v. 18). What matters, therefore, either way, is that we please God.

Some Christians today, such as the Salvation Army, permanently abstain from alcohol because they are reaching out to and working with those afflicted by alcohol addiction; others such as missionaries in societies suffering with alcohol problems temporarily abstain. Paul commended this behaviour to the 1st Century Romans but added it is to be a matter of personal conscience, i.e. optional (Rom 14:20-23).

3. Pilgrimages

Pilgrims 'journey to sacred places as an act of religious devotion'[136] and, in support of this practice, some today quote:

> Blessed are those whose strength is in You,
> Who have set their hearts on pilgrimage. (Psa 84:5, *NIV*)

Pilgrimages were required under the Old Covenant: three times a year, all the men of Israel were to stand before the Tabernacle in Shiloh or Temple in Jerusalem (Ex 23:17, 34:23). We can easily forget that Israel had very few books and no means of mass communication other than to gather to hear the Law being read aloud and explained, as in Ezra's time (Neh 13:1-8), or the latest word of the Lord through His prophets. This is why Jeremiah stood at the gate of the Lord's house to prophesy (Jer 7:2), Jesus taught daily at the Temple (Mark 14:49), and the apostles went there daily to preach and teach (Acts 5:19-21, 42).

Those who 'set their hearts on pilgrimage' were therefore the ones doing everything they could to hear God. However, as we saw earlier, Jesus told the Samaritan woman:

> 21. "Woman, believe Me, an hour is coming when neither in this

---

136 *The Concise Oxford Dictionary*, 7th Edition; Oxford University Press, 1985, p. 776.

> mountain nor in Jerusalem will you worship the Father...
> 23. "...an hour is coming, and now is, when the true worshipers will worship the Father in spirit and truth; for such people the Father seeks to be His worshipers." (John 4:21-23)

We no longer have to travel three times a year to Jerusalem to hear the word of God nor, as in Catholic tradition, make pilgrimages to Rome or Santiago de Compostela, nor as required by Muhammad, to Mecca. We are instead to listen to the Spirit of God every day.[137]

We are also free to take time out from our busyness or daily cares to seek God in good company while, for example, hiking the Carmino de Santiago, as dramatised in the popular movie, *The Way*.[138]

4. Festivals

The festivals were all amazing prophetic dramas which for almost 1,500 years were to graphically demonstrate in every Jewish home what Messiah would do when He came and how we should respond to Him (1 Cor 5:7-8, Col 2:16-17).

While these festivals are wonderful to celebrate as studies in typology, God does not require us to keep them but to trust in Jesus who fulfills them all. Paul wrote that anyone who believes otherwise has seriously misunderstood the gospel:

> 9. But now that you have come to know God, or rather to be known by God, how is it that you turn back again to the weak and worthless elemental things, to which you desire to be enslaved all over again?
> 10. You observe days and months and seasons and years.
> 11. I fear for you, that perhaps I have labored over you in vain.
> (Gal 4:9-11)

---

137 It may be that Zechariah predicts a future requirement for pilgrimage (Zech 14:16-19) but I read it as being metaphorically fulfilled in the New Covenant.
138 From Jack Hitt's book, *The Way*, produced and directed by Emilio Estevez, 2010, Filmax Entertainment, Icon Entertainment International, and Elixir Films, Spain and USA.

Their fulfilments are outside the scope of this study but, if the reader is interested, I have written about them in detail in *The Red Heifer's Ashes*.[139]

5. Sabbaths

The Sabbaths were not only days but whole years. As well as every seventh day, they were to be kept at every new moon (Amos 8:5, Col 2:16-17), on the first and last days of the festivals of Unleavened Bread and Tabernacles, and on the Days of Pentecost, Trumpets, and Atonement. Every seventh year was likewise a Sabbath, as was every fiftieth.

These were all to foreshadow the rest we are to come into when we cease trusting in our own works and trust instead in His:

> 9. So there remains a Sabbath rest for the people of God.
> 10. For the one who has entered His rest has himself also rested from his works, as God did from His.
> 11. Therefore let us be diligent to enter that rest… (Heb 4:9-11)

Accordingly, Paul says, the literal Sabbath is now optional:

> 5. One person regards one day above another, another regards every day alike. Each person must be fully convinced in his own mind.
> 6. He who observes the day, observes it for the Lord, and he who eats, does so for the Lord, for he gives thanks to God; and he who eats not, for the Lord he does not eat, and gives thanks to God. (Rom 14:5-6)

6. Giving

Under the Law of Moses, Israel was required to set aside a tenth of their harvest every year, the tithe, to be spent on celebrating the Feast of Tabernacles with family and friends for two years and given to the Levites in the third year (Deut

---

139 *The Red Heifer's Ashes: Mysteries of Ancient Israel*, Emmaus Road Publishing, 2001.

14:22-29, 26:12). If they disobeyed, they incurred the curse of the Law (Mal 3:9-10). Again, if the reader is interested, I have written about tithing elsewhere.[140]

Under the New Covenant, however, we are firstly to give everything, to surrender ownership of ourselves and our possessions to Jesus Himself:

> "So then, none of you can be My disciple who does not give up all his own possessions. (Luke 14:33)

Then, as stewards of His possessions, we are to consider what we should give to others. All giving is therefore optional:

> Each one must do just as he has purposed in his heart, not grudgingly or under compulsion, for God loves a cheerful giver. (2 Cor 9:7)

We are to give because we love (1 John 3:17-18), and while the Law could set standards for Israel, its compulsion could never make them loving. As Paul wrote to Philemon:

> ...without your consent I did not want to do anything, so that your goodness would not be, in effect, by compulsion but of your own free will. (Phm 1:14)

7. Penalties

Nowhere do we see the shadow of the Law in starker contrast to the reality of Jesus and the New Covenant than in the penalties for transgressions such as Sabbath-breaking and occult practices.[141] Under the Law, Sabbath-breaking is punishable by death (Ex 31:14-15, 35:2); under the New Covenant, there is neither offence nor penalty. Under the Law, occultism is punishable by death (Lev 20:27); under the New Covenant, practitioners are forgiven on the basis of repentance and faith in Jesus' substitutionary death (Acts 19:18-19, Gal 5:20-25).

---

140 *Eating Sacred Cows: A Closer Look at Tithing*, Emmaus Road Publishing, 1988. Revised 2015.
141 These are spelled out in Deuteronomy 18:9-14.

It was failing to recognise this distinction that caused the infamous witch-hunts in Christian nations in Europe and North America between the 15th and 17th Centuries and which continue to this day in Latin America[142] and Sub-Saharan Africa.[143] It was not only witches who were killed in Europe during those centuries. As covered in *Slouching Towards Bethlehem*,[144] Catholic and Protestant kings were urged by their respective clerics to execute dissenting citizens. Reformers drowned the Anabaptists for teaching 'believers' baptism' instead of infant baptism, calling the sentence 'the third baptism'.[145] Other heretics were burnt at the stake. Michael Servetus, for example, was sentenced to be burned alive in 'a slow fire' by the Catholic Inquisition in Lyons, France, for denying the Trinity and infant baptism. He fled to the Reformers' stronghold in Geneva, Switzerland, only to be arrested and condemned by them in 1553. John Calvin argued for him to be more mercifully beheaded for his heresy but the majority of the leaders of the churches of Geneva, Zurich, Berne, Basle, and Schaffhausen ensured he was slowly burned with green wood, adding a garland of sulphur. As Blaise Pascal observed, 'Men never do evil so completely and cheerfully as when they do it from religious conviction'.

Three hundred and fifty years later this execution was formally renounced on a monument erected on the site:

> Dutiful and grateful followers of Calvin our great Reformer, yet condemning an error which was that of his age, and strongly attached to liberty of conscience, according to the true principles of the Reformation and of the Gospel, we have erected this expiatory monument.

---

142 www.nytimes.com/2014/07/05/opinion/the-persecution-of-witches-21st-century-style.html?_r=0, 27 Feb, 2017.
143 www.dailymaverick.co.za/article/2012-05-30-witch-hunts-the-darkness-that-wont-go-away/#.WLOeG_mGNit, 27 Feb, 2017.
144 *STB*, pp. 60-65.
145 www.cob-net.org/anabaptism.htm, 3 May, 2008.

October 27th, 1903.[146]

The Law's death penalty had a twofold purpose – to demonstrate to Israel God's attitude and to foreshadow for all of us the reality of the second death:

> 7. "He who overcomes will inherit [a new heaven and a new earth]...
> 8. "But for the cowardly and unbelieving and abominable and murderers and immoral persons and *sorcerers* and *idolaters* and all liars... *the second death*". (Rev 21:7-8, emphasis added)

Accordingly, we are not to promote the shadow but to proclaim the reality of Jesus and forgiveness of all sins on the basis of His substitutionary death.

All or Nothing

This tragic confusion was caused by theologians dividing the Law into moral, ceremonial, and civil (or judicial) requirements, arguing that the ceremonial and civil have become obsolete, but not the moral, which includes the Ten Commandments.[147]

For example, Thomas Aquinas wrote in 1270:

> We must therefore distinguish three kinds of precept in the Old Law; viz. 'moral' precepts, which are dictated by the natural law; 'ceremonial' precepts, which are determinations of the Divine worship; and 'judicial' precepts, which are determinations of the justice to be maintained among men.[148]

Three hundred years later, during the Reformation, John Calvin wrote:

> We must attend to the well-known division which

---

146   www.banneroftruth.org/pages/articles/article_detail.php?457, 3 May, 2008.
147   Augustine, however, excluded the Sabbath commandment on the basis of Romans 14:5.
148   Thomas Aquinas, *Summa Theologica*, 2a, Question 99, Art. 4.

distributes the whole law of God, as promulgated by Moses, into the moral, the ceremonial, and the judicial law.[149]

The Westminster Confession of Faith stated in 1646 that the moral law was given first to Adam, then to Israel at Mt Sinai in the Ten Commandments:

> III. Beside this law, commonly called moral, God was pleased to give to the people of Israel, as a church under age, ceremonial laws… All which ceremonial laws are now abrogated, under the new testament.
>
> IV. To them also, as a body politic, He gave sundry judicial laws, which expired together with the State of that people…
>
> V. The moral law doth forever bind all, as well justified persons as others, to the obedience thereof.[150]

Sabbath-keeping, being the fourth of the Ten Commandments, was therefore held to be mandatory by both Catholics and Protestants. They also changed it from the Law's injunction and today's Jewish observance, i.e. Friday sundown to Saturday sundown (Gen 1:31-2:3), to Saturday midnight to Sunday midnight.

However, Jesus explicitly forbids us to change or divide the Law like this:

> 18. "For truly I say to you, until heaven and earth pass away, not the smallest letter or stroke shall pass from the Law until all is accomplished.
> 19. "Whoever then annuls one of the least of these commandments, and teaches others to do the same, shall be called least in the kingdom of heaven; but whoever keeps and teaches them, he shall be called great in the kingdom of

---

149 John Calvin, *Institutes of the Christian Religion*, tr. Henry Beveridge, Cambridge; James Clark & Co., 1962, Vol 2, Bk 4, Chap 20, Sec 14, p. 663.
150 *Westminster Confession*, Chap XIX, Of the Law of God.

heaven." (Matt 5:18-19)

The Law is a complete package, i.e. it is all or nothing:

> For whoever keeps the whole law and yet stumbles in one point, he has become guilty of all. (Jas 2:10)

It still applies today in its entirety to every Jew who is not yet trusting in Jesus, and it does not apply to any Gentile, nor to anyone in Christ, whether Jew or Gentile. Every Jew trusting in Jesus, however, does not cease to be Jewish and is free to enjoy as much of Jewish culture as they want, as Paul did (1 Cor 9:20).

As Christians, therefore, we are not allowed to pick and choose from the Law but have to establish our morality entirely from the New Covenant.

New Covenant Morality

The Merriam-Webster Dictionary defines moral law as:

> such a rule or group of rules conceived as universal and unchanging and as having the sanction of God's will, of conscience, of man's moral nature, or of natural justice as revealed to human reason.[151]

It is this universal sense of right and wrong that Paul describes:

> 14. ...when Gentiles who do not have the Law do instinctively the things of the Law, these, not having the Law, are a law to themselves,
> 15. in that they show the work of the Law written in their hearts, their conscience bearing witness and their thoughts alternately accusing or else defending them (Rom 2:14-15)

Morality transcends us all and is written in every heart. From the very beginning, when Cain killed Abel, everyone knew that murder was wrong – he complained that "whoever finds me will kill me" (Gen 4:14). Everyone knew Lamech was unjust and vindictive when he boasted of avenging himself

---

[151] www.merriam-webster.com/dictionary/moral%20law, 22 Feb, 2017.

'seventy-seven fold' by killing even a boy who struck him (Gen 4:23-24).[152] Noah's sons recognised his drunkenness and his humiliation (Gen 9:21-23).

When Jesus explained to the Jews the Law's teaching about divorce and remarriage, He reminded them of God's original intention for all mankind that a man and a woman should become 'one flesh' and remain loving and faithful (Matt 19:3-9).

However, we can deceive ourselves and dull our consciences so when God established the nation of Israel, He gave them the Law to mediate justice for all. If anyone attacked another, for example:

> 23. "...you shall appoint as a penalty life for life,
> 24. eye for eye, tooth for tooth, hand for hand, foot for foot,
> 25. burn for burn, wound for wound, bruise for bruise."
> (Exo 21:23-25)

The Law is perfectly just – the perpetrator should receive as due penalty exactly the damage he inflicted.[153]

Jesus, however, calls us to be more than just, responding instead with grace:

> 38. "You have heard that it was said, 'AN EYE FOR AN EYE, AND A TOOTH FOR A TOOTH.'
> 39. "But I say to you, do not resist an evil person; but whoever slaps you on your right cheek, turn the other to him also."
> (Matt 5:38-39)

We must also set aside the teaching of Aquinas, Calvin, and the Westminster Confession that we have to keep the Sabbath, albeit on the first day rather than the last day of week. As mentioned earlier, the Law's Sabbath-keeping was to foreshadow the very real rest we come into as soon as we cease trusting in our own works and trust instead in His:

---

152 See Jesus' response to this explained in *GSS*, pp. 148-149.
153 Property crimes are punished by proportionate fines (e.g. Ex 22:1).

> 9. So there remains a Sabbath rest for the people of God.
> 10. For the one who has entered His rest has himself also rested from his works, as God did from His.
> 11. Therefore let us be diligent to enter that rest… (Heb 4:9-11)

Accordingly, Paul concludes:

> One person regards one day above another, another regards every day alike. Each person must be fully convinced in his own mind. (Rom 14:5)

Under the New Covenant, there is neither offence nor penalty here.

What then of other moral issues such as pride, hatred, greed, covetousness, dishonesty, envy, and sexual immorality? All of these are plainly addressed by Jesus[154] and throughout the New Testament.[155] Sexual immorality, however, needs more explanation. For example, where exactly should we start, with Jesus or Paul?

With Jesus…?

What is often confusing is that while Jesus made the New Covenant, it was not inaugurated until He died and rose again; as long as Jesus was alive, He was Himself under the Old, Mosaic Covenant. He not only perfectly kept the Law, He taught His fellow-Jews to keep the Law. When He healed lepers, for example, He told them:

> "…show yourself to the priest and present the offering that Moses commanded…" (Matt 8:4, Mark 1:40, Luke 7:14)

What then did He teach about sexual immorality? Some claim today that Jesus was non-specific regarding immorality because He was redefining it, or deliberately vague so the church could redefine it. However, if you remember He was a 1st Century Jew, Jesus was actually very specific – every time He spoke on

---

154 e.g. Mark 7:20-23.
155 e.g. 1 Corinthians 6:9-11, Galatians 5:19-21, 1 Peter 5:5-6, James 3:13-18.

sexual immorality,[156] it was in relation to the Law's definitions which His Jewish listeners already knew.

God had spelled out the defiling sexual practices of the Egyptians and Canaanites (Lev 18:3) and the dire consequences:

> 24. "Do not defile yourselves by any of these things; for by all these the nations which I am casting out before you have become defiled.
> 25. "For the land has become defiled, therefore I have brought its punishment upon it, so the land has spewed out its inhabitants.
> 26. "But as for you, you are to keep My statutes and My judgments and shall not do any of these abominations...
> 28. so that the land will not spew you out, should you defile it, as it has spewed out the nation which has been before you."
> (Lev 18:24-28)

The practices listed there were incest (vv. 6-17), adultery (v. 20), idolatry (v. 21), homosexuality (v. 22), and bestiality (v. 23). Idolatry often involved male and female temple prostitution (Deut 23:17) and the Law also forbade heterosexual rape (Deut 22:25) while Genesis 19:5-7 condemned homosexual rape (Jude 1:7).

We see then that God not only forbade these sexual practices to Israel but He was judging the Canaanites to be so defiled by them that they had defiled the land of Canaan and forfeited their right to it.

There was no vagueness when Jesus taught on sexual immorality to those under the Law. He even tightened the Law's morality in several instances. Whereas the Law allowed polygamy,[157] Jesus upheld God's original intention that marriage should be two becoming one (Matt 19:6). He also taught that adultery is not only wrong in practice but also in looking with lust (Matt 5:27-28), that all defiling behaviour

---

156 e.g. Matthew 5:32, 15:19, 19:9, Mark 7:21.
157 Leviticus 18:18 forbids marrying two sisters simultaneously, tightening up on Jacob's marrying Leah and Rachel.

comes from within:

> 19. "...out of the heart come evil thoughts, murders, adulteries, fornications [Grk. *porneia*], thefts, false witness, slanders.
> 20. "These are the things which defile the man; but to eat with unwashed hands does not defile the man" (Matt 15:19-20)

The *NASB* translates the Greek, *porneia*, as "fornications" here, as "unchastity" in Matthew 5:32, and as "immorality" in Matthew 19:9. It was a generic term for all "sexual immorality".

What therefore did His 1st Century Jewish listeners understand Him to be including as evil and defiling? Sexual immorality as defined by the Law, the basis for all His teaching:

> 18. "For truly I say to you, until heaven and earth pass away, not the smallest letter or stroke shall pass from the Law until all is accomplished.
> 19. "Whoever then annuls one of the least of these commandments, and teaches others to do the same, shall be called least in the kingdom of heaven; but whoever keeps and teaches them, he shall be called great in the kingdom of heaven." (Matt 5:18-19)

So, because Jesus upheld the Law's definitions of sexual immorality, we have to turn to Paul to establish the New Covenant's definitions of sexual immorality.

...or Paul?

Jesus had spoken of the time coming when the Law would not apply to His disciples, when, for example, the food laws would no longer be God's will (Mark 7:19). His teaching of new wineskins being essential for new wine (Matt 9:17) was to illustrate that the New Covenant would be more effective than the Old. Then, at the Last Supper, He introduced the New Covenant which offers the necessary new heart and new spirit (Jer 31:31-34, Ezek 36:26-27).

Paul therefore preached the New Covenant to the Gentiles

but, given that they did not have a Jewish education, he spelled out some issues for them:

> 9. Or do you not know that the unrighteous will not inherit the kingdom of God? Do not be deceived; neither *fornicators*, nor *idolaters*, nor *adulterers*, nor *effeminate*, nor *homosexuals*,
> 10. nor thieves, nor the covetous, nor drunkards, nor revilers, nor swindlers, will inherit the kingdom of God.
> 11. Such were some of you; but you were washed, but you were sanctified, but you were justified in the name of the Lord Jesus Christ and in the Spirit of our God. (1 Cor 6:9-11, emphasis added)

Paul was not alone in writing of the New Covenant's standards of morality: Peter wrote similarly (1 Pet 4:3-5); Jude, the Lord's brother, described God's justice in judging the 'gross immorality' (Grk, *ekporneuo*) of Sodom and Gomorrah (Jude v. 7); John warned that the immoral will end up in the lake of fire (Rev 21:8).

We need to be very clear. The New Covenant provides the ultimate means of atonement (Jesus' death and resurrection) and of overcoming sin (the power of the Spirit) but it does not change the definitions of behaviour such as theft, greed, drunkenness, fraud, or sexual immorality. It also does not change the definitions of murder (Rom 1:29, Rev 21:8), lying (Rom 9:1, Rev 21:8), or incest (1 Cor 5:1).

Thankfully, the good news is that we can all be washed of our defiling sins, forgiven, restored, and sanctified in Christ.

The Law and the Spirit

We must always remember that the New Covenant grants us the means by which we are empowered to please God – the Holy Spirit living within us. It is not to be by our obeying every written command, which was required by the Law, but by firstly trusting in Jesus who fulfilled the Law and then by following the Spirit's prompting within each of us:

> But now we have been released from the Law, having died to that by which we were bound, so that we serve in newness of the Spirit and not in oldness of the letter. (Rom 7:6)

We are to be:

> servants of a new covenant, not of the letter but of the Spirit; for the letter kills, but the Spirit gives life. (2 Cor 3:6)

Of course, this inner prompting must be carefully distinguished from our own sinful desires but this is the essence of true spirituality:

> 12. So then, brethren, we are under obligation, not to the flesh, to live according to the flesh -
> 13. for if you are living according to the flesh, you must die; but if by the Spirit you are putting to death the deeds of the body, you will live.
> 14. For all who are being led by the Spirit of God, these are sons of God. (Rom 8:12-14)

This distinction is also addressed in the New Covenant section in Appendix A – God's Covenants.

Summary of the Law and Christians

We see then that:

(i) Christians, whether Jew or Gentile, need to learn and maintain the distinction between the Old and New Covenants.

(ii) The Law, or Old Covenant, still applies to every descendant of Abraham, Isaac, and Jacob who does not yet trust in Jesus fulfilling it as Messiah.

(iii) The Law does not apply to any Jew who has entered the New Covenant through trusting in Jesus as Messiah. However, they are no less Jewish and can freely enjoy as much Jewish culture as they want.

(iv) The Law's priests, garments, altars, sacrifices, buildings, pilgrimages, and festivals all foreshadow the reality of Jesus, what He has done, is doing, and will do for us, and how we should respond to Him.

(v) We need to clear up any confusion over 'clean' and 'unclean' foods, alcohol, festivals, Sabbaths, giving, and sexual morality; each of these issues must be understood according to the New rather than the Old Covenant.

(vi) Some church traditions hold that we are to divide the Law into moral, ceremonial, and judicial commandments, then set aside the ceremonial and judicial but keep the moral commandments, including the Ten. However, Jesus taught that the Law cannot be divided or altered in any way. As Christians, therefore, we have to establish our morality from the New Covenant.

(vii) Jesus always referred to the Law's definitions of sexual morality when He was Himself under the Law and He spoke to Jews who had all grown up under the Law and knew those definitions. The Law condemned the Egyptians' and Canaanites' sexual immorality and forbade Israel behaving like them.

(viii) When Paul wrote to Gentiles in Rome and Corinth, he had to spell it all out to those not knowing God's standards of morality. He made it clear the New Covenant does not change the definitions of theft, murder, greed, lying, drunkenness, fraud, or sexual immorality. However, he also focused on the New Covenant's provision of the power of Holy Spirit to overcome sin.

7
Obsolete and Disappearing?
Means of Atonement

What then are we to make of Hebrews 8:13 which seems to say the Law is 'obsolete' and 'ready to disappear'? Quoting Jeremiah 31:31, the writer of Hebrews comments:

> When He said, "A new covenant", He has made the first obsolete. But whatever is becoming obsolete and growing old is ready to disappear. (Heb 8:13)

As we saw earlier, the Westminster Confession took this to mean that all the 'ceremonial laws are now abrogated' and 'sundry judicial laws… expired together with the State of that people [the Jews]'.[158] Others today teach this means the whole old covenant is 'no longer valid or effective'[159] and that 'it was the divine intention that it should be superseded by the new covenant and itself cease to be'.[160]

What then are we to make of Jesus' teaching in the Sermon on the Mount?

> 17. "Do not think that I came to abolish the Law or the Prophets; I did not come to abolish but to fulfill.
> 18. "For truly I say to you, until heaven and earth pass away, not the smallest letter or stroke shall pass from the Law until all is accomplished". (Matt 5:17-18)

There is quite a difference between abolishing and fulfilling – Jesus fulfilled the Law and the Prophets in 30 AD, but He has left the Law intact until "all is accomplished" when "heaven and earth pass away" on Judgment Day. Those teaching it

---

158 *Westminster Confession*, Chap XIX, Of the Law of God, Sec III-IV.
159 *NASB Study Bible*, p. 1792.
160 *New Bible Commentary*, Third Edition, p. 1205.

'ceased to be' are simply unable to explain:

> These verses [Matt 5:17-18] have caused considerable difficulty because they seem to demand a total acceptance of the OT law in a way which was neither practised by the early church nor apparently advocated in the rest of the Sermon on the Mount.[161]

Others add that along with its covenant, the nation of Israel also became obsolete and ready to disappear.

Sun, Moon, Stars, and Sea

A better understanding comes from reading Jeremiah's new covenant promise in context. The well-known portion of Jeremiah 31 begins with:

> 31. "Behold, days are coming," declares the LORD, "when I will make a new covenant with the house of Israel and with the house of Judah,
> 32. not like the covenant which I made with their fathers in the day I took them by the hand to bring them out of the land of Egypt, My covenant which they broke, although I was a husband to them," declares the LORD.
> 33. "But this is the covenant which I will make with the house of Israel after those days," declares the LORD, "I will put My law within them and on their heart I will write it; and I will be their God, and they shall be My people.
> 34. "They will not teach again, each man his neighbor and each man his brother, saying, 'Know the LORD,' for they will all know Me, from the least of them to the greatest of them," declares the LORD, "for I will forgive their iniquity, and their sin I will remember no more". (Jer 31:31-34)

Hebrews 8:8-12 is a direct quote of this. However, Jeremiah continues in a lesser known portion:

> 35. Thus says the LORD,
> Who gives the sun for light by day

---

161 Ibid., p. 1205.

> And the fixed order of the moon and the stars for light by night,
> Who stirs up the sea so that its waves roar;
> The LORD of hosts is His name:
> 36. "If this fixed order departs from before Me," declares the LORD, "then the offspring of Israel also will *cease from being a nation* before Me forever."
> 37. Thus says the LORD,
> "If the heavens above can be measured
> And the foundations of the earth searched out below,
> Then I will also cast off all the offspring of Israel
> For all that they have done," declares the LORD.
> (Jer 31:35-37, emphasis added)

Has the "fixed order" of sun, moon, stars, and sea departed yet? Of course not.

The "new covenant" (v. 31) does not mean the end of His covenant with Israel as "a nation" (v. 36). God actually couples the nation's existence to that of heaven and earth, matching Jesus' reference to the Law also not passing away, "not the least jot or stroke", until heaven and earth pass away.

He simply will not "cast off all the offspring of Israel", no matter what they do (v. 37).

Israel's Covenant

We need to remember the Mosaic Covenant was made with a whole nation and applied to everyone born into that nation:

> "Now then, if you will indeed obey My voice and keep *My covenant*, then you shall be My own possession... a kingdom of priests and *a holy nation*"... (Ex 19:5-6, emphasis added)

Accordingly, Paul wrote of Jesus as 'born under the Law' (Gal 4:4).

When Israel continually disobeyed God in the wilderness and broke His covenant, He did not cast them off – He waited until that unfaithful generation died before starting again with the faithful few, like Joshua and Caleb, and the next generation:

> "So the LORD'S anger burned against Israel, and He made them wander in the wilderness forty years, until the entire generation of those who had done evil… was destroyed." (Num 32:13)

Seven hundred years later, when the northern kingdom of Israel again worshipped the golden calves, He divorced them for "all the adulteries" (Jer 3:8) and left them to the Assyrian invaders. Faithful individuals, however, rejoined the southern kingdom:

> He [King Asa] gathered all Judah and Benjamin and those from Ephraim, Manasseh and Simeon who resided with them, for many defected to him from Israel when they saw that the LORD his God was with him. (2 Chron 15:9)[162]

One hundred and forty years later, when the southern kingdom was similarly unfaithful, God exiled them to Babylon for seventy years before bringing back another generation.

Israel's restoration in 1948 was God again bringing back another generation, demonstrating He is still faithful to this covenant, just as He promised He will be until the sun, moon, and stars stop shining, and the waves cease to roar (Jer 31:35-37).

The Mosaic Covenant being a national covenant also means that Gentiles such as Rahab and Ruth (Matt 1:5) were able to be grafted in when they committed themselves to the nation and the God of Israel. Conversely, disobedient Jews were to be 'cut off from the people' (e.g. Lev 7:20-21, Rom 11:17-23).

We see then that from the time of the Exodus, every descendant of Abraham, Isaac, and Jacob was born into the Mosaic Covenant but could opt out. With the New Covenant, however, every Jew and every Gentile is born outside it and has to opt in. As Jesus explained to Nicodemus:

> 5. … "Truly, truly, I say to you, unless one is born of water and the Spirit he cannot enter into the kingdom of God.

---

[162] Many more rejoined Judah and the house of David during the reforms of Hezekiah (2 Chron 30:1-11) and Josiah (2 Chron 35:18).

6. "That which is born of the flesh is flesh, and that which is born of the Spirit is spirit.
7. "Do not be amazed that I said to you, 'You must be born again'...
10. "Are you the teacher of Israel and do not understand these things?" (John 3:5-7, 10)

Obsolete to Whom?

Returning to Hebrews 8:13 then, we need a closer look:

> When He said, "A new covenant", He has made the first obsolete. But whatever is becoming obsolete and growing old is ready to disappear (Heb 8:13)

If, as we are told, the Old Covenant was 'abrogated' and 'ceased to be' when Jesus established the New Covenant, why was it still '*becoming* obsolete' and '*growing* old' over thirty years later?[163] What exactly was '*ready* to disappear' then?

The writer is recognising a process here, that the transition from the Old to the New is not, and never could be, a one off, all-inclusive event for the Jewish nation, as the making of the Old had been. The New Covenant requires each and every individual descendant of Abraham, Isaac, and Jacob to choose for him or herself – born under the Old, he or she has to be born again to enter the New. Remember Paul's words to his Jewish brethren:

> ...you were made *to die to the Law* through the body of Christ, so that you might be joined to another, to Him who was raised from the dead... (Rom 7:4, emphasis added)

> ...now we have been released from the Law, *having died* to that by which we were bound, so that we serve in newness of the Spirit... (Rom 7:6, emphasis added)

---

163 It is estimated Hebrews was written c. 63-64 AD. *Zondervan Pictorial Encyclopedia*, Vol 3, p. 87-88.

Only individual Jews can make this choice to die to the Law and be born again. Whenever they do, 'a new covenant' makes 'the first obsolete' *for them*. Jesus did not 'abolish' the Law but 'fulfilled' it *for them* so it still applies to any Jew not yet trusting in Him.

We see a similar process in Paul's description of everyone, Jew or Gentile, who has come to Christ:

> ...He [God] rescued us from the domain [Grk, *exousias*, authority] of darkness, and transferred us to the kingdom of His beloved Son (Col 1:13)

The 'domain of darkness' has not been destroyed – many still live there and it will last until Satan is stripped of his power on Judgement Day – but as soon as anyone believes in Jesus, they change kingdoms.

'Ready to Disappear'?

So what exactly was 'ready to disappear'? The Temple, the altar, and all of its sacrifices (which takes us back to where we started, with John being sent to measure their new form).

Consider the immediate context of Hebrews 8:13.

In chapter 7, the Hebrews were reminded that the temporal Temple, the mortal Levitical priesthood, and the animal sacrifices were only 'shadows', foreshadowing Jesus who fulfilled all of that work for all eternity for all who trust in Him (Heb 7:23-25, 8:5. Also Heb 10:12). The Temple, the altar, and all its sacrifices thereby became obsolete in 30 AD, but did not disappear until 70 AD when Jerusalem was razed by Titus and his army.

This transition from the old *means of atonement* to the new is spelled out in chapters 9 and 10:

> 8. The Holy Spirit is signifying this, that the way into the holy place has not yet been disclosed while the outer tabernacle is still standing,

> 9. which is a symbol *for the present time*. Accordingly both gifts and sacrifices are offered which cannot make the worshiper perfect in conscience… (Heb 9:8-9, emphasis added)

At that time, 'the outer tabernacle' was 'still standing' (v. 8) but demonstrating its ineffectiveness:

> 1. For the Law…can never, by the same sacrifices which they offer continually year by year, make perfect those who draw near.
> 2. Otherwise, would they not have ceased to be offered…?
> 3. But in those sacrifices there is a reminder of sins year by year. (Heb 10:1-3)

The New Covenant did not mean the abolition of the Law and Prophets for the Jewish nation but the end of the Old Covenant as their means of atonement. The destruction of the Temple, the altar, and the sacrifices demonstrated once and for all that the only means left standing is Jesus Himself. He perfectly fulfilled all of the Law's requirements and offers forgiveness to everyone, Jew or Gentile, who trusts in Him.

For any Jew who chooses not to trust in Him, the Law will continue to be the standard by which God will hold them accountable until the sea dries up and the sun, moon, and stars stop shining.

'The End of the Law'?

Some believe the Law has been abolished,[164] based on their understanding of Romans 10:4:

> For Christ is the *end of the law* for righteousness to everyone who believes.

This is a reasonable interpretation because the Greek word here translated as 'end', *telos*, can mean 'termination' or 'cessation'.[165] However, like 'end' in English, it can also mean

---

164 e.g. *NEB*, IVP's *New Bible Commentary*.
165 e.g. Hebrews 7:3, 2 Corinthians 3:13, Luke 1:33.

'goal' or 'fulfilment', as in 'the end justifies the means'.

Kittel's Theological Dictionary of the New Testament explains: 'to understand *telos*... one must remember [its] dynamic character [which] denotes "fulfilment" (cf. Luke 22:37)', based on achievement, success, completion, totality or perfection.[166] Accordingly, it is translated as 'goal' in 1 Timothy 1:5, where love is clearly the goal of instruction, rather than its cessation; also in 1 Peter 1:9 where salvation is the 'goal' of faith in Christ, rather than its nullification.

Accordingly, *The New Oxford Annotated Bible* concludes:

> *The end of the law* almost certainly means its goal, not its termination (see also Rom 3.31, 7.12, 16, 22; 9.30-32).[167]

Paul is explicit:

> Do we then nullify the Law through faith? May it never be! On the contrary, we establish the Law. (Rom 3:31)

Add to this Jesus' words as quoted above from Matthew 5:17-18 and it becomes plain that the Law has not been terminated or nullified. It still applies to all the descendants of Abraham, Isaac, and Jacob unless they have been born again in Christ.

The Role of the Temple

The Tabernacle of Moses (1446 - c. 1000 BC) and the two Temples (the First, c. 1000 - 586 BC; the Second, 516 BC - 70 AD) were God's dwelling place in the midst of His people. At the very heart of these dwellings, in the Holy of Holies, was the ark of the covenant, the container of the two stone tablets of the Ten Commandments (Ex 25:21), which symbolised the Law (Deut 4:13).

---

166 *Kittel's Theological Dictionary of the New Testament*, abridged by G.W. Bromiley, Grand Rapids; William B. Eerdmans Publishing, 1985, pp. 1161-1162.
167 3rd Edition, *New Testament*, p. 257. So too Zondervan's *NASB Study Bible*, William Barclay's translation, and *The Message*.

From the very beginning of God dwelling among the people of Israel, He promised to meet with them on the basis of atonement, or propitiation, i.e. that they would address all violations of the covenant by sprinkling blood on the lid of the ark. Made of solid gold, it measured 2.5 x 1.5 cubits (approx. 1.1 x 0.7 metres) and its only ornamentation was two overshadowing golden cherubim (Exodus 25:17-20):

> 21. "You shall put the mercy seat on top of the ark, and in the ark you shall put the testimony which I will give to you.
> 22. "*There I will meet with you*; and from above the mercy seat, from between the two cherubim which are upon the ark of the testimony, I will speak to you about all that I will give you in commandment for the sons of Israel." (Ex 25:21-22, emphasis added)

The term 'mercy seat' was coined by Tyndale to translate the Hebrew noun *kapporeth*, which came from *kippur* (atonement) and *kopher* (the price of a life, or ransom).[168] Accordingly, the *NIV* translates it as 'the atonement cover'. The point is, it was the means of mercy.[169]

Every year, on the holiest day of the year, the Day of Atonement, Yom Kippur, the High Priest was to enter the Holy of Holies and sprinkle the blood that made propitiation or atoned for all the sins of Israel that year.

This is why the Pharisees were so outraged at Jesus forgiving people:

> 2. And they brought to Him a paralytic lying on a bed. Seeing their faith, Jesus said to the paralytic, "Take courage, son; your sins are forgiven."
> 3. And some of the scribes said to themselves, "This fellow blasphemes." (Matt 9:2-3)

---

168 *Strongs Hebrew Dictionary*, p. 1538
169 Paul wrote that that 'God publicly displayed [Jesus] as a propitiation [Gk, *hilasterion*] in His blood' (Rom 3:24-25). This Greek word is used by the Septuagint for the 'mercy seat' or 'atonement cover' (Ex 25:17-22) so Paul is explaining that Jesus is the real atonement cover, not hidden behind the veil but 'publicly displayed'.

They thought forgiveness of sins could only come through the Temple's atonement ritual. Jesus therefore answered their objections:

> 4. And Jesus knowing their thoughts said, "Why are you thinking evil in your hearts?
> 5. "Which is easier, to say, 'Your sins are forgiven,' or to say, 'Get up, and walk'?
> 6. "But so that you may know that the Son of Man has authority on earth to forgive sins" – then He said to the paralytic, "Get up, pick up your bed and go home."
> 7. And he got up and went home. (Matt 9:4-7)

He proves He is Messiah by fulfilling the predicted works of Messiah (Isa 29:18-21, 35:5-6) but He is also telling them that He is replacing the Second Temple and its means of atonement so He can forgive the man.

All the dwellings of God in ancient Israel, the Tabernacle and both of the Temples, were only ever temporary. Their real role was actually to foreshadow God coming to dwell among us in person, in the flesh:

> For a child will be born to us, a son will be given to us;
> And the government will rest on His shoulders;
> And His name will be called Wonderful Counselor, Mighty God, Eternal Father, Prince of Peace. (Is 9:6)

Messiah is the Eternal Father in human form. In John's words:

> In the beginning was the Word, and the Word was with God, and the Word was God… And the Word became flesh, and dwelt [lit. tabernacled] among us… (John 1:1 and 14)

However, until He came, these "temples made with hands" (Acts 7:48) and their sacrifices were the only means of atonement for the Jews.

Destroying the Temples

When God allowed His temples to be defiled by Gentile invaders, it was to send an unambiguous and terrible message to Israel: He was leaving His dwelling place amongst them; their sins were no longer being forgiven; they were being judged.

I established in Book 2 that this has occurred five times, in each of Israel's temples.[170] We saw there that each time, it was because Israel had committed an "abomination of desolation", i.e. an appalling sin in a long line of appalling sins that would be the ultimate, the last straw. The first instance was at Shiloh in about 1050 BC and, some four hundred and forty years later, God reminded the people through Jeremiah:

> "But go now to My place which was in Shiloh, where I made My name dwell at the first, and see what I did to it because of the wickedness of My people Israel." (Jer 7:12)

He warned them of their misplaced trust in the Temple:

> 4. "Do not trust in deceptive words, saying, 'This is the temple of the LORD, the temple of the LORD, the temple of the LORD.'
> 5. "For if you truly amend your ways and your deeds, if you truly practice justice between a man and his neighbor,
> 6. if you do not oppress the alien, the orphan, or the widow, and do not shed innocent blood in this place, nor walk after other gods to your own ruin,
> 7. then I will let you dwell in this place, in the land that I gave to your fathers forever and ever.
> 8. "Behold, you are trusting in deceptive words to no avail. (Jer 7:4-8)

Israel had been abusing God's grace, assuming that because they could be forgiven, they could sin with impunity. The "deceptive words" (v. 4) were in their misunderstanding the

---

170 *STB*, pp. 265-283: (i) the Tabernacle in Shiloh (c. 1050 BC); (ii) the First Temple in Jerusalem (586 BC); (iii) the Second Temple in Jerusalem (167 BC); (iv) The Crucifixion (30 A.D); (v) Herod's Temple (70 AD).

Temple as their means of being saved or "delivered" (v. 10):

> 9. "Will you steal, murder, and commit adultery and swear falsely, and offer sacrifices to Baal and walk after other gods that you have not known,
> 10. then come and stand before Me in this house, which is called by My name, and say, 'We are *delivered!*' – that you may do all these abominations? (Jer 7:9-10, emphasis added)

God was therefore about to remove the means of His grace or forgiveness, reminding them of how He had had to do this before, destroying the sanctuary at Shiloh:

> 11. "*Has this house, which is called by My name, become a den of robbers in your sight?* Behold, I, even I, have seen it," declares the LORD.
> 12. "But go now to My place which was in Shiloh..." (Jer 7:11-12, emphasis added)

Dens were where robbers went to hide after they had committed their robberies. God's answer was to destroy the Temple as Israel's hiding place and to judge them, just as He had at Shiloh.

This is also why Jesus was quoting Jeremiah's "den of robbers" when He cleansed the Temple in 30 AD (Matt 21:12-13).

Did the disappearance of the Tabernacle from Shiloh or the First and Second Temples in Jerusalem mean the end of the Law and the Prophets? No. With the removal of Israel's means of forgiveness, they were then judged according to the Law and the Prophets.

They spent seventy years in Babylon without the Temple, the priests and the sacrifices while the Mosaic Covenant remained in full force. In fact, as Jeremiah and Daniel recognised, they lost the Temple, priests and sacrifices because of the Mosaic Covenant.

Hosea's Prediction

This situation was not wholly unexpected. Hosea had predicted several hundred years before Jeremiah that it would happen:

> 4. For the sons of Israel will remain for many days without king or prince, *without sacrifice* or sacred pillar and *without ephod* or household idols.
> 5. Afterward the sons of Israel will return and seek the LORD their God and David their king; and they will come trembling to the LORD and to His goodness in the last days.
> (Hos 3:4-5, emphasis added)

To be 'without king or prince' (v. 4) meant that David's dynasty would be suspended 'for many days' (v. 4) but restored in 'the last days' (v. 5), i.e. in the time of Messiah as a descendant of David. Amos also predicted this restoration:

> "In that day I will raise up the fallen booth of David,
> And wall up its breaches;
> I will also raise up its ruins
> And rebuild it as in the days of old..." (Amos 9:11)

The "booth of David" is a metaphor for his dynasty rather than his literal sukkah, i.e. tent or tabernacle.[171]

Hosea's and Amos's original listeners were their countrymen of the northern kingdom who had forsaken both the house of David and the house of God in Jerusalem. God was therefore about to abandon them to the Assyrian invaders (722 BC) but their time of restoration was not until after the southern kingdom had been in captivity in Babylon for seventy years and the Second Temple was dedicated in 516 BC. Then the two kingdoms were to be reunited under 'My servant David' (Ezek 37:15-28), i.e. Messiah.[172]

---

[171] There is popular teaching that David's tabernacle refers to the worship David instituted in Jerusalem which I briefly address in Chapter 12 – David's Legacy.

[172] It was recognising that Jesus was fulfilling Amos 9:11 and reigning over Gentiles (Amos 9:12) that convinced James to withdraw his objection to Gentile believers not being circumcised (Acts 15:13-19).

For those two hundred years, the northern kingdom were 'without sacrifice or sacred pillar and without ephod or household idols', i.e. no means of atonement or divine guidance, either from the Temple or their idolatrous shrines in Bethel and Gilgal.

In other words, Hosea's prophecy was fulfilled and yet, throughout this time, all of Israel, whether of the northern or southern kingdoms, remained under the Law of Moses.

Some Messianic prophecies are recapitulated, or repeated. For example, Matthew recorded in the 1st Century that Isaiah 7:14 was again being fulfilled (Matt 1:22-23), as was Hosea 11:1 (Matt 2:15) and Jeremiah 31:35 (Matt 2:17-18). I believe this prophecy of Hosea 3:3-5 of Israel remaining many days 'without king or prince, without sacrifice or sacred pillar and without ephod or household idols' was likewise recapitulated, from 70 AD to the present day. Whether it was or not, we know that the Second Temple was destroyed in 70 AD because, as Israel's means of forgiveness, it had again become obsolete and ready to disappear (Heb 8:13).

Did this mean the end of the Law and the Prophets? Not according to Jesus in Matthew 5:17-18.

His prediction regarding Jerusalem's destruction forty years later demonstrates that even after the New Covenant was established by His death and resurrection, the Mosaic Covenant was still being enforced for those still under it.

"So... What's Left of Moses?"

Given that so much of the Law concerns the Tabernacle or Temple, the priests and the sacrificial system, what exactly is left when these are taken away?

Well, consider how Israel kept the Law while in exile in Babylon.

They kept the food-laws (Dan 1:8), fasted and prayed (Dan 9:3, Est 4:3, Zech 7:5), gave 'for the house of God' to be rebuilt

(Ezra 1:4, 2:68), and registered tribal genealogies (Neh 7:5ff.). To these we can add the unstated but everyday essentials – male circumcision,[173] keeping the Sabbath[174] and at least the Ten Commandments:

> "So He declared to you His covenant which He commanded you to perform, that is, the Ten Commandments; and He wrote them on two tablets of stone". (Deut 4:13)

These observances ensured they maintained their national identity, which was the primary purpose of the covenant:

> "Now then, if you will indeed obey My voice and keep My covenant, then you shall be *My own possession* among all the peoples, for all the earth is Mine…" (Ex 19:5, emphasis added)

Accordingly, as soon as they returned from Babylon, they rebuilt the Temple, financially supported the priesthood, and restored the sacrifices as the Law required:

> 2. Then… the priests… arose and built the altar of the God of Israel to offer burnt offerings on it, as it is written in *the Law of Moses, the man of God*.
> 3. So they set up the altar on its foundation, for they were terrified because of the peoples of the lands; and they offered burnt offerings on it to the LORD, burnt offerings morning and evening. (Ezra 3:2-3, emphasis added)

They also renewed the covenant:

> 28. Now the rest of the people, the priests, the Levites, the gatekeepers, the singers, the temple servants and all those who had separated themselves from the peoples of the lands to the Law of God, their wives, their sons and their daughters, all those who had knowledge and understanding,
> 29. are joining with their kinsmen, their nobles, and are taking on themselves a curse and an oath to walk in God's law, which was given through Moses, God's servant, and to keep and

---

173 The sign of both the Abrahamic and the Mosaic Covenants (Gen 17:10, Ex 4:26, Josh 5:2).
174 Exodus 31:12-17.

> to observe all the commandments of GOD our Lord, and His ordinances and His statutes… (Neh 10:28-29)

To protect their endangered identity as Israel, they committed to stop intermarrying:

> 30. and that we will not give our daughters to the peoples of the land or take their daughters for our sons. (Neh 10:30)

Lastly, the Law guaranteed the Promised Land, first promised by the Abrahamic Covenant:

> 42. …then I will remember My covenant with Jacob, and I will remember also My covenant with Isaac, and My covenant with Abraham as well, and *I will remember the land*.
> 43. "For the land will be abandoned by them, and will make up for its Sabbaths while it is made desolate without them….
> 45. "But *I will remember* for them *the covenant* with their ancestors, whom I brought out of the land of Egypt [i.e. the Mosaic Covenant] in the sight of the nations, that I might be their God. I am the LORD." (Lev 26:42-45, emphasis added)

As long as sun, moon, stars, and sea endure, the people of Israel will always be restored to the land that has been "desolate without them" (v. 43), because God promised, not only in the Abrahamic Covenant (v. 42) but also in the Mosaic Covenant (v. 45), to always "remember the land" (v. 42).

Always to Be Restored

The Babylonian exile was to allow the land "to make up for its Sabbaths" (v. 43), as promised under the Law (Lev 25:2-7) and as Jeremiah prophesied (2 Chron 36:21). When the seventy years of judgement were fulfilled, God fulfilled the Law's promise of restoration.

This happened despite their unbelief:

> 22. "Therefore say to the house of Israel, 'Thus says the Lord GOD, "*It is not for your sake, O house of Israel,* that I am about to act, but for My holy name, which you have profaned among the

> nations where you went...
> 24. "For I will take you from the nations, gather you from all the lands and bring you into your own land.
> 25. "Then I will sprinkle clean water on you, and you will be clean; I will cleanse you from all your filthiness and from all your idols."'" (Ezek 36:22-25, emphasis added)

The order is important here – God promised to first gather them and then cleanse them. It was not because of their faith, as we will consider soon, but because of His own plan (v. 22).

The Romans driving them out of the land again in 70 AD again fulfilled the curse of the Law (Lev 26:31-33), and the promise of the Law is why the people of Israel are back in the land of Israel today:

> 44. "Yet in spite of this, when they are in the land of their enemies, *I will not reject them*, nor will I so abhor them as to destroy them, breaking My covenant with them; for I am the LORD their God.
> 45. "But *I will remember* for them *the covenant* with their ancestors, whom I brought out of the land of Egypt in the sight of the nations, that I might be their God. I am the LORD."
> (Lev 26:44-45, emphasis added)

This may also be why Jesus was so sure that Israel would be restored before He returned:

> 23. "...there will be great distress upon the land and wrath to this people;
> 24. and they will fall by the edge of the sword, and will be led captive into all the nations; and Jerusalem will be trampled underfoot by the Gentiles *until* the times of the Gentiles are fulfilled." (Luke 21:23-24, emphasis added)

He clearly did not know the exact timing because, when the disciples asked Him, "when will these things happen, and what will be the sign of Your coming, and of the end of the age?" (Matt 24:3), He only gave them signs to look for, explaining:

> "But of that day and hour no one knows, not even the angels of

heaven, nor the Son, but the Father alone." (Matt 24:36)

However, He did know that Israel would regain Jerusalem when "the times of the Gentiles are fulfilled".

Summary of the Temple and Atonement

Contrary to what many believe today:

(i) The Law did not become 'obsolete and grow old', 'ready to disappear' but its means of atonement did. The Temple and its altar were demolished in 70 AD, having become obsolete as the only place where Israel's sins could be atoned for when Jesus fulfilled the Law 'once for all' in 30 AD for all who trust in Him.

(ii) This was why John was sent in 95-96 AD to 'measure the temple of God and the altar, and those who worship in it' (Rev 11:1), twenty-five years after the Temple and the altar had been obliterated. His measuring was not literal, nor were any results recorded; he was instead to understand and report that 'a spiritual house' was being built of 'living stones' for 'a royal priesthood' and that the new altar was metaphorical – the cross.

(iii) The Romans' destruction of the Second Temple in 70 AD was the third time that God had removed the means of Israel's atonement, the first two being when the Philistines captured the ark of the covenant in about 1050 BC, and the Babylonians destroyed the First Temple in 586 BC.

(iv) We see therefore that the loss of the ark and the destruction of the First Temple did not mean the end of the Law and the Prophets. Instead, with the removal of Israel's means of atonement, Israel were being judged according to the Law and the Prophets.

(v) Even without the Temple and its sacrifices, the Law

ruled Israel while they were in Babylon: they kept the food-laws, fasted and prayed, gave for rebuilding the Temple, registered tribal genealogies, circumcised their sons, kept the Sabbath, and obeyed the Ten Commandments.

(vi) The Romans driving Israel out of the land, forty years after the new covenant had been made, was fulfilling the Law and the Prophets. Israel's return in 1948 also fulfilled the Law and the Prophets and Jesus' prediction (Luke 21:24).

8
The Law's Curse
Duly Caused

The promise of always being restored, even if it took almost two millennia, has never lessened the consequences of Israel's disobedience. As we saw in Chapter 5, Israel has been struck throughout these 'twelve hundred and sixty days' (Rev 11:3) by the two witnesses who…:

> 6. …have the power to shut up the sky, so that rain will not fall during the days of their prophesying; and they have power over the waters to turn them into blood, and to strike the earth with every plague, as often as they desire. (Rev 11:6)

Israel were always taught about the Law's consequences. As just quoted in Chapter 7, Nehemiah described them as:

> …taking on themselves a curse and an oath to walk in God's law, which was given through Moses… (Neh 10:29)

'Taking on themselves a curse' can seem strange to modern ears, even superstitious, but in those days, it simply demonstrated their willingness to accept the penalty or due consequence of breaking a covenant. This understanding can also be seen in Proverbs 26:2:

> Like a sparrow in its flitting, like a swallow in its flying,
> So a curse without cause does not alight.

There is no thought of superstition or arbitrariness here – a curse always has a cause. This is perfectly logical because it is a consequence.

From its very beginning as a nation, God had covenanted to bless Israel by living amongst them as their king:

> 4. "You yourselves have seen… how I bore you on eagles' wings, and brought you to Myself.
> 5. "Now then, if you will indeed obey My voice and keep My covenant, then you shall be My own possession among all the peoples, for all the earth is Mine;
> 6. and you shall be to Me a kingdom of priests and a holy nation". (Ex 19:4-6)

He would not only bring them into His land (Jer 2:7), but He would also bless and protect them. However, if Israel disobeyed and broke the covenant, He would initially "turn away" from them (Deut 23:14). If they continued in disobedience, He would increasingly remove His blessings and, ultimately, His protection and their right to the land. If that happened, whenever a nation or empire arose who wanted Israel's land or wealth, they would be on their own until they had "made amends for their iniquity" by paying the due penalty (Lev 26:43).

Most of us today read about this curse in Paul's letter to the Galatians and think no more about it because it was only for the Jews under the Law:

> Christ redeemed us from the curse of the Law, having become a curse for us – for it is written, "CURSED IS EVERYONE WHO HANGS ON A TREE…" (Gal 3:13, quoting Deut 21:23)

That is a reasonable personal response for Gentiles but if we want to properly understand Jewish history, we have to understand the curse as spelled out in Leviticus 26 and Deuteronomy 28, and as clearly recognised and understood by David, Isaiah, Josiah, Huldah,[175] Jeremiah, Daniel, the writer of Chronicles, Nehemiah, Ezra, and Malachi. We will look at their responses soon, but focus on Daniel's because his is the most explicit.

---

[175] Not well known as a prophetess today but her prophecy to Josiah confirmed his reforms (2 Kings 22:13-23:3).

Terrible Consequences

We have already looked briefly at Leviticus 26. In Book 3,[176] we saw the metaphorical meaning of the number seven as 'perfect, complete or just'; in this book, we have been referencing Leviticus 26's covenantal promise of the land. Now we need to consider its predictions of Jewish history.

God had clearly warned Israel of the consequences if they were to turn away from Him:

> 17. "I will set My face against you so that you will be struck down before your enemies; and those who hate you will rule over you, and you will flee when no one is pursuing you.
> 18. "If also after these things you do not obey Me, then I will punish you seven times more for your sins.
> 19. "I will also break down your pride of power; I will also make your sky like iron and your earth like bronze". (Lev 26:17-19)

With God and His protection withdrawn, Israel were on their own. The few that survived would be those who surrendered, as He warned Israel:

> 5. "I have made the earth, the men and the beasts which are on the face of the earth by My great power and by My outstretched arm, and I will give it to the one who is pleasing in My sight.
> 6. "Now I have given all these lands into the hand of Nebuchadnezzar king of Babylon, My servant, and I have given him also the wild animals of the field to serve him.
> 7. "All the nations shall serve him and his son and his grandson until the time of his own land comes; then many nations and great kings will make him their servant.
> 8. "It will be, that the nation or the kingdom which will not serve him, Nebuchadnezzar king of Babylon, and which will not put its neck under the yoke of the king of Babylon, I will punish that nation with the sword, with famine and with pestilence," declares the LORD, "until I have destroyed it by his hand."
> (Jer 27:5-8)

---

176 *GSS*, p. 147.

Those who did not surrender faced "the sword, with famine and with pestilence" (v. 8).

Leviticus 26 adds that drought, plundering, slavery, and despair would follow for Israel's men, women, and children, and even the holy places and the land of Israel would be desolate:

> 31. "I will lay waste your cities as well and will make your sanctuaries desolate, and I will not smell your soothing aromas.
> 32. "I will make the land desolate so that your enemies who settle in it will be appalled over it.
> 33. "You, however, I will scatter among the nations and will draw out a sword after you, as your land becomes desolate and your cities become waste.
> 34. "Then the land will enjoy its sabbaths all the days of the desolation, while you are in your enemies' land; then the land will rest and enjoy its sabbaths." (Lev 26:31-38)

Deuteronomy 28 confirms that the curse will include losing battles (vv. 25-26), disease (vv. 21, 27, 35), drought (vv. 23-24), famine (v. 21), plagues (vv. 22, 38-40, 42), despair (vv. 28-29, 34), persecution (vv. 29 and 33), rape (v. 30), plundering (vv. 30-31, 33, 43-44), slavery (vv. 32, 36, 41), and cruel mockery (v. 37).

Daniel's Insight

As we saw in Book 1,[177] Daniel recognised in about 538 BC that everything that had happened and was happening to Israel was due to the curse of the Law. He also clearly saw the cause, beginning his extraordinary prayer with the covenant and confessing Israel's sinfulness:

> 4. I prayed to the LORD my God and confessed and said, "Alas, O Lord, the great and awesome God, who keeps His covenant and loving-kindness for those who love Him and keep His commandments,
> 5. we have sinned, committed iniquity, acted wickedly and

---

177 *DDJ*, pp. 154-155.

> rebelled, even turning aside from Your commandments and ordinances.
> 6. "Moreover, we have not listened to Your servants the prophets, who spoke in Your name to our kings, our princes, our fathers and all the people of the land." (Dan 9:4-6)

He acknowledges that God has been acting perfectly justly:

> 7. "Righteousness belongs to You, O Lord, but to us open shame, as it is this day – to the men of Judah, the inhabitants of Jerusalem and all Israel, those who are nearby and those who are far away in all the countries to which You have driven them, because of their unfaithful deeds which they have committed against You". (Dan 9:7)

He specifically includes all in Israel, those from the southern kingdom, Judah, and those from the northern kingdom, Israel (v. 7). Some are "nearby" in Babylon with him, after the destruction of Jerusalem in 586 BC; some are "far away" after they were scattered throughout the Assyrian Empire, when Samaria was captured in 721 BC. He confesses their disobedience to the covenant-enforcers, the prophets:

> 8. "Open shame belongs to us, O Lord, to our kings, our princes and our fathers, because we have sinned against You.
> 9. "To the Lord our God belong compassion and forgiveness, for we have rebelled against Him;
> 10. nor have we obeyed the voice of the LORD our God, to walk in His teachings which He set before us through His servants the prophets". (Dan 9:8-10)

He summarises all of Israel's calamities as due to the curse of the Law:

> 11. "Indeed all Israel has transgressed Your law and turned aside, not obeying Your voice; *so the curse has been poured out on us, along with the oath which is written in the law of Moses* the servant of God, for we have sinned against Him. (Dan 9:11, emphasis added)

He also sees this as due to God's faithfulness to this covenant:

12. "Thus He has confirmed His words which He had spoken against us and against our rulers who ruled us, to bring on us great calamity; for under the whole heaven there has not been done anything like what was done to Jerusalem.
13. "As it is written in the law of Moses, all this calamity has come on us; yet we have not sought the favor of the LORD our God by turning from our iniquity and giving attention to Your truth.
14. "Therefore the LORD has kept the calamity in store and brought it on us; for the LORD our God is righteous with respect to all His deeds which He has done, but we have not obeyed His voice." (Dan 9:12-14)

Thus what many might see as a fault in God in judging severely, Daniel recognises as His goodness and faithfulness to the explicit provisions of the Law and due entirely to Israel's breaking of the Mosaic Covenant. This included the 8th Century BC siege and capture of Samaria and the exile of the ten tribes, as well as the 6th Century BC sacking of Jerusalem by Nebuchadnezzar and Daniel's own exile in Babylon.

Recognising Curse and Cause

Daniel was not unique. As we will see next, from the beginning of Israel as a nation, many godly leaders recognised the curse of the Law when they saw it and addressed the cause appropriately.

However, Eli, the high priest in about 1100 BC, was a tragic exception. Even though he held the primary responsibility for teaching the Law (Lev 10:8-11), he signally failed in his responsibility. Israel was a nation in crisis at the time, as can be seen throughout the book of Judges and summarised in the last verse:

In those days there was no king in Israel; everyone did what was right in his own eyes. (Judg 21:25)

Right at home in the anarchy, Eli's sons, Israel's priests, were adulterous and corrupt, taking whatever they wanted from the sacrifices (1 Sam 2:12-17). God sent a prophet to rebuke Eli for honouring his sons more than the Lord (1 Sam 2:27-30) but when he still refused to act, the Lord raised up Samuel to replace them (1 Sam 2:34-35). Until he became old enough, God stood back from Israel:

> Now the boy Samuel was ministering to the LORD before Eli. And word from the LORD was rare in those days, visions were infrequent. (1 Sam 3:1)

The silence was God turning away from Israel but, despite many warnings, Eli did not recognise the curse and its cause. Accordingly, Samuel's first prophecy, given when he was a child, was the final warning:

> 12. "In that day I will carry out against Eli *all that I have spoken* concerning his house, from beginning to end.
> 13. "For I have told him that I am about to judge his house forever for the iniquity which he knew, because his sons *brought a curse on themselves* and he did not rebuke them.
> 14. "Therefore I have sworn to the house of Eli that the iniquity of Eli's house shall not be atoned for by sacrifice or offering forever." (1 Sam 3:12-14, emphasis added)

The elders of Israel were no better than Eli. Even though they recognised God was refusing to protect them (1 Sam 4:3), i.e. that they were under the curse of the Law, they ignored the cause as being the nation's sinfulness and tried instead to use the ark of the covenant as a talisman:

> When the people came into the camp, the elders of Israel said, "Why has the LORD defeated us today before the Philistines? Let us take to ourselves from Shiloh the ark of the covenant of the LORD, that *it may come* among us and *deliver us* from the power of our enemies" (1 Sam 4:3, emphasis added)

This was the first 'abomination of desolation', as we established in Book 2.[178] The outcome was an unmitigated disaster:

---

178 *STB*, pp. 265-266.

> 10. So the Philistines fought and Israel was defeated, and every man fled to his tent; and the slaughter was very great, for there fell of Israel thirty thousand foot soldiers.
> 11. And the ark of God was taken; and the two sons of Eli, Hophni and Phinehas, died. (1 Sam 4:10-11)

Eli fell and died, and the sanctuary at Shiloh was left desolate (Jer 7:12).

David, Amos, and Isaiah

David knew to pray:

> Now there was a famine in the days of David for three years, year after year; and David sought the presence of the LORD. And the LORD said, "It is for Saul and his bloody house, because he put the Gibeonites to death." (2 Sam 21:1)

David thought there might be a cause for the famine so he prayed and the Lord answered him. He also recognised his son Absalom's rebellion as the curse due to his own adultery with Bathsheba and his killing of her husband, Uriah (2 Sam 16:5-13).

Two hundred and fifty years later, around 755-750 BC,[179] Amos spelled out the increasing severity of the curse on the northern kingdom:

> 6. "But I gave you also famine in all your cities
> And lack of bread in all your places,
> *Yet you have not returned to Me,"* declares the LORD.
> 7. "Furthermore, I withheld the rain from you...
> *Yet you have not returned to Me,"* declares the LORD...
> 9. "I smote you with scorching wind and mildew;
> And the caterpillar was devouring Your many gardens...
> *Yet you have not returned to Me,"* declares the LORD.
> 10. "I sent a plague among you after the manner of Egypt;
> I slew your young men by the sword along with your captured

---

[179] David Allan Hubbard, *Joel and Amos (Tyndale Old Testament Commentary)*, Leicester; InterVarsity Press, 1989, p. 90.

horses…
Yet you have not returned to Me," declares the LORD.
11. "I overthrew you, as God overthrew Sodom and Gomorrah,
And you were like a firebrand snatched from a blaze;
Yet you have not returned to Me," declares the LORD.
12. "Therefore thus I will do to you, O Israel;
Because I will do this to you,
Prepare to meet your God, O Israel." (Amos 4:6-12, emphasis added)

They indeed met their God when the Assyrians invaded in 722 BC.

Soon after, in about 700 BC,[180] Isaiah spelled out the cause of the Assyrian invasion:

> Behold, the LORD lays the earth waste, devastates it, distorts its surface and scatters its inhabitants… for they transgressed laws, violated statutes, broke the everlasting covenant. *Therefore, a curse* devours the earth, and those who live in it are held guilty. Therefore, the inhabitants of the earth are burned, and few men are left. (Isa 24:1-6, emphasis added)

Josiah, Huldah, and Jeremiah

Eighty years later, in 622 BC (2 Kin 22:3),[181] the godly young king Josiah recognised an imminent danger to his kingdom, sending Hilkiah the high priest to the prophetess Huldah:

> 13. "Go, inquire of the LORD for me and the people and all Judah concerning the words of this book that has been found, for great is the wrath of the LORD that burns against us, because our fathers have not listened to the words of this book, to do according to all that is written concerning us." (2 Kin 22:13)

Because he responded by leading Judah to repentance, Huldah prophesied he would be spared the curse of the Law in his

---
180 Ibid.
181 Paul R. House, *The New American Commentary*, 1-2 Kings, Vol 8, Nashville, TN; B and H Publishing Group, 1995, pp. 350-351.

generation:

> 19. "…because your heart was tender and you humbled yourself before the LORD when you heard what I spoke against this place and against its inhabitants that they should become *a desolation and a curse*, and you have torn your clothes and wept before Me, I truly have heard you," declares the LORD.
> 20. "Therefore, behold, I will gather you to your fathers, and you will be gathered to your grave in peace, and your eyes will not see all the evil which I will bring on this place." (2 Kin 22:19-20, emphasis added)

Notice God "spoke" regarding the curse (v. 19) through "the words of this book" (v. 13). Josiah's listening to Leviticus 26, or Deuteronomy 28, or both, pleased God and He listened to him in return.

Thirty years later, Jeremiah recognised what was about to happen to Israel at the hand of the Babylonians but he could not persuade his hearers:

> For the land is full of adulterers;
> For the land mourns *because of the curse*.
> The pastures of the wilderness have dried up.
> Their course also is evil
> And their might is not right. (Jer 23:10, emphasis added)

In his Lamentations, he acknowledged the justice of God:

> 64. You will recompense them, O LORD,
> According to the work of their hands.
> 65. You will give them hardness of heart,
> *Your curse* will be on them. (Lam 3:64-65, emphasis added)

Not spared himself, he recorded the effects:

> 9. We get our bread at the risk of our lives
> Because of the sword in the wilderness.
> 10. Our skin has become as hot as an oven,
> Because of the burning heat of famine.
> 11. They ravished the women in Zion,
> The virgins in the cities of Judah.

> 12. Princes were hung by their hands;
> Elders were not respected.
> 13. Young men worked at the grinding mill,
> And youths stumbled under loads of wood. (Lam 5:9-13)

Just as Moses had stipulated, the curse included the sword (v.9), famine (v. 10), rape (v. 11), torture and abuse (v. 12), and slavery (v. 13).

With the wisdom of hindsight, the writer of Chronicles acknowledged God's extraordinary patience until "there was no other remedy" than judgement:

> 15. The LORD, the God of their fathers, sent word to them again and again by His messengers, because He had compassion on His people and on His dwelling place;
> 16. but they continually mocked the messengers of God, despised His words and scoffed at His prophets, until the wrath of the LORD arose against His people, until *there was no remedy*.
> 17. Therefore He brought up against them the king of the Chaldeans who slew their young men with the sword in the house of their sanctuary, and had *no compassion on young man or virgin, old man or infirm; He gave them all into his hand.*
> (2 Chron 36:15-17, emphasis added)

Nehemiah and the Returnees

In 444 BC,[182] after hearing Ezra and the Levitical scribes read out and explain 'the book of the Law of Moses' (Neh 8:1), the returnees recalled their nation's one thousand year history of disobedience to the Law and the prophets. Nehemiah recorded it:

> 25. "They [the forefathers] captured fortified cities and a fertile land.
> They took possession of houses full of every good thing,
> Hewn cisterns, vineyards, olive groves,
> Fruit trees in abundance.

---

[182] *Zondervan Pictorial Encyclopedia of the Bible*, Vol. 2, p. 471.

> So they ate, were filled and grew fat,
> And revelled in Your great goodness.
> 26. "But they became disobedient and rebelled against You,
> And cast Your law behind their backs
> And killed Your prophets who had admonished them
> So that they might return to You,
> And they committed great blasphemies.
> 27. "Therefore You delivered them into the hand of their oppressors who oppressed them…" (Neh 9:25-27)

The four hundred years from Joshua to Solomon had been troubled by Canaanite, Moabite, Midianite, Ammonite and Philistine invasions and the returnees recognised His help:

> 27. …But when they cried to You in the time of their distress,
> You heard from heaven, and according to Your great compassion
> You gave them deliverers who delivered them from the hand of their oppressors. (Neh 9:27)

These deliverers were the judges and military leaders like Othniel, Ehud, Shamgar, Deborah, Barak, Gideon, Jephthah, and Samson. However, each succeeding generation abused His grace and turned away from Him:

> 28. "But as soon as they had rest, they did evil again before You;
> Therefore You abandoned them to the hand of their enemies, so that they ruled over them. When they cried again to You, You heard from heaven,
> And many times You rescued them according to Your compassion,
> 29. And admonished them in order to turn them back to Your law.
> Yet they acted arrogantly and did not listen to Your commandments but sinned against Your ordinances,
> By which if a man observes them he shall live.
> And they turned a stubborn shoulder and stiffened their neck, and would not listen". (Neh 9:28-29)

The prayer goes on to marvel at God's patience and forgiveness:

> 30. "However, You bore with them for many years,
> And admonished them by Your Spirit through Your prophets,
> Yet they would not give ear.
> Therefore You gave them into the hand of the peoples of the lands.
> 31. "Nevertheless, in Your great compassion You did not make an end of them or forsake them, For You are a gracious and compassionate God." (Neh 9:30-31)

Like Daniel, these returnees openly confessed their sins, their trust in God, and in His faithfulness to His covenants with Abraham (Neh 9:7-8) and their nation through Moses (Neh 9:13-14). They ended in confession:

> 33. "However, You are just in all that has come upon us;
> For You have dealt faithfully, but we have acted wickedly.
> 34. "For our kings, our leaders, our priests and our fathers have not kept Your law
> Or paid attention to Your commandments and Your admonitions with which You have admonished them.
> 35. "But they, in their own kingdom,
> With Your great goodness which You gave them,
> With the broad and rich land which You set before them,
> Did not serve You or turn from their evil deeds." (Neh 9:33-35)

Clearly seeing their national ingratitude, they recommit themselves to God by renewing the covenant (Neh 9:38-10:29), as mentioned earlier.

Malachi's Curse

Fourteen years later, in 430 BC,[183] God has to remind them through Malachi:

> 8. "Will a man rob God? Yet you are robbing Me! But you say, 'How have we robbed You?' In tithes and offerings.
> 9. "*You are cursed with a curse*, for you are robbing Me, the whole nation of you!

---

183 *The Jewish Encyclopedia*, 1906. www.jewishencyclopedia.com/articles/10321-malachi-book-of, 18 Oct, 2016.

> 10. "Bring the whole tithe into the storehouse, so that there may be food in My house, and test Me now in this," says the LORD of hosts, "if I will not open for you the windows of heaven and pour out for you a blessing until it overflows.
> 11. "Then I will rebuke the devourer for you, so that it will not destroy the fruits of the ground; nor will your vine in the field cast its grapes," says the LORD of hosts."
> (Mal 3:8-11, emphasis added)

Israel's failure to give the Levites the third year tithe, as required in Deuteronomy 26:12-15, meant they could not claim the associated blessing, which left them with the curse instead.[184]

And, of course, Malachi ends with:

> 4. "Remember the law of Moses My servant, even the statutes and ordinances which I commanded him in Horeb for all Israel.
> 5. "Behold, I am going to send you Elijah the prophet…
> 6. "… lest I come and smite the land with *a curse*."
> (Mal 4:4-6, emphasis added)

So, throughout the entire Hebrew Bible, i.e. until about 400 BC, Israel's godly leaders and prophets helped them to recognise when the curse of the Law was operating and why, and how to avoid or recover from it. So why do so few today?

The Expositor's Bible

The Expositor's Bible is one of the recognised standards of expository commentaries. Published in 1906, its comments on Leviticus were written by Samuel H. Kellogg.[185] He saw Leviticus chapter 26 as not only the basis for all the predictions by Israel's prophets regarding their nation, but also as an astonishing overview of Israel's three and a half thousand year history as a nation:

---

[184] For the other two years, the tithe provided the feast for the Feast of Tabernacles (Deut 14:22-29). For more details, see my *Eating Sacred Cows (A Closer Look at Tithing)*, Emmaus Road Publishing, 2016.
[185] Samuel H. Kellogg D.D., LL.D. (1839-1899), taught Didactic Theology at Western Theological Seminary in Chicago.

> ...not only is it an epitome of all later prophecy of Holy Scripture concerning Israel, but, no less truly, an epitome of Israel's history. So strictly true is this that we may accurately describe the history of that nation, from the days of Moses until now, as but the translation of this chapter from the language of prediction into that of history.[186]

Throughout Israel's first fifteen hundred years as a nation, he wrote, the curse of the Law was evident as punishment:

> The numerous visitations in the days of the Judges, when again and again the people were given into the hands of their enemies for their sins, and so often as then they repented, were again and again delivered; the heavier judgements of later days, ...culminating in the captivity of the ten tribes, following the siege and capture of Samaria, 721 BC; and still later, the terrible siege and capture of Jerusalem by Nebuchadnezzar, 586 BC, ...What were all these events... but an historical unfolding of this twenty-sixth chapter of Leviticus?
>
> As apostasy has succeeded to apostasy, judgement has followed upon judgement. To a Nebuchadnezzar succeeded an Antiochus Epiphanes; and, after the Greco-Syrian judgement, then, following the supreme national crime of the rejection and crucifixion of their promised Messiah, came the Roman captivity, the most terrible of all...[187]

Unlike many today, Dr Kellogg realised the Law was not abolished at the cross for the nation of Israel. He recognised the curse was still in effect in his day, in the 19th Century's Russian, Ukrainian, and Polish pogroms:

> ...a judgement continued even until now in the eighteen hundred years of Israel's exile from the land of the covenant, and their scattering among the nations –

---

186 *The Expositor's Bible*, p. 528, emphasis added.
187 Ibid., pp. 528-529.

eighteen hundred years of tragic suffering, such as no other nation has ever known, or, knowing, has yet survived; sufferings which are still exhibited before the eyes of all the world to-day in the bitter experiences of the four millions of Jews in the Empire of the Czar, and the persecutions of Anti-Shemitism [sic] in other lands.[188]

Like Mark Twain in 1867,[189] and Sir Frederick Treve in 1913,[190] Dr Kellogg remarked on the fertility of the land of Israel:

> And, strangest of all, throughout this time the once fertile land has lain desolate, for the Gentiles have never settled in it in any great number; and in place of a population of five hundred to the square mile in the days of Solomon, we find now [in 1899] only a few hundred thousand miserable people, and the most of the land, for lack of cultivation, in such a condition that nothing can easily exceed its desolation… [Lev 26:31-34] have in the fullest possible sense become historical fact.[191]

He concluded there were two clearly supernatural phenomena evident throughout this eighteen hundred years, from 70 AD until the 1890s:

> One is the predicted survival of exiled Israel as a nation in the land of their enemies, their indestructibility throughout centuries of unequalled suffering; the other, the extraordinary fact that their land, so rich and fertile, which was at that time and for centuries afterwards one of the principal highways of the world's commerce and travel, the coveted possession of many nations from a remote antiquity, should during the whole period of Israel's banishment remain comparatively unoccupied

---

188 Ibid.
189 Twain wrote of 'miles of desolate country whose soil is rich enough, but is given over wholly to weeds'. Details in *DDJ*, pp. 141-142.
190 Treve wrote of Galilee being 'still fertile and even luxuriant, but neglected and forsaken like the rest of the land that surrounds the sea'. Ibid., Reference and quotations on pp. 271-272.
191 *The Expositor's Bible*, p. 529.

and untilled… Surely, one would have expected that if Israel should be cast out of such a land, it would at once and always be occupied by others who should cultivate its proverbially productive soil. But it was not to be so, for it had been otherwise written…

He finished his commentary on Leviticus 26, saying it…:

…contains unmistakable predictions regarding the nation and the land; predictions which, if fulfilled, no doubt, in a degree, in the days of the Babylonian exile and the return, were yet to receive a fulfilment far more minute, exhaustive, and impressive, in centuries which then were still *in a far distant future.*[192]

Is it not remarkable that Dr Kellogg wrote this at the end of the 19th Century (he died in 1899), before both the Holocaust and Israel's rebirth?

In summary, he says: the curse in Leviticus 26 has been enacted throughout Israel's 3,500 year history; it was not abrogated or nullified by the Crucifixion in 30 AD but, forty years later, caused the Roman exile; it also caused the next eighteen hundred years of tragic suffering, including the pogroms of his day.

Summary of the Curse

We see then that:

(i) Ancient Israel understood that the Law included awful consequences for breaking it. These were called the curse of the Law and were always perfectly just, never coming without a cause.

(ii) The Law promised the land to Israel but if God withdrew from them, which necessarily included His blessing and protection, any Gentile empire that wanted to could invade it. The consequences as spelled

---

192 Ibid., p. 530. emphasis added

out in Leviticus 26 and Deuteronomy 28 included war, disease, drought, famine, plagues, plundering, rape, slavery, and the desolation of their holy places and the land.

(iii) Many leaders in Israel including David, Amos, Isaiah, Josiah, Huldah, Jeremiah, the Chronicler, Daniel, Nehemiah, Ezra, and Malachi recognised both the curse and its cause in their times and responded accordingly.

(iv) While some may think God judged Israel too severely, Daniel recognised it as His goodness and faithfulness to the explicit provisions of the Law and due entirely to Israel's breaking of the Mosaic Covenant. This included the 8th Century BC destruction of Samaria and the exile of the ten tribes as well as the 6th Century BC sacking of Jerusalem and Daniel's own exile in Babylon.

(v) Tragically, other leaders in Israel did not recognise the curse or its cause. In about 1050 BC, Eli the high priest, who held primary responsibility for teaching the Law, failed to recognise the curse of the Law that he, his sons, and Israel were bringing on themselves; the nation's elders did not recognise it either, and this led to the first abomination of desolation, as covered in Book 2.

(vi) Throughout the Hebrew Bible, Israel's godly leaders and prophets helped them to recognise when the curse of the Law was operating and why, and how to avoid or recover from it by repenting and recommitting themselves to God via the covenant.

(vii) At the end of the 19th Century, Samuel H. Kellogg's commentary on Leviticus 26 recognised the curse of the Law as operating throughout Israel's 3,400 year history, including the then-current desolation of the otherwise "rich and fertile land" of Palestine. He also recognised that Leviticus 26 predicted not only Israel's survival but their exile by the Romans in 70 AD and future return to the land.

9
20th Century Jewish Leaders
Suspending the Law

In the last chapter, we saw that many leaders in ancient Israel recognised the curse of the Law and its cause in their times and responded accordingly. What then of more recent times? In his *Holocaust: Where Was God? An Appeal for Jewish Consideration*, Jewish intellectual Art Katz observes:

> There has not been any event in recent history that has prompted more writing, more research and more literature. It is voluminous and would take libraries of libraries to contain the exhaustive works that have sifted through the Holocaust… But there is very little literature at all on the question of, "Where was God and why did He allow it?" We can say *how* it was performed but we cannot say *why*.[193]

For example, Elie Wiesel was perhaps the most well-known and respected survivor and commentator on the Holocaust and he wrote that it…:

> …could not have been without God, nor could it have been with God. It cannot be conceived on any level.[194]

> Perhaps someday someone will explain how, on the level of man, Auschwitz was possible; but on the level of God, it will forever remain the most disturbing of mysteries.[195]

---

193   Arthur Katz, *Holocaust: Where was God?* 4th Edition, Singapore; Genesis One Media Pte Ltd, 2001, p. iv, emphasis in original.
194   Eliezer Wiesel, *Freedom of Conscience – A Jewish Commentary*, Journal of Ecumenical Studies 14 (Autumn 1977): 643.
195   Eliezer Wiesel, *Legends of Our Time*, New York; Avon, 1968, p. 20.

Katz, however, lays bare the heart of the issue according to the Scriptures:

> There is very little thought on the part of Jewish commentators to examine the meaning of the Holocaust in the context of Israel's prophetic past. We have suffered previous calamities, judgements and expulsions from the Land, but our first disposition as man has been to seek a secular, sociological or political explanation rather than to find the answer in God. We have turned to human analysis rather than to Divine revelation, and we have chosen to suspect the defects of men and of nations rather than seek the cause *in ourselves and in our own sin*.[196]

"Our Own Sin"

Just after the war, Katz was visiting Dachau as an atheist and 'an indignant, self-righteous Jew, having a fervent hatred for Germans'[197] when he had a devastating revelation:

> Something blew in me. I could no longer go on with the naïve view of "good guys" and "bad guys"... Up to that moment, I was convinced I had understood the Holocaust because I was always deeply concerned about it. But now, I had touched a horror that eclipsed those naïve categories. For me, thereafter, it was only all "bad guys" – *and I was one of them*.[198]

In 1961, Yehiel Dinur had a similarly devastating revelation. A survivor of Auschwitz, he was a witness in the trial of Adolf Eichmann, one of the major organisers of the Holocaust. When Dinur saw the mild-looking Eichmann sitting in the dock, he collapsed sobbing. Everyone assumed he was overcome by his memories of Eichmann's evil but to the astonishment of all, he later explained:

---

196   Katz, p. 17, emphasis in original.
197   Ibid., p. 1.
198   Ibid., p. 2, emphasis in original.

> I was afraid about myself. I saw that I am capable to do this… exactly like he. Eichmann is in all of us.[199]

Political theorist Hannah Arendt covered the trial for The New Yorker and wrote of the 'conspicuous helplessness the judges experienced' while trying to understand Eichmann:

> The trouble with Eichmann was [not that he was a unique monster but] precisely that so many were like him, and that the many were neither perverted nor sadistic, that they were, and still are terribly and terrifyingly normal.[200]

Her report was controversial at the time because she also strongly criticised Jewish leaders including Chaim Rumkowski, the dictatorial head of the Jewish authorities in the Lodz ghetto, who was later revealed to have been corrupt and sexually abusive.

Her experience of the Eichmann trial caused her to change her mind regarding what she had described in 1951 in *The Origins of Totalitarianism* as 'radical evil', seeing instead 'the fearsome, word-and-thought-defying banality of evil'.[201] She persuasively argued that evil possesses 'neither depth nor any demonic dimension' but 'overgrowing and laying waste the whole world because it spreads like a fungus on the surface'.[202]

However, as we saw in Book 1,[203] there is almost always a demonic dimension – the dragon tempts, inspires, anoints, and empowers us to do evil – which in no way diminishes our sinfulness, any more than Adam's was diminished in Eden.

Accordingly, Art Katz believed in both 'radical evil' and the 'demonic dimension', realising that the Holocaust…:

---

199 CBS *60-Minutes* interview by Mike Wallace, broadcast February 6, 1983.
200 *Eichmann And The Holocaust*, Penguin Books, 2005, p. 103
201 Ibid., p. 90
202 Quoted by Idith Zertal, *Israel's Holocaust And The Politics of Nationhood*, Cambridge Middle East Studies 21, Cambridge University Press, 2005, p. 136.
203 *DDJ*.

...is not a new phenomenon except in its magnitude and contemporary horror. Its radical evil reveals hitherto concealed dimensions of the demonic and satanic. It requires us, as Jews, to bring into consideration dimensions of understanding of the spirit realm that are uncomfortable for rational and secular consideration.[204]

Ignoring the Two Witnesses

Katz also saw a particular failure in Jewish leaders:

> It would not be an exaggeration to say that our finest and ablest spokesmen, under the compulsion of trying to understand the most devastating tragedy of our national experience, make little or no attempt to find explanation in any reference to Scripture at all.[205]

He quotes Emil L. Fackenheim, noted Jewish philosopher of the University of Toronto, who wrote:

> As we have seen, even the ancient rabbis were forced to suspend the biblical 'for our sins are we punished'... We too may at most only suspend the biblical doctrine, if only because we, no more than the rabbis, dare either to deny our own sinfulness or to disconnect it from history. Yet, *suspend it we must*.[206]

Obviously, not everything that goes wrong is God's punishment for our sins but to rule out the possibility altogether regarding the Holocaust? This is surely to ignore Leviticus 26 and Deuteronomy 28, clinging instead to religious traditions which invalidate the very word of God Himself (Matt 15:6).

Katz further writes:

> I once had the privilege of meeting the distinguished author, Elie Wiesel, a Romanian Jew and famed winner

---

204 Arthur Katz, *Holocaust: Where Was God?* Singapore; Genesis One Media, 1998, p. 3.
205 Ibid., p. 25.
206 Ibid., p. 107, emphasis added.

of a Nobel Peace Prize. He himself is a survivor of the Holocaust, and is probably one of the greatest spokesmen on the subject of the Holocaust. He is a beautifully eloquent man…[207] At the conclusion of his public address, I asked him privately: "Mr. Wiesel, to what degree would you be willing to acknowledge that the sufferings that we have experienced as Jews, in all the calamities of our history and especially the Holocaust, are the fulfilment of God's judgements forewarned prophetically in the concluding chapters of the books of Leviticus and Deuteronomy?" He looked at me for a moment in a kind of shocked silence and then answered, "*I refuse to consider that.*"[208]

Ironically, many 20th Century Jewish leaders nevertheless saw the hand of God in restoring them to the land. Irving Greenberg,[209] for example:

> If the experience of Auschwitz symbolizes that we are cut off from God and hope, and that the covenant may be destroyed, then the experience of Jerusalem symbolizes that God's promises are faithful and His people live on… If Treblinka makes human hope an illusion, then the Western Wall asserts that human dreams are more real than force and facts. Israel's faith in the God of history demands that an unprecedented event of destruction be matched by an unprecedented act of redemption, and this has happened.[210]

However, rather than a divine redressing of the balance, this

---

[207] For example, *The Testament*, New York; Bantam Books, 1982, and *Night*, New York; Hill and Wang, 2006.
[208] *Holocaust: Where was God?* p. 11, emphasis in original.
[209] Founder and director of the USA's National Jewish Center for Learning and Leadership; co-founder with Elie Wiesel of the Holocaust memorial organization, Zachor, and advisor to the USA's Holocaust Memorial Musuem.
[210] Irving Greenberg, *Auschwitz: Beginning of a New Era?* Reflections on the Holocaust, ed. Eva Fleischner, New York: KTAV Publishing House, Inc., 1977, p. 32.

redemption was explicitly promised in Leviticus 26, as we saw earlier:

> 42. "...I will remember My covenant with Jacob, and I will remember also My covenant with Isaac, and My covenant with Abraham as well, and I will remember the land.
> 43. "For the land will be abandoned by them, and will make up for its sabbaths while it is made desolate without them. They, meanwhile, will be making amends for their iniquity, because they rejected My ordinances and their soul abhorred My statutes.
> 44. "Yet in spite of this, when they are in the land of their enemies, I will not reject them, nor will I so abhor them as to destroy them, breaking My covenant with them; for I am the LORD their God.
> 45. "But I will remember for them the covenant with their ancestors, whom I brought out of the land of Egypt in the sight of the nations, that I might be their God. I am the LORD."
> (Lev 26:42-45)

Israel's Holocaust Museum in Jerusalem, Yad Vashem, freely acknowledges God's hand. Over its portals is inscribed a portion of Ezekiel's promise of national resurrection and restoration:

> "I will put My breath in you and you shall live again, and I will set you upon your own soil..." (Ezek 37:14)

Half a Verse

This is only half the verse. Ezekiel 37:14 continues:

> "Then you will know that I, the LORD, have spoken and done it," declares the LORD.

Israel's restoration and survival are so miraculous[211] that anyone can see God's hand if they want, even though many, even Christian Bible teachers, choose not to.

---

[211] As detailed in Book 1, *DDJ*.

What is also extraordinary, even for the most hardened cynic, is the means by which He did it. When Jesus predicted Israel's 70 AD exile, He was very specific, just as Ahijah,[212] Isaiah,[213] Hosea,[214] and Amos[215] had predicted Israel's assimilation into the Assyrian Empire in 722 BC, and Isaiah,[216] Jeremiah,[217] and Ezekiel[218] predicted Judah's exile into the Babylonian Empire in 586 BC. However, when Jesus predicted Israel's destruction by the Romans, He spoke of a very much wider dispersion:

> "…and they will fall by the edge of the sword, and will be led captive into *all the nations*; and Jerusalem will be trampled under foot by the Gentiles until the times of the Gentiles are fulfilled" (Luke 21:24, emphasis added)

Into "all the nations". Over the last 2,000 years, there have been Jews living in every nation, including here in New Zealand in the uttermost parts of the earth from their land. There is therefore a remarkable symmetry in God using "all the nations" to restore them to their land: the United Nations. The only organisation in all of recorded history to represent all 193 nations on the earth,[219] today the UN is consistently anti-Zionist, as we will consider in Book 5, *Kingdom Come*. However, at just the right time, on 29th November, 1947, the UN was so horrified by the Holocaust that it passed Resolution 181 to legitimise Israel's re-birth as a nation.

Is all this really just a coincidence?

---

[212] 1 Kings 14:15-16.
[213] Isaiah 7:20, 8:4.
[214] Hosea 10:1-7, 11:5.
[215] Amos 5:27.
[216] 2 Kings 20:17.
[217] Jeremiah 20:4.
[218] Ezekiel 12:13.
[219] www.un.org/en/members/growth.shtml, 1 Sept, 2015.

'Time and Chance Overtake All'

We saw above Professor Fackenheim insisting we must 'suspend the Biblical "for our sins are we punished"' and he does so on a perfectly valid point. The vast majority of disasters are clearly not God's punishments, despite their being blamed on Him in the legal term 'act of God', which describes immense natural phenomena such earthquakes, volcanic eruptions, tsunamis, hurricanes, tornadoes, and floods.

Other events such as wars and riots are obviously acts of man, but most disasters are caused by time and chance, as Solomon observed:

> I again saw under the sun that the race is not to the swift and the battle is not to the warriors, and neither is bread to the wise nor wealth to the discerning nor favour to men of ability; for *time and chance overtake them all*. (Eccles 9:11, emphasis added)

A race-winning athlete can stumble, a battle be lost due to bad weather, a child be killed in an accident.

On a personal note, I lost a wonderful young nephew, Sean, who was killed by an avalanche at age eighteen. He was a follower of Jesus and an expert climber who had done everything correctly for his climb – skilled companions, right weather, right equipment, right safety procedures, right techniques – but was taken by freak, unforeseeable snow conditions in one area of the mountain.

Some religions such as Islam and even Christian theologians such as John Calvin deny this, teaching that everything has been eternally predestined, even the fall of Adam.[220] However, Jesus challenges us all to instead think about this:

> 1. Now on the same occasion there were some present who reported to Him about the Galileans whose blood Pilate had mixed with their sacrifices.
> 2. And Jesus said to them, *"Do you suppose* that these Galileans

---

220 *Institutes of the Christian Religion*, Book III, Chap. xxiii, Para. 7.

> were greater sinners than all other Galileans because they suffered this fate?
> 3. "I tell you, no, but unless you repent, you will all likewise perish.
> 4. "Or *do you suppose* that those eighteen on whom the tower in Siloam fell and killed them were worse culprits than all the men who live in Jerusalem?
> 5. "I tell you, no, but unless you repent, you will all likewise perish." (Luke 13:1-5, emphasis added)

The Galileans' tragedy was obviously caused by Pontius Pilate's cruel and abusive rulership[221] and not by their sinfulness. However, the tragedy in Siloam was a matter of time and chance – the eighteen men were just in the wrong place at the wrong time.

Jesus therefore counsels us all to be ever ready because we can all die at any time.

His half-brother James advises us similarly:

> 13. Come now, you who say, "Today or tomorrow we will go to such and such a city, and spend a year there and engage in business and make a profit."
> 14. Yet you do not know what your life will be like tomorrow. You are just a vapour that appears for a little while and then vanishes away.
> 15. Instead, you ought to say, "If the Lord wills, we will live and also do this or that."
> 16. But as it is, you boast in your arrogance; all such boasting is evil. (Jas 4:13-16)

God can supernaturally intervene, as He did when He raised Tabitha from the dead (Acts 9:36-41), Peter from prison (Acts 12:3-10), and Paul and all his shipmates from shipwreck (Acts 27:23-24), but, in the natural order of things, none of us is guaranteed tomorrow.

---

221 Josephus refers to another incident, an ambush ordered by Pilate against protesters, in which 'there were a great number of them slain by this means, and others of them ran away wounded', *Antiquities*, XVIII, chap. 3, v. 2.

Of course, it was Adam's sin (Rom 5:12) that began the decay and crumbling of the entire natural order but Paul takes the long view, seeing Creation's present pains as birth-pangs:

> 20. For the creation was subjected to futility, not willingly, but because of Him who subjected it, in hope
> 21. that the creation itself also will be set free from its slavery to corruption into the freedom of the glory of the children of God.
> 22. For we know that the whole creation groans and suffers the pains of childbirth together until now. (Rom 8:20-22)

Accordingly:

> I consider that the sufferings of this present time are not worthy to be compared with the glory that is to be revealed to us. (Rom 8:18)

The Book of Job clearly established for ancient Israel that the righteous will suffer, even when completely innocent (Job 1:8). James therefore urges us today to learn from Job, and from all the prophets:

> 10. As an example, brethren, of suffering and patience, take the prophets who spoke in the name of the Lord.
> 11. We count those blessed who endured. You have heard of the endurance of Job and have seen the outcome of the Lord's dealings, that the Lord is full of compassion and is merciful. (Jas 5:10-11)

James too takes the long view of 'the outcome' (v. 11).

The Holocaust as the Law's Curse

Returning to the Holocaust, therefore, is it reasonable to rule out Jewish sinfulness as a cause, as Professor Fackenheim does? He reasons:

> ...not a single one of the six million died because they failed to keep the divine-Jewish covenant: they all died because their great-grandparents had kept it, if only to the minimum extent of raising Jewish children [i.e. they were

killed for being Jewish]. Here is the point where we reach radical religious absurdity. Here is the rock on which the "for our sins are we punished" suffers total shipwreck.²²²

He does, however, acknowledge that 2nd Century rabbis accepted some responsibility in their time:

> ...the ancient rabbis were forced to suspend the biblical "for our sins we were punished", *perhaps not in response to the destruction of the temple by Titus* [in 70 AD], *but in response to the paganization of Jerusalem by Hadrian* [in 135 AD].²²³

In other words, the destruction of Jerusalem and the Temple, and the deaths of over a million Jewish men, women, and children, were punishment, but Hadrian's building a temple to Jupiter on the Temple Mount sixty five years later was not. Despite the unanimous judgement of all the prophets and writers of the Scriptures that all the previous desolations of Israel, her land, and her sanctuaries, were for their sins and fulfilling Leviticus 26, Professor Fackenheim assumes everything somehow changed after the 2nd Century.

Along with this inconsistency, he attempts to blame it all on a simplistic sole cause: 'for our sins we were punished'. If it were that simple, we could perhaps all agree but he is also being short-sighted. We are instead called to a multi-layered understanding in the light of the biggest of pictures, in the divine revelation.

As we saw in Book 1,²²⁴ Revelation 12 portrays Israel in the 1st Century as a woman whose purpose, her raison d'etre as a nation from the 15th Century BC, was to bring forth Messiah to redeem all mankind. Viciously attacked by six successive Gentile empires as the dragon, Satan, tried to kill her Child,

---

222 Emil L Fackenheim, *God's Presence in History: Jewish Affirmations and Philosophical Reflections*, New York; Harper & Row, 1970, p. 73, comment inserted.
223 Ibid., dates inserted, emphasis added.
224 *DDJ*.

she survived and successfully gave birth. Tragically, however, she had then rejected her Son, Jesus of Nazareth, and in 70 AD was sent back into the wilderness, Ezekiel's 'wilderness of the peoples'. She remained there until 1948.

We see here at least four layers – Israel's sin and foolishness, Satan's unrelenting vindictiveness, the Gentiles' anti-Semitism, and God's faithfulness and patience:

(i) Israel are not guiltless – the Crucifixion was an abomination of desolation. Given their celebrated national covenant, they could not remain unpunished nor in the land because their Law requires a just penalty. This led directly to the sacking of Jerusalem and the Temple in 70 AD, and even though the 2nd Century rabbis did not see that connection, they did see many other sins as the cause.[225]

(ii) From about 1500 BC, Satan made the most of every opportunity to inspire the murderous, sometimes genocidal, anti-Semitism in six great Gentile empires to prevent the birth of Jesus. He then orchestrated the killing of Jesus by tempting Judas, the majority of the Jewish leaders, and the local Romans, even the lowly-ranked soldiers mocking and abusing Him. Even after Jesus was raised beyond his reach, Satan refocused his hatred on the Jewish exiles among all the nations. His genocidal campaign has therefore lasted over 3,500 years.

(iii) The Gentiles are not guiltless. Our on-going collusion with Satan's temptations and anti-Semitism has had a terrible impact on Israel but also on ourselves, as revealed in Revelation 13.

---

225 At the time, Josephus blamed the disastrous famine that sapped the defenders of Jerusalem on their murderous in-fighting and the setting on-fire of their own grain supplies, which would otherwise have lasted for years.

(iv) Despite all of this, we see that God has never given up, and never will give up, on Israel 'according to the flesh' (Rom 9:3-5), no matter what she does. He will justly punish her but He will not revoke her calling as a nation (Rom 11:29). He has also never given up, and never will give up, on us Gentiles according to the flesh. He loves the world so much that He gave us all His only-begotten Son and He still calls us all to trust in Him.

In Books 2 and 3,[226] I showed how Revelation 13 describes and predicts the consequences to the Gentiles of our rejection of Jesus, i.e. that we have instead worshipped our emperors and received their marks, from the Roman emperors in John's day, to the god-emperors of the 20th Century (Hirohito, Stalin, Mussolini, and Hitler) who provoked World War II. The death toll over the last 2,000 years has been truly appalling – in the last 100 years alone, some 270 million men, women, and children.

In this book on Revelation 11, we are focussed again on Israel 'according to the flesh'; the Law of Moses and 'the sword of vengeance for the covenant' have continued to function over these 2,000 years; Israel is still held accountable to their covenant.

Accordingly, we can conclude that the Holocaust was indeed one more fulfilment of Leviticus 26 and Deuteronomy 28, the consequences of breaking the Law.

The Boasting Axe

Lastly, what is God's attitude to the perpetrators of the Holocaust? Does He excuse Adolf Hitler because he was demonically inspired[227] in his anti-Semitism? Should He

---

226 *STB* and *GSS*.
227 I document Hitler's 'revelations' in *DDJ*, pp. 84-88, and his demonic anointing in *STB*, pp. 85-90.

even reward them because they were inflicting His 'sword of vengeance for the covenant'?

Again, this is multi-layered, according to all the issues of justice, but Isaiah gives God's unequivocal answer. Yes, God was sovereignly punishing Israel with His rod of correction by using the nations, but…:

> 5. "Woe to Assyria, the rod of My anger
> And the staff in whose hands is My indignation…
> 12. "So it will be that when the Lord has completed all His work on Mount Zion and on Jerusalem,
> He will say, 'I will punish the fruit of the arrogant heart of the king of Assyria and the pomp of his haughtiness'…
> 15. "Is the axe to boast itself over the one who chops with it?
> Is the saw to exalt itself over the one who wields it?
> That would be like a club wielding those who lift it,
> Or like a rod lifting him who is not wood". (Isa 10:5-15)

God held accountable all the god-emperors and nations of Egypt, Assyria, Babylon, Medo-Persia, Greece, and Rome, and He will also Hitler, as well as Stalin, Hirohito, Mussolini, Mao, Pol Pot, Kim Il Sung, and all who did their bidding. John saw that day coming:

> "And the nations were enraged, and Your wrath came, and the time came for the dead to be judged, and the time to reward Your bond-servants the prophets and the saints and those who fear Your name, the small and the great, and *to destroy those who destroy the earth*". (Rev 11:18, emphasis added)

Summary of 20th Century Jewish Leaders

(i) Throughout the first two millennia of Jewish history, godly leaders recognised in their time whenever the curse of the Law was operating and sought its cause in their own sinfulness.

Graeme Carlé

(ii) In the 20th Century, Jewish intellectual and commentator Art Katz called on his contemporaries to do the same in regard to the Holocaust, citing Emil L. Fackenheim and even Elie Wiesel as refusing to consider any cause "in ourselves and in our own sin".

(iii) Hannah Arendt also criticised her contemporaries for glossing over Jewish corruption and argued that evil is present in all of us.

(iv) The Holocaust can only be understood as multi-layered, a perfect storm of Israel's sinfulness, Satan's unrelenting vindictiveness, and the Gentiles' continuing anti-Semitism. Most 20th Century Jewish leaders saw only the Gentiles' anti-Semitism and ignored the testimony of the two witnesses regarding Israel's sins, as well as John's revelation of Satan's role.

(v) Many did, however, see the hand of God in the restoration of Israel in 1948. As we will consider later, this perception has continued to grow and will have a wonderful outcome.

10
In Sackcloth in Jerusalem
"O Jerusalem..."

We now turn to the time period, clothing, and location of the two witnesses:

> 3. "And I will grant authority to My two witnesses, and they will prophesy for twelve hundred and sixty days, clothed in sackcloth"...
> 8. [Then] their dead bodies will lie in the street of the great city which mystically is called Sodom and Egypt, where also their Lord was crucified (Rev 11:3, 8)

The Time Period

For the time period, we just have to use the key we obtained in Book I[228] – the "twelve hundred and sixty days" are "the times of the Gentiles" (Luke 21:24), a metaphor for the last 2,000 years, which began at the Crucifixion in 30 AD.

This vision in Revelation 11 is therefore telling us that:

(i) despite Israel's rejection of Jesus as their Messiah

(ii) despite God turning to work among the Gentiles, just as He did during Elijah's twelve hundred and sixty day drought

(iii) He has not left Himself without a witness to the Jews – Moses and Elijah, i.e. the Law and the Prophets, have never ceased testifying to them.

Theologians often divide divine revelation into general and special revelation:

---

228 *DDJ*, pp. 118-138.

> General revelation is God's witness to Himself towards all mankind through creation, history, and the conscience of man... Special revelation is God's disclosure of Himself in salvation history... and in... Scripture.[229]

Barnabas and Paul pointed out this general revelation to the Gentile crowds in Lystra:

> "He permitted all the nations to go their own ways; and yet *He did not leave Himself without witness*, in that He did good and gave you rains from heaven and fruitful seasons, satisfying your hearts with food and gladness." (Act 14:17, emphasis added)

Creation testifies to God's existence, forbearance, love, and goodness and, ultimately, He will judge all unbelieving Gentiles by it, even though they ignore or suppress the evidence:

> 19. because that which is known about God is evident within them; for God made it evident to them.
> 20. For since the creation of the world His invisible attributes, His eternal power and divine nature, have been clearly seen, being understood through what has been made, so that they are without excuse. (Rom 1:19-20)

The Jews, however, have this general revelation and the special revelation of their 'salvation history' – their existence as a people was due to God delivering them from the Egyptians – and the testimony of the Law and the Prophets. Accordingly, if they are not trusting in Jesus, they will be judged by this special revelation:

> 9. There will be tribulation and distress for every soul of man who does evil, of the Jew first and also of the Greek,
> 10. but glory and honor and peace to everyone who does good, to the Jew first and also to the Greek.
> 11. For there is no partiality with God.
> 12. For all who have sinned without the Law will also perish without the Law, and all who have sinned under the Law will be judged by the Law... (Rom 2:9-12)

---

[229] *Zondervan Pictorial Encyclopedia of the Bible*, Vol 5, p. 87.

We will look at the end of this time period in Chapter 13 – Dead in the Street.

'Clothed In Sackcloth…'

The Law and the Prophets will also 'prophesy…, clothed in sackcloth" (v. 3).

In ancient times, sackcloth was the Jewish garb for mourning and lamenting. When Jacob thought that Joseph had been killed, he "tore his clothes, and put sackcloth on his loins and mourned for his son many days" (Gen 37:34). David did likewise, lamenting for Abner (2 Sam 3:31). When Mordecai learned that Haman had persuaded Xerxes to annihilate the Jews…:

> …he tore his clothes, put on sackcloth and ashes, and went out into the midst of the city and wailed loudly and bitterly. (Est 4:1)

It was also for Jews to humble themselves and repent – David and the elders of Israel repented in sackcloth to save Jerusalem (1 Chron 21:16) as did Hezekiah (2 Kin 19:1). Isaiah, Jeremiah, Ezekiel, Daniel, Joel, Amos, Ezra, and Nehemiah called on Israel to don sackcloth because of God's judgment.[230] Jesus spoke of Chorazin and Bethsaida needing to "repent in sackcloth and ashes" (Matt 11:21).

Isaiah prophesied wearing sackcloth (Isa 20:2), as did Jeremiah (Jer 4:8) and Daniel (Dan 9:3), graphically illustrating their message.

In Revelation 11, therefore, we see that the two witnesses prophesying while clothed in sackcloth are mourning and lamenting as they speak. We are not explicitly told their message but, as established in Chapter 4, they began after Jesus was crucified and, in His two Resurrection Day Bible Studies, He ensured that all His disciples understood what

---

230   Isaiah 22:12, Jeremiah 4:8, Ezekiel 7:18, Daniel 9:3, Joel 1:13, Amos 8:10, Nehemiah 9:1.

the Law and the Prophets had always been saying about Him:

(i) that the Christ or Messiah had to die

(ii) that He had to rise from the dead on the third day

(iii) and that His message was to go to every nation, beginning in Jerusalem.

In considering their role as 'witnesses', we have necessarily focused on their testifying rather than their prophesying, and the text uses the expressions interchangeably – their 'prophesying' in v. 3 and 6 is described as 'testimony' in v. 7. However, there is a distinction to be maintained – to testify is to affirm, declare, or give evidence, usually in a courtroom,[231] whereas to prophesy is to speak on behalf of God.[232]

The Hebrew Bible has always borne testimony in its text but, over the last two thousand years, the emphasis has changed significantly. The two witnesses have continued to speak of Jesus but they are now also lamenting as they spell out the awful consequences to all under the Law who have continued to reject Him – no atonement for sins.

When Jesus came, He warned of this:

> 39. "You search the Scriptures because you think that in them you have eternal life; it is these that testify about Me;
> 40. and you are unwilling to come to Me so that you may have life." (John 5:39-40)

And again:

> 23. And He was saying to them, "You are from below, I am from above; you are of this world, I am not of this world.
> 24. "Therefore I said to you that you will die in your sins; for unless you believe that I am He, you will die in your sins." (John 8:23-24)

Let us now look at the witnesses' location.

---

231 *Concise Oxford Dictionary*, p. 1106.
232 Ibid., p. 825.

'... In Jerusalem'

As we saw earlier, opinion is divided as to which city John means. Those expecting a literal future appearance of Moses and Elijah believe this city is literally Jerusalem while those who believe the two witnesses are a metaphor for the church believe the city is also metaphorical. As Michael Wilcock explained:

> The city where their corpses lie exposed to public gaze is no more literal than the rest. It cannot at one and the same time be literally both Sodom and Egypt; and if those names are used metaphorically, why should not 'the city... where their Lord was crucified' be metaphorical also?[233]

I responded to this question earlier, in Chapter 2, pointing out that we are actually told that Sodom and Egypt are metaphorical, whereas the crucifixion of Jesus was in Jerusalem, a literal locality but given two metaphorical names:

> ...the great city which mystically [Grk. *pneumatikos*, spiritually, figuratively] is called Sodom and Egypt, where also their Lord was crucified. (Rev 11:8)

There is a clear precedent when Isaiah began his vision regarding 'Judah and Jerusalem' (Isa 1:1) by rebuking their rulers as "you rulers of Sodom" and the people as "you people of Gomorrah" (Isa 1:10). He was even speaking to the people of the same literal locality using two metaphorical names, so we will establish the meaning of these names soon.

However, what do these commentators mean by Jerusalem in Revelation 11 being metaphorical?

Craig R. Koester's answer is 'the whole realm in which oppression takes place';[234] N.T. Wright says 'the great city' is Rome itself, or maybe in this case the public world of the

---

233 *The Message of Revelation*, p. 106.
234 *Revelation and the End of All Things*, pp. 109-110.

entire Roman Empire';[235] and Laurie Guy calls it 'simply a place of great evil'.[236]

As I see it, they are partly right and partly wrong. As established above, the two witnesses are metaphorical, Moses and Elijah symbolising the Law and the Prophets but the city here is both literal, i.e. where Jesus was crucified, and metaphorical.

This dual meaning is also plainly taught in Galatians 4 where Paul contrasts Abraham's two wives and their sons: Sarah was free and bore the promised child, Isaac, and Hagar was a 'bondwoman', or slave, and bore Ishmael. By divine inspiration, he tells us they symbolise two covenants and two Jerusalems:

> 24. This is allegorically speaking, for these women are two covenants: one proceeding from Mount Sinai bearing children who are to be slaves; she is Hagar.
> 25. Now this Hagar is Mount Sinai in Arabia and corresponds to the present Jerusalem, for she is in slavery with her children.
> 26. But the Jerusalem above is free; she is our mother…
> 31. …we are not children of a bondwoman, but of the free woman. (Gal 4:24-31)

What are 'the present Jerusalem' (v. 25) and 'the Jerusalem above' (v. 26)? 'Present Jerusalem' is the literal, old city, in contrast to the spiritual, 'heavenly Jerusalem' (Heb 12:22) or 'new Jerusalem' (Rev 21:2).

'The present Jerusalem' also symbolises the covenant 'from Mount Sinai bearing children who are slaves' (v. 24). Who are her children? All Jews who reject the New Covenant and therefore remain under the Old, or Mosaic, Covenant.

---

235 *Revelation for Everyone*, pp. 99-100.
236 *Making Sense of Revelation*, p. 107.

Jesus' Lament

We also see this in Jesus' lament:

> "O Jerusalem, Jerusalem, the city that kills the prophets and stones those sent to her! How often I wanted to gather your children together, just as a hen gathers her brood under her wings, and you would not have it! (Luke 13:34)

To whom is He speaking? Who exactly is "Jerusalem" and "your children" (v. 34)? Clearly Jesus does not mean that the literal city kills prophets and apostles but that the nation's leaders who reside there do; Jerusalem's "children" are all who follow them. This is the same as Paul's metaphor (and perhaps its origin) regarding 'the present Jerusalem... with her children'. It means all who remain under the Mt Sinai Covenant because they reject Jesus and the New Covenant.

Jesus warns these adult "children" of the outcome:

> "Behold, your house is left to you desolate; and I say to you, you will not see Me until the time comes when you say, 'BLESSED IS HE WHO COMES IN THE NAME OF THE LORD!'" (Luke 13:35)

"Your house" (v. 35), the Temple, is becoming "desolate" because in rejecting Jesus, these unbelieving Jews are rejecting God Himself, living in their midst.[237] Even so, He makes them a remarkable promise: if any change their mind regarding Him, they will "see" Him.

Why must they "say" that phrase? Because in the 1st Century, this phrase from Psalm 118:26 was commonly understood as a Messianic title, as in the cry of the multitudes when He entered Jerusalem on Palm Sunday:

> "Hosanna! BLESSED IS HE WHO COMES IN THE NAME OF THE LORD, even the King of Israel". (John 12:13)

In what way then would they "see" Him?

---

237 This was the fourth "abomination of desolation", as identified in *STB*, pp. 273-275.

> 19. "After a little while the world will no longer see Me, but you will see Me; because I live, you will live also.
> 20. "In that day you will know that I am in My Father, and you in Me, and I in you." (John 14:19-20)

Jesus will reveal Himself to any who call on Him from a surrendered heart (John 14:22-23).

Returning to our text then, we find that Revelation 11 is illustrating, as John saw in 95 AD, that sixty five years after the Crucifixion, the Law and the Prophets were still testifying to 'the present Jerusalem... with her children', and have continued to do so for the last 2,000 years.

'Sodom and Egypt'

It must have come as a rude shock for many to hear John's description of Jerusalem as:

> ...the great city which mystically [Gk, *pneumatikos*, spiritually] is called Sodom and Egypt, where also their Lord was crucified. (Rev 11:8)

The *NASB* translators used the word 'mystically' where others use 'spiritually',[238] the *NIV* has 'figuratively', the *RSV* reads 'allegorically', the *NRSV*, 'prophetically', and the *ESV*, 'symbolically'. Clearly this is a metaphorical name. So, why is Jerusalem called Sodom and Egypt?

1. Sodom

John was following Isaiah who addressed the rulers of Judah and Jerusalem as "you rulers of Sodom" and the people as "you people of Gomorrah" (Isa 1:10). This is not a hard metaphor to understand. Sodom and Gomorrah were two infamous cities destroyed by God for their wickedness (Gen 18:20). Jesus likewise warned every Jewish city who ignored His messengers:

> "Truly I say to you, it will be more tolerable for the land of

---

238 e.g. *KJV, NKJV, Modern Language*.

Sodom and Gomorrah in the day of judgement than for that city". (Matt 10:15)

Jerusalem is therefore 'mystically', spiritually, metaphorically called Sodom because they rejected His message and crucified Him.

2. Egypt

Again, this is not a hard metaphor. Egypt was infamous to the Jews as the great Gentile empire that had enslaved them; their first annual festival, Passover, celebrated their escape from that slavery. The irony of Jerusalem now being "Egypt"!

Now, Paul says, 'the present Jerusalem' is not only 'in slavery with her children' to the Law (Gal 4:25) but also persecuting the children born 'free' and 'according to the Spirit' (Gal 4:29). He reproves the Galatians for submitting to those trying to circumcise them:

> But now that you have come to know God, or rather to be known by God, how is it that you turn back again to the weak and worthless elemental things, to which you desire to be *enslaved all over again?* (Gal 4:9, emphasis added)

When Israel was born as a nation, Moses called down the plagues of God on Egypt; for the last 2,000 years, it has been Israel 'according to the flesh' suffering these plagues, just as Moses warned them:

> 58. "If you are not careful to observe all the words of this law which are written in this book, to fear this honored and awesome name, the LORD your God,...
> 60. He will bring back on you *all the diseases of Egypt* of which you were afraid, and they will cling to you." (Deut 28:58-60, emphasis added)

In other words, if they turned back to live like the Egyptians, God would punish them just as He had the Egyptians. Stephen too tried to warn those who were about to stone him to learn from history:

> "Our fathers were unwilling to be obedient to him [Moses], but repudiated him and *in their hearts turned back to Egypt..."* (Act 7:39, emphasis added)

'The present Jerusalem' is at heart just like Egypt: disobedient to God and trying to turn back Jewish believers in Jesus to be enslaved again.

Summary of Sackcloth in Jerusalem

In considering the time period, clothing, and location of the two witnesses, we found:

(i) The 1,260 days that the two witnesses prophesy is the metaphorical "times of the Gentiles". They therefore began this ministry from the Crucifixion in 30 AD, continued throughout almost two millennia, and seem to have finished in 1967. We will consider soon what happened in 1967.

(ii) The witnesses are clothed in sackcloth, the garb of lamenting and mourning, because they are testifying to the Jewish people about their sins after they have rejected Jesus as Messiah and about the awful consequences when there is no other means of atonement.

(iii) Their testifying in Jerusalem means they are speaking to 'the present Jerusalem' (Gal 4:25) which, as Paul wrote, is a metaphor for all Jews who have not yet accepted Jesus as Messiah.

(iv) In the 6th Century BC, Isaiah referred to Jerusalem as Sodom; in John's 1st Century vision, God again refers to Jerusalem as Sodom because so many there were wicked and rejecting Jesus as Messiah. He also calls Jerusalem 'Egypt' because their leaders were persecuting Jews who had accepted Jesus, to enslave them again under the Law.

11
Conclusions
So Far...

In Chapter 1, I established that John's being sent in 95 or 96 AD to measure 'the temple of God and the altar, and those who worship in it' (Rev 11:1) had to be metaphorical because the temple in Jerusalem and its altar had been obliterated by the Romans in 70 AD. We saw how this echoed Ezekiel measuring the earlier temple and altar in 573 BC, after it too had been destroyed by the Babylonians, and Zechariah seeing a man being sent 'to measure Jerusalem' (Zech 2:2) in 519 BC. We were able to conclude:

(i) 'Measuring' in this manner was a Jewish metaphor for comprehending, understanding, and judging.

(ii) John was to understand that God was building 'a spiritual house', comprised of 'living stones' for 'a royal priesthood' to offer 'spiritual sacrifices' (1 Pet 2:5 & 9) at a spiritual altar (Heb 13:10).

(iii) The city of Jerusalem was to remain under Gentile domination for "forty-two months" (Rev 11:2), to be "trampled underfoot by the Gentiles until the times of the Gentiles are fulfilled" (Luke 21:24). Jerusalem's being regained by Israel in 1967 points to this time period being a metaphor for the last 2,000 years.

In Chapters 2 to 5, I established that the 'two witnesses' are not literally Moses and Elijah but allusions that personify the Law and the Prophets, i.e. the Hebrew Bible:

(i) Far from becoming irrelevant when Jesus came as

Messiah to fulfill their prophecies in 30 AD, the Law and the Prophets became the primary witnesses to Israel as to the gravity and consequences of their rejection of Him.

(ii) This is why, on the very day of His resurrection from the dead, instead of celebrating, Jesus took first the two disciples on the road to Emmaus, then the apostles and all who had gathered in Jerusalem on the Bible study of all Bible studies. 'He explained to them the things concerning Himself in all the Scriptures' (Luke 24:27); that "all things which are written about Me in the Law of Moses and the Prophets and the Psalms must be fulfilled" (Luke 24:44). The Hebrew Bible never lost its importance; understanding it properly became even more vital.

(iii) The 1,260 days that the two witnesses prophesy (Rev 11:3) is the same metaphorical time period as the forty-two months (Rev 11:2), and the second half of Daniel's 70th Week. They therefore began their testimony in 30 AD, continued throughout the last 2,000 years, and seem to have finished in 1967. We will consider what happened in 1967 soon.

(iv) The two witnesses' testimony is irresistible because it is God's judgement. The fire flowing 'out of their mouth' points us to Moses, whose Israelite opponents were destroyed by the fire of God, and Elijah, who called down the fire of God on two squads of Israelite soldiers sent to arrest him. It is therefore God's vindication of the Law and the Prophets, destroying their unbelieving Jewish opponents over the last 2,000 years.

Chapters 6 and 7 address the common misunderstanding in our churches that what we call the Old or Mosaic Covenant is obsolete:

(i) Jesus made a clear distinction between abolishing and fulfilling, saying He was fulfilling the Law but not abolishing it because even the 'smallest letter and stroke' will endure 'until heaven and earth pass away' and 'all is accomplished' (Matt 5:17-18).

(ii) We need to be clear, however, that the Law only applies to those with whom it was made, all of the descendants of Abraham, Isaac, Jacob, and Jacob's twelve sons 'according to the flesh' who have not yet died and been born again in Christ (Rom 7:4).

(iii) Accordingly, any Christian, whether Jew or Gentile, who tries to be justified by the Law is choosing the wrong covenant and fallen from grace (Gal 5:4).

(iv) We need to understand the issues of priests, garments, altars, sacrifices, buildings, festivals, Sabbaths, food, alcohol, and giving according to the New Covenant and not the Old.

(v) The definition of sexual morality in the Old Covenant has not changed in the New, any more than the definition of murder, rape, theft, drunkenness, or lying.

(vi) However, the means of atonement and how we are to overcome our sinfulness has changed dramatically: instead of going to a priest in a holy building for forgiveness, we are to talk directly to Jesus, our great High Priest, and trust in His completed sacrifice on the cross; to overcome the power of sin, we are to call on the Holy Spirit to give us a new heart and a new spirit, to change our thoughts and desires.

(vii) God allowed the Tabernacle and the First and Second Temples to be destroyed so that Israel's misplaced trust in these structures would be redirected back to Him. Their destruction as the means of atonement did not mean the end of the Law and the Prophets but that Israel was being judged according to the Law and the Prophets.

(viii) Hosea prophesied that Israel would live 'for many days… without sacrifice' and without a priest wearing an ephod (Hos 3:4) but, because of this, would return to God and His Messiah (Hos 3:5). Amos also predicted David's dynasty would be restored by Messiah (Amos 9:11).

(ix) Through all these calamitous times, the Law kept Israel distinct as a nation until Jesus came and has continued to do so until today.

In Chapters 8 and 9, we looked at how ancient Israel's godly leaders recognised the curse of the Law when it came into force, and why:

(i) This is most obvious in the prayers of Daniel (Dan 9:4-14) and Nehemiah (Neh 9:26-35) and in the lives and prophecies of Samuel, David, Amos, Isaiah, Josiah, Huldah, Jeremiah, Nehemiah, Ezra, and Malachi, and in the Chronicles (2 Chron 36:15-17).

(ii) In stark contrast, Israel's national leaders in the 20th Century rejected even the concept of the curse of the Law while often accepting the promise of the restoration of the land.

Chapter 10 therefore argued:
- (i) The two witnesses are dressed in sackcloth, lamenting because they are testifying to Israel's sins and lack of atonement, dramatically illustrated by the destruction of the Temple, the altar, and its sacrifices in 70 AD.
- (ii) Being located in Jerusalem means they have been speaking to 'the present Jerusalem', a metaphor for every Jewish man or woman who has rejected Jesus and His New Covenant, thus remaining under the Mosaic Covenant.
- (iii) Jesus wept, "O Jerusalem, Jerusalem…", because He knew exactly what lay before her and her children.
- (iv) Jerusalem was spiritually called Sodom and Egypt in 95 AD because, as Isaiah and Jesus prophesied, Sodom was a metaphor, a by-word, for great wickedness; Egypt was a metaphor for the disobedient enslavers of God's people.
- (v) The witnesses' message includes the consequences of Israel's rejection of Messiah, the loss of God's kingdom, and the curse of the Law, as spelled out in Leviticus 26 and Deuteronomy 28. However, it also contains the way back for any Jew willing to listen to their testimony that Messiah had to die and rise again on the third day and that His offer of forgiveness of sins was for all the nations.

Relevance for Today

The role of the Law of Moses is often misunderstood today:
- (i) Many Christians believe that when Jesus fulfilled the Law, He also abolished or nullified it, despite Jesus explicitly keeping these two concepts separate. He added that the

Law will not pass away until all is accomplished and heaven and earth pass away (Matt 5:17-18). Paul likewise told us the New Covenant was not 'nullifying' but 'establishing the Law' (Rom 3:31), i.e. vindicating it.

(ii) This means the Law still applies to those who remain under it, i.e. all in Israel 'according to the flesh' who reject Jesus. Paul explicitly taught this in Romans 7:1-4.

(iii) James the Lord's brother confirmed this when testifying at the council in Jerusalem: there was no point in the church "preaching Moses" when the synagogues in every city were already doing so – the church needed to preach Jesus (Acts 15:21). He also affirmed the Law's testimony in his letter (Jas 2:10).

(iv) What became obsolete in 30 AD and then disappeared in 70 AD was not the Law but its means of atonement: the Temple and the sacrificial system. Accordingly, the only means of forgiveness that exists for every Jew, as it is for every Gentile, is faith in Jesus who has fulfilled the Law. This explicitly rules out Dual Covenant Theology, the belief that Jews or Jewish proselytes are still to trust in the Mosaic Covenant for salvation and that it is only Gentiles that are saved through trusting in the New Covenant.

(v) This loss of atonement was also demonstrated in the destruction of the First Temple in 586 BC. Having lost their means of forgiveness, Israel faced the judgement of God for seventy years in the Babylonian exile. While in Babylon, however, they still kept the food laws, fasted, prayed, gave, circumcised their baby boys, registered their genealogies, observed the Sabbath and the Ten Commandments, and never forgot Jerusalem or the Promised Land.

(vi) They have done the same for the last 2,000 years.

The curse of the Law is also often misunderstood today:

(i) In Biblical times, it was not dreaded as arbitrary but seen as the reasonable penalty for breaking the covenant, i.e. God removing His blessing, and eventually His presence.

(ii) When the curse was incurred, the great Gentile empires could do to Israel what they were doing to every other nation around them: killing, plundering, raping, enslaving, and desecrating holy places as they pleased, until the land was left desolate.

(iii) The curse also included natural disasters such as droughts, famines, plagues of insects, and diseases. Godly leaders in ancient Israel recognised when the curse was operating, prayed to find the reason, and responded accordingly.

(iv) In the 20th and 21st Centuries, tragically few Jewish leaders have recognised the curse and its cause. What would Daniel, David, Isaiah, Josiah, Huldah, Jeremiah, Nehemiah, Ezra, and Malachi have thought of our times?

Lastly, we should keep our eyes on Jerusalem in these days, which is not hard because it is often in our news headlines. We need to understand why it is not just Jews, Christians, and Muslims who love the city for its historical significance but God Himself who loves it today and will protect it in the future.

12
David's Legacy
More Than A Song

What is it about Jerusalem? Why is this earthly city so important in God's plans? The answers lie in the 'everlasting covenant' God made with David (2 Sam 23:5).

It is only when we consider this covenant that we can properly understand today's news' headlines about Jerusalem; we will also better understand the priestly order of Melchizedek, the 'royal priesthood' to which all Christians belong (1 Pet 2:9). As we will see, it is no coincidence that Jerusalem was the city of Melchizedek.

It initially seemed wrong to me that, like the Mosaic Covenant, David's covenant would also still be in force today. Many Christians, perhaps most, believe as I did, that there is only one Biblical covenant now, the New and Eternal Covenant. However, when I actually searched out the status of eight covenants God made in the Scriptures, I found that they are all still in force for those under them. In fact, they are all referred to as Eternal or Everlasting (Heb, *ola*; Grk, *aionios*). Their relevance and application today requires quite some explanation so I have given details in Appendix A – God's Covenants.

As for David, we need to first establish his historicity, then the promises God made to him, his capture of Jerusalem, and his prophecy regarding Melchizedek's priesthood.

The Quest for the Historical David

David is a spectacular figure in the Scriptures, mentioned over a thousand times and famed not only for his exploits in battle after his triumph over Goliath, but also as 'the sweet psalmist of Israel' (2 Sam 23:1). Although scholars today debate whether he wrote all seventy three psalms attributed to him, the New Testament names him as author of the Messianic prophecies of Psalms 2, 8, 16, 22, 69 and 110.[239]

Over the last fifty years, some archaeologists have poured scorn on this Biblical record. For example, Israel Finkelstein, Professor of Archaeology at Tel Aviv University, who…:

> … has made a career out of merrily demolishing [the reliability of the Bible as an archaeological and historical guide]. He and other proponents of "low chronology" say that the weight of archaeological evidence in and around Israel suggests the dates posited by biblical scholars are a century off. The "Solomonic" buildings excavated by biblical archaeologists over the past several decades at Hazor, Gezer and Megiddo were not constructed in David and Solomon's time, he says, and so must have been built by kings of the ninth century BC's Omride dynasty, well after David and Solomon's reign.
>
> During David's time, as Finkelstein casts it, Jerusalem was little more than a "hill-country village", David himself a raggedy upstart akin to Pancho Villa, and his legion of followers more like "500 people with sticks in their hands shouting and cursing and spitting – not the stuff of great armies of chariots described in the text".[240]

In his 2001 book, *The Bible Unearthed: Archaeology's New Vision of Ancient Israel and the Origin of Its Sacred Texts*, he and Neil Silberman wrote:

> …an archaeological analysis of the patriarchal conquest, judges, and United Monarchy narratives [shows] that

---

239 Psalm 2 (Acts 4:25), Psalm 8 (Heb 2:6-8), Psalm 16 (Acts 2:25-28), Psalm 22 (Matt 27:46, Mark 15:34, John 19:23-24, 34, 37), Psalm 69 (Rom 11:9), Psalm 110 (Matt 22:43-44, Mark 12:36, Luke 20:42, Acts 2:34-35).
240 Robert Draper, *National Geographic*, Dec, 2010, pp. 73-74.

while there is no compelling archaeological evidence for any of them, there is clear archaeological evidence that places the stories themselves in a late 7th-century BCE context.²⁴¹

However, he spoke too soon.

In 2005, Eilat Mazar of the Hebrew University of Jerusalem unearthed the City of David. At the same time, Yosef Garfinkel, also of the Hebrew University, was excavating the Judaean city of Shaaraim (1 Sam 17:52) in the Elah Valley, where David killed Goliath, and dating it to 10th Century BC. Meanwhile, Thomas Levy, a San Diego professor, was excavating a vast copper-smelting operation just south of the Dead Sea. *National Geographic* reported in December, 2010:

> Levy dates one of the biggest periods of copper production at the site to the tenth century B.C – which, according to the biblical narrative, is when David's antagonists the Edomites dwelled in this region. (However, scholars like Finkelstein maintain that Edom did not emerge until two centuries later.) The very existence of a large mining and smelting operation fully two centuries before Finkelstein's camp maintains the Edomites emerged would imply complex economic activity at the exact time that David and Solomon reigned. "It's possible that this belonged to David and Solomon," Levy says of his discovery. "I mean, the scale of metal production is that of an ancient state or kingdom".
>
> Levy and Garfinkel… support their contentions with a host of scientific data, including pottery remnants and radiocarbon dating of olive and date pits found at the sites… As Eilat Mazar says with palpable satisfaction, "This is the end of Finkelstein's school".²⁴²

---

241 Israel Finkelstein and Neil Asher Silberman, *The Bible Unearthed: Archaeology's New Vision of Ancient Israel and the Origin of Its Sacred Texts*, New York; Free Press, 2001.
242 Robert Draper, *National Geographic*, Dec, 2010, p. 75.

The article fails to note that the Edomites had been David's antagonists but then became his servants:

> He put garrisons in Edom. In all Edom he put garrisons, and all the Edomites became servants to David. And the LORD helped David wherever he went. (2 Sam 8:14)

This means the Edomites would have paid 'tribute, custom and toll' (Ezra 4:20), as did their neighbours, the Moabites (2 Sam 8:2) and the Arameans (2 Sam 8:6), firstly to David, and then to Solomon (1 Kin 4:21).

David's Everlasting Covenant

David was an all too fallible king, his adultery with Bathsheba still being sung about by Leonard Cohen in his celebrated *Hallelujah*:

> Your faith was strong but you needed proof,
> You saw her bathing on the roof,
> Her beauty and the moonlight overthrew you…

However, David was also 'a man after God's own heart' (1 Sam 13:14), because he knew how to repent thoroughly, as we know from his Psalms 32 and 51. His temporary lapse did not negate his otherwise lifelong devotion to God:

> One thing I have asked from the LORD, that I shall seek:
> That I may dwell in the house of the LORD all the days of my life,
> To behold the beauty of the LORD
> And to meditate in His temple. (Psa 27:4)

Though not allowed to build the Temple (1 Chron 28:3), he was inspired to design it (1 Chron 28:19) and provide the materials (1 Chron 29:2-5). As a child looking after sheep in the hills around Bethlehem, David had developed not only his skill as a musician and song-writer, but a compassion and spiritual sensitivity that God appreciated:

> 70. He… chose David His servant

> And took him from the sheepfolds;
> 71. From the care of the ewes with suckling lambs He brought him
> To shepherd Jacob His people,
> And Israel His inheritance.
> 72. So he shepherded them according to the integrity of his heart,
> And guided them with his skilful hands. (Psa 78:70-72)

God also promised David:

> 12. "When your days are complete and you lie down with your fathers, I will raise up your descendant after you, who will come forth from you, and I will establish his kingdom.
> 13. "He shall build a house for My name, and I will establish the throne of his kingdom forever". (2 Sam 7:12-13)

The first part of this promise was fulfilled in Solomon building the First Temple but the latter part grants David an everlasting dynasty. In his last words, David attributes this to an 'everlasting covenant' (2 Sam 23:5), as does a prophecy in Psalm 89:

> 3. "I have made a *covenant* with My chosen;
> I have sworn to David My servant,
> 4. I will establish your seed *forever*
> And build up your throne to all generations…" (Psa 89:3-4, emphasis added)

It is to endure as long as the sun and moon, i.e. until the Last Day:

> 36. "His seed shall endure forever
> And his throne as the sun before Me.
> 37. "It shall be established forever like the moon,
> And the witness in the sky is faithful." (Psa 89:36-37)

This covenant also became a standard of God's faithfulness:

> "Incline your ear and come to Me.
> Listen, that you may live;
> And I will make an everlasting covenant with you,
> According to the faithful mercies shown to David". (Isa 55:3)

David's Fallible Heirs

When his son Solomon turned away from God, Ahijah prophesied to Jeroboam, one of Solomon's officials:

> 31. "...thus says the LORD, the God of Israel, 'Behold, I will tear the kingdom out of the hand of Solomon and give you ten tribes
> 32. (but he will have one tribe, *for the sake of My servant David and for the sake of Jerusalem*, the city which I have chosen from all the tribes of Israel),
> 33. because they have forsaken Me, and have worshiped Ashtoreth the goddess of the Sidonians, Chemosh the god of Moab, and Milcom the god of the sons of Ammon...'" (1 Kin 11:31-33, emphasis added)

Despite Solomon and Israel's idolatry, God honoured David and his city, Jerusalem, by naming it His own:

> 36. But to his son [Rehoboam] I will give one tribe, that My servant David may have a lamp always before Me in Jerusalem, the city where I have chosen for Myself to put My name.'" (1 Kin 11:36)

In the time of Rehoboam, David's grandson, ten tribes abandoned David's dynasty to become the northern kingdom under Jeroboam, retaining the name of Israel; Judah, Benjamin, and the Levites became the southern kingdom, called Judah. Two hundred and fifty years later, in 722 BC, the northern kingdom was destroyed by the Assyrians.

However, Hosea predicted at the time, the survivors of the northern kingdom of Israel would eventually regather to the house of David:

> 4. For the sons of Israel will remain for many days without king or prince, without sacrifice or sacred pillar and without ephod or household idols.
> 5. Afterward the sons of Israel will return and seek the LORD their God and *David their king*; and they will come trembling to the LORD and to His goodness in the last days. (Hos 3:4-5, emphasis added)

Amos had prophesied similarly, predicting the complete destruction of the northern kingdom, followed by the restoration of David's dynasty over the survivors:

> 8. "Behold, the eyes of the Lord GOD are on the sinful kingdom,
> And I will destroy it from the face of the earth;
> Nevertheless, I will not totally destroy the house of Jacob,"
> Declares the LORD.
> 9. "For behold, I am commanding,
> And I will shake the house of Israel among all nations
> As grain is shaken in a sieve,
> But not a kernel will fall to the ground.
> 10. "All the sinners of My people will die by the sword,
> Those who say, 'The calamity will not overtake or confront us.'
> 11. "In that day *I will raise up the fallen tabernacle of David*
> And wall up its breaches;
> I will also raise up its ruins
> And rebuild it as in the days of old" (Amos 9:8-11, emphasis added)

Just as a sieve separated grain from small stones and detritus, God was going to let "all the sinners" (v. 10) fall before the Assyrians but preserve all who remained faithful to Him (v. 9).

The southern kingdom escaped the Assyrians, but in 586 BC they were devastated by the Babylonians. It seemed to many that David's dynasty died then, with Zedekiah and his sons:

> 6. Then they captured the king [Zedekiah] and brought him to the king of Babylon at Riblah, and he passed sentence on him.
> 7. They slaughtered the sons of Zedekiah before his eyes, then put out the eyes of Zedekiah and bound him with bronze fetters and brought him to Babylon. (2 Kin 25:6-7)

However, Zedekiah's predecessor Jehoiachin, who had been exiled to Babylon eleven years earlier in 597 BC, was still being honoured there as the king of Judah in 561 BC (2 Kin 25:27-30). Jehoiachin was therefore the last king of David's dynasty until Jesus came, as Ezekiel prophesied:

> 25. "And you, O slain, wicked one, the prince of Israel, whose day has come, in the time of the punishment of the end,"
> 26. thus says the Lord GOD, "Remove the turban and take off the crown; this will no longer be the same…
> 27. "… This also will be no more *until He comes whose right it is*, and I will give it to Him." (Ezek 21:25-27, emphasis added)

Of Jehoiachin's five sons, none was ever anointed as king but his grandson Zerubbabel (Matt 1:12) did return to Judah as governor, as we saw earlier in Zechariah 4.

Today, the rabbis teach that for the next one and a half thousand years, Israel was led by an Exilarch, i.e. prince of the exiles.[243] The last one, Hezekiah ben David, was executed by a Muslim caliph in 1040 AD. Accordingly, in 2016 they are still waiting for Hosea's prophecy of 'David their king' (Hos 3:5) to be fulfilled.

David's Infallible Heir

In the chaotic aftermath of the Assyrian invasion and the threat of the Babylonian invasion, Isaiah also predicted restoration:

> A throne will even be established in lovingkindness,
> And a judge will sit on it in faithfulness *in the tent of David*;
> Moreover, he will seek justice
> And be prompt in righteousness (Isa 16:5, emphasis added)

Isaiah's more famous Messianic prophecies speak of this as re-establishing David's dynasty:

> 6. For a child will be born to us, a son will be given to us;
> And the government will rest on His shoulders;
> And His name will be called Wonderful Counselor,
> Mighty God, Eternal Father, Prince of Peace.
> 7. There will be no end to the increase of His government or of peace, *on the throne of David* and over *his kingdom*,
> To establish it and to uphold it with justice and righteousness
> From then on and forevermore.
> The zeal of the LORD of hosts will accomplish this.
> (Isa 9:6-7, emphasis added)

---

243 www.jewishencyclopedia.com/articles/5937-exilarch, 2 Jul, 2015.

Not only would Messiah raise up the Davidic dynasty for Israel but also for Gentiles:

> 5. And now says the LORD, who formed Me from the womb to be His Servant,
> To bring Jacob back to Him, so that Israel might be gathered to Him...
> 6. He says, "It is too small a thing that You should be My Servant
> To raise up the tribes of Jacob and to restore the preserved ones of Israel;
> I will also make You a light of the nations
> So that My salvation may reach to the end of the earth."
> (Isa 49:5-6)

David's Tabernacle

Amos's prophecy that God would "raise up the fallen tabernacle of David" (Amos 9:11) is understood by some today as referring to the tent or tabernacle that David set up to house the ark of the covenant in Jerusalem before the First Temple was built (2 Sam 6:17). They therefore believe its rebuilding is a restoration today of the worship that David instituted with the Levite musicians before the ark. While this is possible, all other references to David's dwelling signify his household, or dynasty.[244]

At the council in Jerusalem in about 46 AD, James, the Lord's brother, realised it had just been fulfilled. He remembered Amos's prediction was not only for the wayward children of Israel but also for Gentiles:

> 13. ... "Brethren, listen to me.
> 14. "Simeon has related how God first concerned Himself about taking from among the Gentiles a people for His name.
> 15. "With this the words of the Prophets agree, just as it is written,
> 16. 'AFTER THESE THINGS I will return, AND I WILL REBUILD THE

---

244   1 Kings 12:19; Isaiah 7:2, 7:13, 16:5.

> TABERNACLE OF DAVID WHICH HAS FALLEN, AND I WILL REBUILD ITS RUINS, AND I WILL RESTORE IT,
> 17. SO THAT THE REST OF MANKIND MAY SEEK THE LORD, AND ALL THE GENTILES WHO ARE CALLED BY MY NAME'...
> 19. "Therefore it is my judgement that we do not trouble those who are turning to God from among the Gentiles..."
> (Acts 15:13-19)

As James at last saw, the Gentiles pouring into the Early Church proved Jesus had indeed rebuilt the fallen tabernacle of David so they could remain Gentiles.[245] The resurrection was therefore God fulfilling His promise to David, "I will establish your seed forever" (Psa 89:4) because Jesus can live and reign forever.

Matthew therefore began his gospel:

> The record of the genealogy of Jesus the Messiah, *the son of David*, the son of Abraham (Matt 1:1, emphasis added)

When people recognised Jesus as the Messiah, they often greeted Him as the Son of David.[246] On His final visit to Jerusalem, a great multitude spread His way with their garments and palm branches, crying out:

> "Hosanna to the Son of David! Blessed is he that cometh in the name of the Lord! Hosanna in the highest! (Matt 21:8-9)

We all benefit if we come to David's 'seed', Jesus, who is sitting on the throne of David now and forever. He is, as the hymn writer says, 'great David's greater Son'.[247] Accordingly, anyone who believes in Jesus, whether Jew or Gentile, is still receiving today the benefit of the Davidic Covenant.

But there is another benefit for Israel 'according to the flesh': they have inherited from David his capital city, Jerusalem.

---

245 Prior to this, he had been insisting the Gentiles had to be circumcised as Jews (Gal 2:12) but now he was agreeing with Paul, Barnabas, and Peter.
246 e.g. Matthew 9:27, 12:23, 15:22, 20:30-31.
247 James Montgomery (1771-1854).

David and Mt Zion

When David captured the Jebusite stronghold of Zion[248] in about 1010 BC, it became his own dwelling:

> Then David dwelt in the stronghold; therefore it was called the city of David. (1 Chron 11:7)

The stronghold was on a rise called Mount Zion and its name was then extended from "the city of David" to include the whole city of Jerusalem (2 Kin 19:31, Isa 2:3), the people of Israel (Isa 51:16), and finally, the land of Israel (Zech 9:13).

We use a similar metonym today when we speak of the Kremlin because this is the Russian word for a citadel or fortress within a city. The Moscow Kremlin is the fortified complex in which the President of the Russian Federation lives. The White House serves the identical function in Washington, USA, when we hear news headlines such as, "The White House said today…" or "Washington wants…"

This extension is also Messianic:

> 6. "But as for Me, I have installed My King
> Upon *Zion, My holy mountain."*
> 7. "I will surely tell of the decree of the LORD:
> He said to Me, 'You are My Son,
> Today I have begotten You.
> 8. 'Ask of Me, and I will surely give the nations as Your inheritance,
> And the very ends of the earth as Your possession.'" (Psa 2:6-8, emphasis added)

Messiah reigns from Mt Zion and His kingdom will ultimately fill the whole earth. In the meantime, the Book of Hebrews tells all who are born of the Spirit:

> …you have come to Mount Zion and to the city of the living

---

248 The meaning of Zion is uncertain, being either pre-Israeli Arabic for a ridge, or Hebrew for dry place or fortress (*Zondervan Pictorial Encyclopedia of the Bible*, Vol. 5, p. 1063).

> God, the heavenly Jerusalem… to God, the Judge of all, and…
> to Jesus, the mediator of a new covenant… (Heb 12:22-24)

As we saw earlier in Galatians 4:25-26, there are two Jerusalems: 'the present Jerusalem' (v. 25) and 'the Jerusalem above' (v. 26) which will come 'down out of heaven from God' (Rev 21:2). This means all the promises about Zion have parallel fulfilments, first in 'the natural, then the spiritual' (1 Cor 15:46) but to properly grasp the latter, we need to understand the former.

Part of David's legacy to the Jews is Jerusalem – it was due to him that the earthly Jerusalem became their capital city, and the city of God.

"City of God"

When Jesus spoke of Jerusalem as "the city of the great King" (Matt 5:35), He was quoting from Psalm 48:

> Great is the LORD, and greatly to be praised,
> In *the city of our God*, His holy mountain.
> Beautiful in elevation, the joy of the whole earth,
> Is Mount Zion in the far north,
> *The city of the great King*. (Psa 48:1-2, emphasis added)

However, Jerusalem only became God's city when David captured it. Almost five hundred years earlier, Moses said that God would choose a place:

> "…you shall seek the LORD at the place which the LORD your God *will choose* from all your tribes, to establish His name there for His dwelling…" (Deut 12:5, emphasis added)

> "You shall eat in the presence of the LORD your God, *at the place where He chooses* to establish His name…" (Deut 14:23, emphasis added)

When Israel entered the land, that place was at Shiloh (Josh

18:1, 1 Sam 1:3). However, as we saw in Book 2 of this series,[249] after Israel's first 'abomination that desolates', God left Shiloh desolate:

> ...He abandoned the dwelling place at Shiloh,
> The tent which He had pitched among men... (Psa 78:60)

The bronze altar and the ark of the covenant were removed to Gibeon (1 Chron 21:29) but, soon after, God chose David to be His king for Israel and Jerusalem became His city:

> "Since the day that I brought My people Israel from Egypt, I did not choose a city out of all the tribes of Israel in which to build a house that My name might be there, but I chose David to be over My people Israel." (1 Kin 8:16)

From then on, He acted:

> "... for the sake of My servant David and for the sake of Jerusalem, *the city which I have chosen* from all the tribes of Israel". (1 Kin 11:32, emphasis added)

> "... that My servant David may have a lamp always before Me in Jerusalem, the city where I have chosen for Myself to put My name". (1 Kin 11:36)

We see then that Jerusalem was established as the city of God through the Davidic Covenant. We also see that the many prophecies and promises about Zion being restored,[250] both before Christ and in our day, are God fulfilling His "everlasting covenant" with David.

---

249 *STB*, pp. 211, 265-266.
250 e.g. Isaiah 1:27, 2:3-4, 51:3, 52:1-2, 59:20, 60:14, 66:8; Jeremiah 30:10, 31:12, 50:4-5; Ezekiel 34:23-24, 37:24-25; Micah 4:1-7.

David and Melchizedek

We earlier glanced at the priesthood of Melchizedek but we need to appreciate what a truly startling development David was prophesying some 3,000 years ago:

> 1. The LORD says to my Lord:
> "Sit at My right hand
> Until I make Your enemies a footstool for Your feet."
> 2. The LORD will stretch forth Your strong scepter from Zion, saying,
> "Rule in the midst of Your enemies"...
> 4. The LORD has sworn and will not change His mind,
> "You are a priest forever
> According to the order of Melchizedek." (Psa 110:1-2, 4)

Ever since, the rabbis of Israel have debated what this means.[251]

In the 1st Century, Jesus asked the scribes to explain the identity of Messiah from this psalm:

> 41. Then He said to them, "How is it that they say the Christ is David's son?
> 42. "For David himself says in the book of Psalms, 'THE LORD SAID TO MY LORD, "SIT AT MY RIGHT HAND,
> 43. UNTIL I MAKE YOUR ENEMIES A FOOTSTOOL FOR YOUR FEET."'
> 44. "Therefore David calls Him 'Lord,' and how is He his son?"
> (Luke 20:41-44)

---

251 The Talmud scholars (3rd to 5th Century AD) thought that "according to the order of" should be translated as "because of the speech of" Melchizedek and that he sinned when he blessed Abraham before blessing God (Gen 14:19-20) so his priesthood was removed and given to Abraham (Talmud, Nedarim 32b). However, *Avot de-Rabbi Nathan* (7th-8th Century), chap 34, says it refers to Messiah. In the 11th Century, Rashi, one of Israel's most acclaimed sages, taught that Melchizedek was appointing Abraham to be his successor as priest and therefore Levi as well (www.chabad.org/library/bible_cdo/aid/16331/jewish/Chapter-110.htm#showrashi=true&v=4, 12 Jul, 2015). Today, the *Jewish Study Bible* avoids the issue altogether by treating the name Melchizedek as impersonal: "You are a priest forever, a rightful king by My decree" (JPS 1985).

David was saying that his ultimate son, Messiah, would be far greater than he – not only would Messiah be a great king but also "a priest forever, according to the order of Melchizedek" who was greater than Abraham and Levi.

We see therefore that this new order of priests is part of the 'everlasting covenant' of David. It is his Seed who is to reign forever (Psa 89:36-37) and to be a priest forever (Psa 110:4).

So who was Melchizedek, why was he important and why was his priesthood needed as well as Levi's?

Prior to David's prophecy, there were only three verses in the Bible referring to him (Gen 14:18-20) but a thousand years after David, the Book of Hebrews explains them. The rabbis today have yet to accept this as revelation, but it is also often misunderstood by Christians too, so let us consider it carefully.

Hebrews 7

The chapter begins with the historical event:

> 1. For this Melchizedek, king of Salem, priest of the Most High God, who met Abraham as he was returning from the slaughter of the kings and blessed him,
> 2. to whom also Abraham apportioned a tenth part of all the spoils, was first of all, by the translation of his name, king of righteousness, and then also king of Salem, which is king of peace. (Heb 7:1-2)

Melchizedek was the Canaanite king of Salem, the city that later became known as Jebus and then Jerusalem, as we saw earlier. He was also a 'priest of the Most High God' to whom Abraham paid tribute. In other words, he was a man of God, residing in the land of God, before Abraham.

The writer of Hebrews translates his name for us: Melchi meaning king, and zedek meaning righteousness, hence the 'king of righteousness', and Salem, meaning peace.

Hebrews 7 continues:

> 3. Without father, without mother, without genealogy, having neither beginning of days nor end of life, but made like the Son of God, he remains a priest perpetually. (Heb 7:3)

As 21st Century Gentiles, we can easily misunderstand this description, thinking it means he was not human ('without father, without mother, without genealogy'), that he was immortal ('having neither beginning of days nor end of life') and must therefore still be alive today. Believing this, some teach he must be Jesus in pre-existent form.[252]

However, this letter was written to Jews[253] who, to this day, are only to accept as priests and Levites those who can prove their genealogical descent from Aaron and Levi (Ezra 8:15-20). Accordingly, Melchizedek was remarkable in that his priesthood is not based on his parentage or genealogy. Nothing is known of his birth or death either but he was not immortal because, almost five hundred years later, one of his successors as King of Jerusalem, Adoni-Zedek (which means 'Lord of Righteousness'), was put to death by Joshua (Josh 10:1, 26). Hebrews 7 is referring to the typology of his role as a stand-alone priest in Abraham's time:

> 4. Now observe how great this man was to whom Abraham, the patriarch, gave a tenth of the choicest spoils.
> 5. And those indeed of the sons of Levi who receive the priest's office have commandment in the Law to collect a tenth from the people…
> 8. In this case mortal men receive tithes, but in that case one receives them, of whom it is witnessed that he lives on.
> 9. And, so to speak, through Abraham even Levi, who received tithes, paid tithes,

---

[252] e.g. www.cgg.org/index.cfm/fuseaction/Library.sr/CT/HWA/k/745/Mystery-Melchizedek-Solved.htm, 14 Jul, 2015.
[253] Abraham and his descendants were originally referred to as Hebrews (e.g. Gen 14:13, 39:14); the name 'Jew' was first used after the northern kingdom was destroyed (e.g. 2 King 25:25, Jer 34:9) and had become a synonym for Israelite by New Testament times (Acts 21:39 cf. Rom 11:1).

> 10. for he was still in the loins of his father when Melchizedek met him. (Heb 7:4-5, 8-10)

Levi's priestly sons were born over four hundred years later so they did not literally pay a tithe to Melchizedek but did typologically through Abraham. Melchizedek did not literally 'live on' (v. 8) but was 'like the Son of God' in typologically foreshadowing Jesus, the King of New Jerusalem, who does live on, and will forever be our High Priest (Heb 6:20).

So why was there a need for this priesthood? Because there was to be a new covenant.

The Old Covenant, the Law of Moses, could not and still cannot change anyone internally but, as we will consider in the next section, the New Covenant can. Hebrews 7 explains:

> 11. Now if perfection was through the Levitical priesthood (for on the basis of it the people received the Law), what further need was there for another priest to arise according to the order of Melchizedek, and not be designated according to the order of Aaron?
> 12. For when the priesthood is changed, of necessity there takes place a change of law also...
> 14. ... our Lord was descended from Judah, a tribe with reference to which Moses spoke nothing concerning priests.
> 15. And this is clearer still, if another priest arises according to the likeness of Melchizedek,
> 16. who has become such not on the basis of a law of physical requirement, but according to the power of an indestructible life.
> 17. For it is attested of Him, "YOU ARE A PRIEST FOREVER ACCORDING TO THE ORDER OF MELCHIZEDEK"...
> 19. (for the Law made nothing perfect), and... there is a bringing in of a better hope, through which we draw near to God. (Heb 7:11-19)

This 'better hope, through which we draw near to God' is the New Covenant. Hebrews 7 therefore points out the covenantal promise and oath made to Messiah as Melchizedek's heir:

> 20. And inasmuch as it [the Law] was not without an oath
> 21. (for they indeed became priests without an oath, but He *with an oath* through the One who said to Him, "THE LORD HAS SWORN AND WILL NOT CHANGE HIS MIND, 'YOU ARE A PRIEST FOREVER'");
> 22. so much the more also Jesus has become the guarantee of a better covenant…
> 28. For the Law appoints men as high priests who are weak, but the *word of the oath*, which came after the Law, appoints a Son, made perfect forever. (Heb 7:20-22, 28, emphasis added)

This promise and oath regarding the priesthood of Melchizedek is all David's legacy.

We who belong to Jesus today likewise belong to this royal priesthood:

> But you are a chosen race, *a royal priesthood*, a holy nation, a people for God's own possession… (1 Pet 2:9, emphasis added)

There is only one royal priesthood, the order of Melchizedek.

Summary of David's Legacy

David's capturing of Zion in 1010 BC set in motion 3,000 years of consequences for the locality:

(i) This Jebusite city, formerly called Salem, Uru-shalim, and Jebus, became the holy city of Jerusalem.

(ii) The Law of Moses had only referred to a future "place where He chooses to establish His name" (Deut 14:23); through David, Jerusalem became the City of God.

(iii) In the time of Abraham, Salem was the city ruled by Melchizedek; a thousand years later, David prophesied that a new order of priest, 'according to the order of Melchizedek', i.e. a royal priesthood, would be established by Messiah. All of us who trust in Him, whether Jew or Gentile, belong to this order (1 Pet 2:9).

(iv) Although Jerusalem was devastated and defiled by the

Babylonians (586 BC), the Greeks (178 BC), and the Romans (70 AD), Jesus taught that after the times of the Gentiles had been fulfilled, Israel would regain it (Luke 21:24). This seems to have happened in 1967[254] so this 'trampling underfoot' or defiling by the Gentiles is over and Jerusalem is again the 'holy city'.

David's legacy to us is everlasting:

(i) Jesus is 'great David's greater Son' and sits on the throne of David forever. All who trust in Him therefore are benefitting from David's 'everlasting covenant'.

(ii) David left us his inspired psalms, prayers, and Messianic prophecies, as well as his personal example in faith, spirituality, creativity, repentance, and restoration.

(iii) To the earthly descendants of Abraham, Isaac and Jacob, i.e. Israel 'according to the flesh', he bequeathed the earthly city of Jerusalem which they regained in June, 1967, and possess today.

(iv) For the spiritual descendants of Abraham, all in Christ whether Jew or Gentile, he created a type, a foreshadowing, of the new, heavenly Jerusalem to which we belong today (Heb 12:22).

(v) He revealed the royal priesthood, the order of Melchizedek, of which Jesus is the High Priest and to which all of us who trust in Him belong today.

---

254 There is a doubt about this timing because the Israelis handed back the heart of Jerusalem, the Temple Mount, to the Islamic authorities.

13
Dead in the Street
Temporarily Silenced

There comes the time when the two witnesses complete their task:

> 3. "And I will grant authority to my two witnesses, and they will prophesy for twelve hundred and sixty days, clothed in sackcloth"...
> 7. When they have *finished their testimony*, the beast that comes up out of the abyss will make war with them, and overcome them and kill them. (Rev 11:3 & 7, emphasis added)

Not only are the two witnesses to be killed but their bodies defiled and their deaths celebrated:

> 8. And their dead bodies will lie in the street of the great city which mystically is called Sodom and Egypt, where also their Lord was crucified.
> 9. Those from the peoples and tribes and tongues and nations will look at their dead bodies for three and a half days, and will not permit their dead bodies to be laid in a tomb.
> 10. And those who dwell on the earth will rejoice over them and celebrate; and they will send gifts to one another, because these two prophets tormented those who dwell on the earth. (Rev 11:8-10)

To those who choose the partially literal/partially metaphorical interpretation, this beast from the abyss is a metaphor for a man, the final Antichrist, and he literally kills two men, Moses and Elijah, who have returned to earth after thousands of years. For example, Tim LaHaye and Jerry Jenkins have their fictional futuristic Nicolae Carpathia shooting them down in cold blood at the Wailing Wall.[255]

---

255 Book 6, *Assassins (Assignment: Jerusalem, Target: Antichrist)*,

Those preferring the fully metaphorical freely admit their task is difficult. N.T. Wright, for example:

> Now – this is the part which many find particularly difficult – it appears that the 'two witnesses' of verses 3-13 *are a symbol for the whole church in its prophetic witness, its faithful death, and its vindication by God.* ... What John is saying is that the prophetic witness of the church, in the great tradition of Moses and Elijah, will perform powerful signs and thereby torment the surrounding unbelievers, but that the climax of their work will be their martyr-death...
>
> The point is this. [Our calling] will not mean one is spared from suffering and death, but rather that this suffering and death itself... will be the ultimate prophetic sign through which the world will be brought to glorify God... The vindication of the church after its martyrdom will complete the prophetic witness...
>
> This most puzzling passage in this most puzzling book, then, turns out to be one of the most important and central statements of what John wants to say to the churches to whom he is writing.[256]

Professor Wright sees this martyrdom as beginning in the 1st Century but William Hendriksen sees it as mostly still future:

> This gospel age is... going to come to an end (cf. Matt 24:14). The Church, as a mighty missionary organization, shall finish its testimony. The beast... shall battle against the Church and destroy it... So when we

---

Tyndale, 1999, p. 389.
256 N.T. Wright, *Revelation For All*, pp. 99-100, emphasis in original. Craig Koestler summarises it similarly: 'In this passage we see an image of the suffering and vindication of the people of God', *Revelation and the End of All Things*, p. 110. So does Laurie Guy, *Making Sense of the Book of Revelation*, p. 107-108, and William Hendriksen, *More Than Conquerors*, p. 129-131.

read that the corpse of the Church is laying on the broad avenues of the great city, this simply means that in the midst of the world the Church is dead: it no longer exists as an influential and powerful institution! Its leaders have been slaughtered; its voice has been silenced.[257]

Michael Wilcock sees it similarly:

> For Scripture does seem to envisage a time... when at the very end of history an unexampled onslaught will be mounted against the church, and she will to all appearances 'go under'... But it will be brief; and at the end of it the church will rise again to meet its Lord, and the world in confusion will at last give worship to its Maker...[258]

These exegetes have to use 'it appears' and 'does seem' because of irresolvable difficulties caused by choosing the wrong metaphor of the two witnesses being the church. This is where all the hard work we have done in establishing better metaphorical understandings of the two witnesses and of Revelation 12 and 13 will repay our labour – these can now take us in another direction through the maze.

Another Metaphorical Direction

Firstly, who is 'the beast that comes out of the abyss' (v. 7), or sea?[259] John does not describe it here in Revelation 11, leaving

---

257 William Hendriksen, *More Than Conquerors*, p. 130-131.
258 Michael Wilcock, *The Message of Revelation*, p. 106.
259 The abyss, from the Greek, *abussos*, meaning 'bottomless', means the depths of the sea and, in Hebrew thinking, symbolised the place of the dead (Rom 10:7, Rev 20:13) and of evil spirits (Luke 8:31, Rev 9:11). Accordingly, the dead are raised from 'the sea' as well as from 'death and Hades' (Rev 20:13) and 'there is no longer any sea' in the new heaven and new earth (Rev 21:1). I see this as symbolic, signifying not that God will change His mind about saltwater or surfing but that evil will no longer have a hiding place. The sea also symbolises "peoples and multitudes and nations and tongues" (Rev 17:15. Also Dan 7:3 & 17), i.e. ungodly Gentiles.

that instead until Revelation 13 – it is the beast with seven heads and ten horns, which looks like a leopard, with feet like a bear's, and a mouth like a lion's (Rev 13:1-2).

In Book 2 of this series,[260] we established this beast is not a flesh and blood man – it is not mortal because it has existed for the last 2,000 years – but a principality and power, the geo-political entity we call the state. However, it is not just any state – John sees it as a wild beast, a God-ordained institution that has gone feral, demanding to be worshipped.

We also established that it looks like a leopard, a bear, and a lion because it manifested in three great Gentile empires that Daniel saw and described in his chapters 2 and 7: the leopard signifies the Greek Empire, the bear the Medo-Persian Empire, and the lion the Babylonian Empire. Each of them had been assigned by God to rule over Israel and, although very different people and cultures, they had committed the same crime: they had abandoned their God-given task of maintaining a just society and tried instead to destroy Israel and her coming Child. I set this out in detail in Book 1.[261]

So, when John saw this principality and power crawling out of the abyss, it was in his day, in the time of the sixth head, i.e. the Roman Empire.

Also in Revelation 13, John saw a second beast, the spirit of antichrist, which caused the people to not only worship the first beast, their empire, but to also worship the living image of it, the emperor. This is why the Romans built temples to *Dea Roma et Augustus* (the goddess who is Rome and Augustus Caesar) such as those in Pergamum in Asia Minor and in Caesarea Philippi and Caesarea Maritima in northern Israel.

Following John's lead, we were then able to identify both beasts manifesting in the 20th Century, in Stalin's USSR, Mussolini's Italy, Hirohito's Japan, Hitler's Germany, Mao's

---

260 *STB, pp. 16-19.*
261 *DDJ*, pp. 28-32.

China, Kim Il Sung's North Korea, and Pol Pot's Cambodia, as well as in Islam in our time.

In this book, I have established that in Revelation 11 the two witnesses allude to Moses and Elijah, who represent the Law and the Prophets, or the Old Testament.

How then does the first beast (the feral state), kill the two witnesses (the Hebrew Bible), i.e. that their dead bodies 'lie in the street of the great city' (v. 8)? And when will all this happen? Let us begin with the city.

'The Great City'

As we established in chapter 10, the 'great city' is not the whole world but Jerusalem. This is to be understood both literally and metaphorically because:

(i) Jerusalem is the literal, geographical location where Jesus was crucified, and which was trodden underfoot, or occupied, by the Gentiles from 70 AD until 1967, when the Jews recaptured it.

(ii) Jerusalem is also a metaphor for the Jews, who were metaphorically trodden underfoot, or despised, by the Gentiles for 'twelve hundred and sixty days', i.e. 'a time, times and half a time', 'the times of the Gentiles', i.e. the last 2,000 years.

As we saw earlier, this dual meaning is spelled out by Paul in Galatians 4 where he writes of two Jerusalems, 'the present Jerusalem' and 'the Jerusalem above', which 'correspond' to Abraham's two wives and their sons. Noting that Sarah was free and bore the promised child, Isaac, whereas Hagar was a 'bondwoman', or slave, and bore Ishmael, Paul explains:

> 24. This is allegorically speaking, for these women are two covenants: one proceeding from Mount Sinai bearing children who are to be slaves; she is Hagar.
> 25. Now this Hagar is Mount Sinai in Arabia and corresponds to

> the present Jerusalem, for she is in slavery with her children.
> 26. But the Jerusalem above is free; she is our mother…
> 31. …we are not children of a bondwoman, but of the free woman. (Gal 4:24-31)

This is a complex allegory but essential to our understanding so let us refresh our memories.

What is 'the present Jerusalem' (v. 25)? The literal ancient city, which Paul and John knew and loved.

What is 'the Jerusalem above' (v. 26)? The metaphorical or spiritual city, which is elsewhere called 'the heavenly Jerusalem' (Heb 12:22) or 'new Jerusalem' (Rev 21:2).

Hagar and 'the present Jerusalem' also represent the covenant 'from Mount Sinai bearing children who are slaves' (v. 24), the Mosaic Covenant. Who are these children? All in Israel 'according to the flesh' (Rom 9:3-5) who reject the New Covenant and therefore *remain* under the Mosaic Covenant.

Here in Revelation 11, therefore, 'the great city' refers to both the literal ancient city, with its devastated Temple Mount, and to the metaphorical 'present Jerusalem', with her still enslaved children: Israel 'according to the flesh'.

How then can the two witnesses, the Law and the Prophets, or the Hebrew Bible, prophesy in "the great city"? Which of the dual meanings of Jerusalem is intended? Both. The Hebrew Bible has always been studied in 'old' Jerusalem *and* by Israel 'according to the flesh'.

However, as Paul tells us:

> 14. …until this very day at the reading of the old covenant the same veil remains unlifted, because it is removed in Christ.
> 15. But to this day whenever Moses is read, a veil lies over their heart;
> 16. but whenever a person turns to the Lord, the veil is taken away.
> 17. Now the Lord is the Spirit… (2 Cor 3:14-17)

This simply cannot be understated – the only way any Jewish

teacher or student of Moses, studying the Torah or Law, can understand the text is by softening, by turning away from tradition and calling on the Holy Spirit who will reveal Christ 'in all the Scriptures' (Luke 24:27), i.e. the Hebrew Bible.

The Beast That Kills Them

> 7. When they have finished their testimony, the beast that comes up out of the abyss will make war with them, and overcome them and kill them. (Rev 11:7)

This beast from the abyss[262] cannot be a literal man, the Antichrist, because it is described as having seven heads and ten horns (Rev 13:1), each of which are 'kings' (Rev 17:10, 17:12). This beast is a 'principality and power'.[263] It manifests whenever any legitimate state leaves its proper function and becomes, like a domesticated animal that has gone feral, a *therion*, a wild beast.

It has seven heads because it had already manifested in the six Gentile states that had ruled over Israel over the previous 2,000 years (Egypt, Assyria, Babylon, Medo-Persia, Greece, and Rome), with the seventh yet to come (Rev 17:10).

In the 1st Century, John could see it manifesting within the sixth, the Roman Empire, killing all who refused to worship it, *Dea Roma*, and its living image, the emperor, i.e. every Roman emperor from Augustus to Diocletian. It has appeared many times throughout the last 2,000 years – in the last 100 years alone, the beast manifested in Stalin's Russia, Mussolini's Italy, Hirohito's Japan, Hitler's Germany, Mao's China, Kim Il Sung's Korea, and Pol Pot's Cambodia.

Its political views and preferences are irrelevant – these regimes covered the whole spectrum from extreme right wing

---

262 The word 'abyss' is Anglicised Greek and means literally, the bottomless pit (Luke 8:31, Rev 20:3).
263 As established in Book 2, *STB*.

(Fascist) to extreme left wing (Marxist Communist). Religious beliefs are likewise irrelevant, since this beast was Shintoist in Japan, Hindu and Buddhist in India and Nepal, and atheistic in China, Russia, Albania, and Romania. In Christian history, it manifested in the Roman Catholic Church until the Second Vatican Council[264] and Reformed Protestant European nations until the 18th Century.[265]

In the 21st Century, it is manifesting most obviously in Kim Jong-Un's North Korea and in the Islamic nations, when they enforce the blasphemy laws for any perceived criticism of Islam or Muhammad.

This beast, as depicted in Revelation 13, has therefore been active among "all the nations" for 2,000 years, so what is different in Revelation 11? The answer is to be seen in the location and the timing.

Loosed in Jerusalem

In distinct contrast to the beast's havoc among the Gentiles in all the nations, this vision is set among the Jews in Jerusalem, i.e. in the land of Israel and amongst all Jews who do not yet believe in Jesus as Messiah. There is only one state that can kill the two witnesses in 'the great city' of Jerusalem – the government of Israel. The manifestation of the beast in Revelation 11 is the secular state of Israel: it is Jewish, but not ruling according to the Law and the Prophets.

In 1896, Theodor Herzl deliberately aimed for secularism, writing in *Der Judenstaat*,[266] his Zionist blueprint:

> Faith unites us, knowledge gives us freedom. We shall

---

264 Details in *STB*, pp. 60-63, 143-146. In 1965, Pope Paul VI officially removed his triregnum, or three-tiered crown, symbol of his being 'king of heaven and of earth and of the lower regions' (Ibid., p. 141-142).
265 Ibid., pp. 63-65, 142.
266 Pamphlet in German, lit. *The Jews' State*, usually referred to as The Jewish State.

> therefore prevent any theocratic tendencies from coming to the fore on the part of our priesthood. We shall keep our priests within the confines of their temples in the same way as we shall keep our professional army within the confines of their barracks.

Israel's first Prime Minister, David Ben Gurion, tried for part-secular, part-Halachic[267] government, negotiating a deal with ultra-Orthodox rabbi-politicians in 1948:

> Kashrut [kosher] in all public institutions, Shabbat as the day of rest, rabbinic control of marriage and divorce, and the exemption of full-time yeshiva students, who at the time numbered only in the hundreds, from army service.[268]

In other words, the government committed to keeping the food laws and the Sabbath, left all matters of marriage and divorce to the rabbis and excused religious students from conscription. Ben Gurion's negotiator, later to be President, Shimon Peres explained this was "because the number of people in Israel who defined themselves as people of faith was large" but he added:

> Israel is a secular state. The Orthodox have bargaining power, so everything has to be done by compromise. But Israel is not under religious control: it's not a halachic country, it's not a theocracy. Ben-Gurion opposed religious coercion and opposed anti-religious coercion.[269]

In July 1958, Ben Gurion spelled this out to Rabbi Judah L. Maimon, the first Minister of Religions in Israel. The Cabinet was in crisis over official state identification of Jewish status for citizenship:

> The Prime Minister added in his letter that Israel's

---

267 Halacha is Orthodox tradition.
268 Shimon Peres & David Landau, *Ben-Gurion: A Political Life*, Nextbook Press, 1998.
269 http://tabletmag.com/jewish-news-and-politics/81660/raw-deal, 27 May, 2015.

Declaration of Independence defined Israel as a country ruled by law and not by the laws of Halacha, the Jewish legal tradition.[270]

While reassuring Rabbi Maimon that 'the government decision is not binding on rabbis in matters of marriage and divorce', Ben Gurion added that the Declaration included freedom of religion and conscience as among the basic principles of the State of Israel. This meant the Jewish State would not be governed by religious law nor theocratic:

> "It is a fact," Mr. Ben Gurion wrote, "perhaps a bitter fact that in matters of religion and religious law there is no unity among the Jewish people and in America there are Orthodox, Conservative, Liberal and Reform rabbis. There are many Jews who belong to neither one nor the other, but are in my opinion Jews as long as they do not become converted to another religion."
>
> The letter concluded by stating that many persons believe that they belong to the Jewish people although they do not observe Jewish law. As long as he remains in the government, Mr. Ben Gurion pledged, he would endeavor to prevent strife over religion. "I see danger in a war against religion and in a war for religion," he warned.[271]

Today in Israel, the *Jerusalem Post* reports that many fear a halachic state:

> Former justice minister Yossi Sarid expressed his fear that if Israel is turned into a state ruled by Halacha, there would be public stonings or burnings in cases of those who dared desecrate the Shabbat or were unfaithful to their spouse, or if two homosexual men had sexual intercourse…
>
> A lot of secular Israelis are afraid that if tomorrow Israel

---

270 www.jta.org/1958/07/03/archive/ben-gurion-gives-his-own-definition-of-who-is-a-jew-draws-on-psalms, 27 May, 2015.
271 Ibid.

becomes a state ruled by Halacha, people will be stoned or burned to death for transgressing sacred laws, or at the very least will be prevented from driving a car, going to a coffee shop, having a barbecue in their backyard or doing anything else that is forbidden on Shabbat.[272]

Indeed, while a few small Orthodox political parties advocate for it, usually with the proviso of capital punishment being set aside, others argue against it as explicitly forbidden until Messiah comes. The latter include the Hasidics, the largest Jewish religious movement in the world, led by their Lubavitcher Rebbe.

As Ben Gurion concluded, there is no, and probably never will be, agreement over what it even means to be Jewish, let alone which Jewish tradition should govern. Israel is firmly committed to be and to remain a secular state, at least until Messiah comes.

Of course, for those of us trusting in Jesus as Messiah already come, whether Jew or Gentile, there is no problem at all; this impossible dilemma is only for those Jews who refuse to trust in Him.[273] Indeed, it may have been the hand of God that Moshe Dayan handed over the Temple Mount in 1967 and thus prevented another Temple being built on the site or a civil war between secular and Orthodox Jews.

The Timing

When John was prophesying, the Romans were still trampling Jerusalem; there had been no Jewish state in Israel from 70 AD. The Bar Kokhba Revolt tried to re-establish it in 132 AD but was

---

272 www.jpost.com/Features/Religious-Affairs-Whos-afraid-of-a-halachic-state, 27 May, 2015.
273 Some today believe, based on their reading of Revelation 20, that when Jesus returns, He will rebuild the Temple in Jerusalem and reinstate the Law to be kept for a thousand years, i.e. during the Millennium. I do not believe this and will explain what I consider to be a better way of understanding Revelation in the next book in this series.

crushed by Hadrian's legions. Israel did not exist as a sovereign nation until its resurrection on 14th May, 1948.

Now observe the beast's timing:

> 3. "And I will grant authority to my two witnesses, and they will prophesy for twelve hundred and sixty days, clothed in sackcloth"...
> 7. When they have finished their testimony, the beast that comes up out of the abyss will make war with them, and overcome them and kill them. (Rev 11:3 & 7)

It attacks the two witnesses at the end of the 1,260 days.

As established in Book 1, this is not a literal three and a half years, but rather a metaphorical time period; it is also known as the "times of the Gentiles" and is based on the mystery of Elijah and his literal three and a half year drought.[274] It began in 30 AD at the crucifixion of Jesus and, He taught, its endpoint is to be determined by the status of Jerusalem, i.e. when the city is again back in Jewish hands (Luke 21:24).

Israel's recapturing of Jerusalem in the Six Day War of 1967 could therefore mean the two witnesses finished their testimony in 1967, the beast has made war with them, overcome, and killed them. This conclusion must be held lightly, however, because the victorious Israeli general Moshe Dayan, trying to be conciliatory, handed back the very heart of the old city, the Temple Mount, to the Islamic Waqf, or authority.

In the eyes of many Orthodox Jews, such as Rabbi Moshe Tsvi Segal, this was handing back Israel's sovereignty:

> ...we can restore our sovereignty only by having the Temple Mount in our hands. Sovereignty over the Land of Israel is impossible while the Temple Mount is in the hands of a (any) foreign religion. The Temple Mount must be in the hands of a Sovereign Kingdom of Israel, to give expression to G-d's sovereignty over Israel. This is brought

---

274 *DDJ*, pp. 118-138.

out all through the Bible, all through our literature and thought.[275]

I am very glad we cannot be dogmatic either way, because it stops us setting exact End Time dates.

However, my personal view is that Israel has regained sovereignty as a nation and over Jerusalem, which means "the times of the Gentiles" ended in 1967 and we are living in momentous times. It also seems to me, as argued in Book 2,[276] that the Temple Mount being held by the Islamic Empire is of profound significance, as it enables the sixth and final 'abomination of desolation' to now stand at any time in the holy place (Matt 24:15).

So, what was happening then, in 1967, among Jerusalem's Jewish inhabitants and all the children of the 'present Jerusalem' in the Diaspora? What was their attitude towards the two metaphorical witnesses, Moses and Elijah, i.e. the Law and the Prophets, or the Hebrew Bible?

The majority left it lying in the street.

'In the Street'?

> And their dead bodies will lie in the street of the great city which mystically is called Sodom and Egypt, where also their Lord was crucified. (Rev 11:8)

Is 'the street of the great city' literal, metaphorical, or both?

Today we use "the street" as an idiom with both meanings. 'Dancing in the street', for example, can mean literally dancing outside rather than inside, in public celebration, or it can be a metaphor for being 'extremely happy', as in, "Not many people will be dancing in the streets about a two percent pay rise".[277]

---

275 www.saveisrael.com/segal/segalmount.htm, 8 Jun, 2015.
276 *STB*, pp. 212-218
277 http://dictionary.cambridge.org/dictionary/british/be-dancing-in-the-streets, 25 May, 2015.

'The man in the street' is not a particular man in a particular street but 'any ordinary, average person whose opinions are considered to represent most people'.[278]

So too in Biblical days: 'wisdom shouts in the street' (Prov 1:20); 'truth has stumbled in the street' (Isa 59:14); 'in the street the sword slays; in the house it is like death' (Lam 1:20). This metaphorical street means all public places or thoroughfares.

Metaphorically then, 'the street of the great city' is the main street, the High Street, the most public of places in Jerusalem, including the Temple Mount where all roads converge. Today, only Muslims are allowed to pray on the Temple Mount – Jews and Christians are forbidden and are arrested if seen praying there because it upsets the Islamic authorities.

This image of the two witnesses' bodies left lying in the street is deliberately shocking. To the Jewish mind, as in most cultures today, this was the ultimate shaming of the dead. At the end of life, the righteous were honoured with proper burial and mourning: the patriarchs were 'gathered to their people' (Gen 25:8, 25:17, 35:29 & 49:33); kings were 'buried with their fathers' (1 Kin 14:31, 15:24 & 22:50); Joseph made his brothers swear to take his bones from Egypt to be buried with his fathers in the Promised Land (Gen 50:25).

At the other extreme, the disgraced Ahab and Jezebel were to be food for dogs (1 Kin 21:19 & 23) and their descendants for birds of prey (1 Kin 21:24).

Accordingly, for those in Jerusalem to leave the two witnesses unburied means they were treating them with utter contempt, just as they had treated Jesus when He was publicly crucified:

> And their dead bodies will lie in the street of the great city which mystically is called Sodom and Egypt, where also their Lord was crucified. (Rev 11:8)

---

278   http://dictionary.cambridge.org/dictionary/british/the-man-woman-person-in-on-the-street, 25 May, 2015.

What does this mean within our metaphorical understanding? Who would allow the sacred scrolls of the Law and the Prophets to be discarded, lying as trash in the gutters of Jerusalem, even on the Temple Mount?!

Sadly, the Jewish people of the 20th and 21st Centuries should be shocked – they have done exactly that, again not literally but metaphorically. For 2,000 years, their ancestors mourned the holy city being "trampled underfoot by the Gentiles", longing and praying for restoration, but when God answered them, instead of renewing His covenant they cast it aside.

Renewing the Covenant

Consider all of Israel's seven earlier restorations:[279]

1. Joshua, 1406 BC
Israel's national covenant with God was cut[280] by Moses at Mt Sinai (Ex 19:1-6) in 1446 BC, but that generation broke it (Num 32:13). Accordingly, after the forty years in the wilderness, Joshua led the nation to renew the covenant, circumcising the next generation (Josh 5:2-10).

2. Joshua, c. 1381 BC
Twenty five years later, after conquering the land, Joshua again renewed the covenant (Josh 24:1-28).

3. Jehoiada, 835 BC
After the death of the wicked queen Athaliah, Jehoiada the high priest led the nation to destroy their idols and renew the covenant (2 Kin 11:17-18).

---

279 The following dates are derived from the *Zondervan NASB Study Bible*, pp. 478-479.
280 The Hebrew expression for covenant-making is *karat beriyt*, lit. to cut a covenant, hence the requirement to cut an animal in half (Gen 15:9-10, 18; Jer 34:15 and 18) and to circumcise sons (Gen 17:10-14).

4. Hezekiah, 715 BC

After the northern kingdom's destruction and southern kingdom's devotion to the Assyrian gods, Hezekiah reformed Judah and renewed the covenant for all Israel (2 Chr 29:10-30:1).

5. Josiah, 622 BC

Josiah likewise 'removed all the abominations from all the lands belonging to the sons of Israel' (2 Chr 34:33) and renewed the covenant (2 Chr 34:29-33).

6. Ezra and Nehemiah, 444 BC[281]

Returning from the Babylonian exile, Ezra and Nehemiah led Israel in renewing the covenant (Neh 10:28-29).

7. Judas Maccabee, 164 BC[282]

Antiochus Epiphanes had desecrated the Temple in 167 BC so Judas Maccabee led Israel to rededicate it, as still celebrated annually at Hanukkah, and to renew the covenant (1 Mac 4:41-59).

After each of these restorations over 1,200 years, Israel recommitted to Moses and the Prophets, but not so in 1948 or 1967. As Shimon Peres declared, "Israel is a secular state... Israel is not under religious control: it's not a halachic country, it's not a theocracy".[283]

Even the idea of a theocracy, i.e. government by God, seems either quaint to our secular mindset or tainted by the abuses that usually occur at the hands of popes, pastors, imams, or mullahs.

For whatever reason, the outcome is clear – in the land of Israel today, the majority of political leaders and the Jewish

---

[281] *Zondervan Pictorial Encyclopedia of the Bible*, Vol. 2, p. 471.
[282] *New Oxford Annotated Bible*, Apocrypha, p. 215.
[283] http://tabletmag.com/jewish-news-and-politics/81660/raw-deal, 27 May, 2015.

people have rejected not only Jesus as Messiah, but also Moses and Elijah who testified about Him:

> 45. "Do not think that I will accuse you before the Father; the one who accuses you is Moses, in whom you have set your hope.
> 46. "For if you believed Moses, you would believe Me, for he wrote about Me.
> 47. "But if you do not believe his writings, how will you believe My words?" (John 5:45-47)

The people of Israel really should be shocked.

We see then in Revelation 11, John was predicting that the people of Israel would be restored to both the land of Israel and Jerusalem while the people were still failing to believe Jesus and Moses. And that happened in 1948, regarding the land, and in 1967, regarding Jerusalem.

Finally Silenced

With the two witnesses dead, it seems they have at last been silenced.

Initially, no one could harm the two witnesses and their testimony was irresistible. They had been testifying since 30 AD but, for the most part, their words had been falling on deaf Jewish ears. The effects were a tragic repeat of Zechariah's prophecy of the Babylonian exile in the 6th Century BC:

> 11. "But they refused to pay attention and turned a stubborn shoulder and *stopped their ears* from hearing.
> 12. "They *made their hearts like flint* so that they could not hear the Law and the words which the LORD of hosts had sent by His Spirit through the former prophets; therefore great wrath came from the LORD of hosts.
> 13. "And just as He called and they would not listen, so they called and I would not listen," says the LORD of hosts;
> 14. "but I scattered them with a storm wind among all the nations whom they have not known. Thus the land is desolated behind them so that no one went back and forth, for they made

the pleasant land desolate." (Zech 7:11-14, emphasis added)

In 70 AD, the Jewish people's again refusing to listen and making 'their hearts like flint' led again to their being physically 'scattered with a storm wind among all the nations' while their land again became 'desolate'. Paul described their spiritual state accordingly:

> For I do not want you, brethren, to be uninformed of this mystery... that *a partial hardening* has happened to Israel *until* the fullness of the Gentiles has come in (Rom 11:25, emphasis added)

As covered in Book 1,[284] this 'hardening' being only 'partial' meant that if any individual wanted to turn to Jesus, he or she could, and many have over the centuries. Most have not, however, often because of a misguided group loyalty ('We are Jews and we do not accept Jesus') or the belief that those who call themselves Christians – like the Crusaders, the Grand Inquisitor, or Adolf Hitler – accurately represent Him.

However, this 'hardening' was also only to last as long as "the times of the Gentiles", when all the nations have been reached with the gospel as Jesus predicted:

> "This gospel of the kingdom shall be preached in the whole world as a testimony to all the nations, and *then* the end will come." (Matt 24:14, emphasis added)

Today, there are very few Gentile nations yet to be reached.[285]

The end of the two witnesses' ministry in 1967 should therefore not be surprising, even if the means is - the secular government of Israel.

> When they have finished their testimony, the beast that comes up out of the abyss will make war with them, and overcome them and kill them. (Rev 11:7)

---

284 *DDJ*, pp.176-178.
285 Ibid.

This ascent of state-mandated secularism in Israel in 1948 ensured that when Jerusalem was finally regained in 1967, the two witnesses were silenced – the Law and the Prophets were no longer to testify 'in the street of the great city' (Rev 11:8).

Summary of the Killing (Rev 11:3, 7-10)

Revelation 11 is a very difficult passage with several possible approaches to understanding it:

(i) Many believe that the two witnesses will be literally Moses and Elijah, returning at a future time to the earth after thousands of years in heaven; they will then be literally killed by a metaphorical beast, the human Antichrist, in literal Jerusalem.

(ii) Others believe the passage is more metaphorical: the two witnesses are a metaphor for the church testifying and facing literal martyrdom, in the 1st Century, throughout the ages, or in the future; the beast represents 'the dark power of pagan empire',[286] or 'the principle of power politics: the state';[287] 'the great city' is a metaphor for Rome or the whole fallen world.

(iii) My approach has been to unpack these Jewish metaphors a little more carefully.

I have shown that:

(i) The two witnesses are metaphorical, being personifications of the Law and the Prophets, i.e. the Christian Old Testament or the Hebrew Bible, which continues testifying to this day to all in Israel who have not yet accepted Jesus and the New Covenant.

(ii) The beast is metaphorical but cannot be the literal

---

286 N.T. Wright, *Revelation For All*, p. 116.
287 Michael Wilcock, *The Message of Revelation*, p. 124.

Antichrist because it has seven heads and ten horns, which are all themselves 'kings' (Rev 17:10, 17:12). As seen in Revelation 13:2, it has elements of the four beasts Daniel saw (Dan 7:1-7) which were the empires of the Babylonians, the Medo-Persians, the Greeks, and the Romans. The beast is the state turned feral, a political power; it is the principality and power behind all of the Gentile states that had ruled over Israel for the previous seven hundred years, by John's time, from 586 BC to 95 AD.

(iii) This interpretation is confirmed by its having seven heads which are 'seven kings; five have fallen, one is, and the other has not yet come' (Rev 17:10). As any Jew knew in the 1st Century, there were two other Gentile empires who had ruled over Israel before Daniel's time: the Egyptians and the Assyrians. This meant for any Jew that five had already ruled them but fallen; 'one is' refers to Rome's ruling over Israel in John's time. The seventh yet to come must therefore rule over Israel sometime after 95 AD.

(iv) It is described as a wild beast, in Greek, *therion*, because it abandoned its calling as a domesticated beast of burden to faithfully administer justice for all as a servant of God (Rom 13:1-4) – these empires all went feral. Instead of serving God, these empires claimed ultimate authority, i.e. worship, for themselves and their emperors, i.e. the living image of the beast. There have been numerous other manifestations throughout the last 2,000 years.

(v) The 'great city' is Jerusalem which Paul tells us is a metaphor for the Old Covenant and all those still under it (Gal 4:24-25).

(vi) When Israel became a state in 1948, it was as a secular state. Whereas every other restoration in Israel's 3,500 year history had been accompanied by a renewing of the Mosaic Covenant, this time it was not. This meant that the same principality and power that ruled in the Gentile states was now being allowed to rule in Israel.

(vii) In 1967, Israel finally regained Jerusalem, seemingly ending the "times of the Gentiles", but handed back the Temple Mount to the Islamic authorities. Thus the beast killed the two witnesses in Jerusalem in 1967 by setting aside the Law and the Prophets: no Temple, no altar, no animal sacrifices. Not even Jewish prayers are allowed there. The two witnesses' bodies have been left lying in the street.

14
Gentiles Rejoicing
Secularism Triumphs

While Israel has left 'the two witnesses', the Law and the Prophets, lying dishonoured in the street since they recaptured Jerusalem in 1967, there is also a Gentile response to consider. Returning to Revelation 11:

> 9. Those from the peoples and tribes and tongues and nations will look at their dead bodies for three and a half days, and will not permit their dead bodies to be laid in a tomb.
> 10. And those who dwell on the earth will rejoice over them and celebrate; and they will send gifts to one another, because these two prophets tormented those who dwell on the earth. (Rev 11:9-10)

These 'peoples and tribes and tongues and nations' (v. 9) are Gentiles who refuse to trust in Jesus. They too want to dishonour Moses and Elijah – they 'will not permit their dead bodies to be laid in a tomb' (v. 9) and so leave them lying in the street. Gentiles 'rejoice over them and celebrate… because these two prophets tormented' not only the Jews but all 'those who dwell on the earth' (v. 10).

Why would that be? Remember David's prophecy:

> 1. Why are the nations in an uproar
> And the peoples devising a vain thing?
> 2. The kings of the earth take their stand
> And the rulers take counsel together
> Against the LORD and against His Anointed, saying,
> 3. "Let us tear their fetters apart
> And cast away their cords from us!" (Psa 2:1-3)

When David wrote this three thousand years ago, he was initially referring to the nations around Israel who resented his ruling over them as the anointed king of Israel but, two thousand years ago, the Early Church saw it also being fulfilled as a Messianic prophecy. They prayed:

> 25. "…our father David Your servant, said, 'WHY DID THE GENTILES RAGE, AND THE PEOPLES DEVISE FUTILE THINGS?
> 26. 'THE KINGS OF THE EARTH TOOK THEIR STAND, AND THE RULERS WERE GATHERED TOGETHER AGAINST THE LORD AND AGAINST HIS CHRIST.'
> 27. "For truly in this city there were gathered together against Your holy servant Jesus, whom You anointed, both Herod and Pontius Pilate, along with the Gentiles and the peoples of Israel…" (Acts 4:25-27, capitals showing the quotation)

We still see it whenever our society boasts in its secularism and rails against our Judaeo-Christian heritage and 1967 was particularly significant. In 1967, the Gentile world was in the throes of an astonishing transformation. What is particularly astonishing to me is that I did not realise the significance of what I was witnessing, and I suspect this is true for most people who lived through it all.

Let us begin by defining our terms more clearly.

Secularism

As mentioned earlier, in 1948 Israel chose to be a secular state. The original meaning of 'secular' was:

> Concerned with the affairs of this world, not sacred or monastic or ecclesiastical.[288]

Secular courts, for example, were to settle criminal and civil cases rather than religious disputes. Israel's secularism meant that it was set up as a Jewish state for the mostly Jewish people but not for the Jewish religion; it was not halachic, i.e. not ruled according to the Law and the Prophets.

However, 'secular' has also come to mean:

---

288 *Concise Oxford Dictionary*, Oxford University Press, 1985, p. 950.

> Sceptical of religious truth or opposed to religious education etc, hence secularism.[289]

Secularisation is therefore the transformation of a society from religious values and institutions to non-religious values and secular institutions, to even anti-religious values and institutions. Many today believe it is almost inevitable that, as people groups progress through modernising and reasoning, religion will lose its impact in all aspects of society.

It is ironic that secularism has become opposed to its own foundation. Despite the popular myth that the concept of separating powers, especially church and state, originated in 18th Century Europe's Enlightenment, Moses was actually codifying it for Israel in the Arabian wilderness, more than three thousand years earlier. The Enlightenment merely served to popularise it in Europe in the 18th Century, one hundred years after the Mayflower's Pilgrims fled being persecuted by state churches, to outwork this separation in the New World.

The Hidden Kingdom

In Book 2 in this series,[290] in the chapter entitled God's Hidden Kingdom, I argued that all five of the essential elements of today's liberal democracies[291] originated in the revelations of Moses and were affirmed by Jesus and Paul:

(i) The intrinsic worth of every individual as made in the image of God (Gen 9:6, Matt 10:29-31).

(ii) The supremacy of justice, hence the rule of law over kings (Deut 17:18-20).

(iii) The separation of powers, including an independent judiciary (Deut 16:18-20) and a free press (Deut 18:15).

---

289 Ibid.
290 *STB*, pp.231-237.
291 A 'liberal democracy' is a country or state based on the liberty and equal rights of all citizens and governed by elected representatives.

(iv) Freedom of conscience (Ex 23:2, 1 Cor 10:29, Rom 14:4 and 22).

(v) Elected representative leaders (Deut 1:13).

This is freely acknowledged by Jürgen Habermas, described by the Stanford Encyclopedia of Philosophy as 'one of the most influential philosophers in the world'[292] today:

> Universalistic egalitarianism, from which sprang the ideals of freedom and a collective life in solidarity, the autonomous conduct of life and emancipation, the individual morality of conscience, human rights and democracy, is the direct legacy of the Judaic ethic of justice and the Christian ethic of love. This legacy, substantially unchanged, has been the object of continual critical appropriation and reinterpretation. To this day, there is no alternative to it. And in light of the current challenges of a post-national constellation, we continue to draw on the substance of this heritage. Everything else is just idle postmodern talk.[293]

Bruce Sheiman, in his book *An Atheist Defends Religion*, also says of Judaism and Christianity:

> A commitment to human dignity, personal liberty, and individual equality did not previously appear in any other culture.[294]

As we saw in Chapter 6 – The Law and Christians, followers of Jesus are not under the Mosaic or Old Covenant but under the New Covenant. However, while the New gave us a better way of pleasing the Father by trusting in Jesus and walking in the Spirit, it did not reinvent the definitions of murder, or

---

292 http://plato.stanford.edu/entries/habermas/, 7 Oct, 2011.
293 Translation of an interview in 1999. Jürgen Habermas, *Time of Transitions*, Cambridge; Polity Press, 2006, pp. 150-151.
294 Bruce Sheiman, *An Atheist Defends Religion: Why Humanity is Better Off with Religion than without It*, Alpha, 2009. Also www.thechurchofnopeople.com/2010/02/atheist-interview-bruce-sheiman, 13 Sep, 2016.

theft, or dishonesty, or greed, or sexual immorality. Wherever the Christian faith spread, it promoted moral purity as well. As Peter wrote, 'having escaped the corruption in the world' (2 Pet 1:4), we are to stay free:

> Now for this very reason also, applying all diligence, in your faith supply moral excellence... (2 Pet 1:5, emphasis added)

Historically, therefore, the Law of Moses provided the basis not only for the West's justice systems, but also our traditional definitions of ethics, or morality. The New Covenant, in turn, provided the necessary new heart and indwelling Holy Spirit to enlighten and motivate all who receive Him (Ezek 36:26-27, Acts 1:4-8).

While it may be hard for us living in the West to recognise the origin and value of our society's ethics, it is not so for many in the East. David Aikman, former Beijing Bureau Chief of Time magazine, writes of Western visitors at one of China's premier academic research institutes, the Chinese Academy of Social Sciences,[295] being astonished when told by their Chinese lecturer:

> One of the things we were asked to look into was what accounted for the success, in fact, the pre-eminence of the West all over the world. We studied everything we could from the historical, political, economic, and cultural perspective. At first, we thought it was because you had more powerful guns than we had. Then we thought it was because you had the best political system. Next we focused on your economic system. But in the past twenty years, we have realized that the heart of your culture is your religion: Christianity. That is why the West has been so powerful. The Christian moral foundation of social and cultural life was what made possible the emergence of capitalism and then the successful transition to democratic politics. We

---

295 Considered the leading think-tank in China, it was founded in 1977 to advance and innovate in the scientific researches of philosophy, social sciences, and policies.

don't have any doubt about this.²⁹⁶

Political scientist Robert Woodberry of the National University of Singapore concludes of the 19th and early 20th Centuries:

> Christianity profoundly shaped both the development and global spread of stable liberal democracy. Some of these religious influences were direct, shaping the ideas and institutions that made stable liberal democracy more likely; some influences were indirect, shaping mass education, mass printing, voluntary associations, nonviolent social movement tactics, and particular types of reform which dispersed power beyond traditional elites and allowed a broader segment of the population to influence politics.²⁹⁷

Woodberry's conclusion was based on an extraordinarily broad analysis of historical data.²⁹⁸ He adds:

> Areas where Protestant missionaries had a significant presence in the past are on average more economically developed today, with comparatively better health, lower infant mortality, lower corruption, greater literacy, higher educational attainment (especially for women), and more robust membership in nongovernmental associations.²⁹⁹

For more, see Appendix B – Grown from 'Missionary Roots'.

Secularism, therefore, did not create itself, nor appear as self-evident, but is an over-extension of the 17th Century Pilgrims' concept of separating church and state, which originated in the Law of Moses in the 15th Century BC. Like a cuckoo chick in another bird's nest, secularism often seeks to evict all the eggs or chicks of its host.

---

296 David Aikman, *Jesus in Beijing: How Christianity is Transforming China and Changing the Global Balance of Power*, Washington D.C.; Regnery Publishing, 2003, p. 5.
297 http://kellogg.nd.edu/vfellowships/woodberry.shtml, 4 May, 2016.
298 When Woodberry and his fifty research assistants presented their conclusions to be published by the *American Political Science Review* (Vol. 106, No. 2, 2012), they provided 192 pages of supporting material.
299 *Christianity Today*, Jan/Feb, 2014.

Conflicting Values and Means

Those opposing the Lord and His Anointed are, of course, wildly overstating their cause when they say:

> "Let us tear their fetters apart and cast away their cords from us!" (Psa 2:3)

The secularists do not want a world where murder, theft, rape, kidnapping, or sex trafficking are legalised – rather, they aim to drive out any vestige of religion, whether good or bad. Accordingly, there are many areas where the values of secularism are congruent with the Law and the Prophets.

There is also much legitimate debate as to what part the laws of any nation can or should play in curbing particular behaviours. While everyone agrees that murder, theft, rape, kidnapping, and sex-trafficking should be illegal, few today would argue for the criminalising of sexual immorality other than for incest, rape, and bestiality, and to set the age of consent. I certainly would not. As Paul says, the Law of Moses set a standard but only the indwelling Holy Spirit can enable us to live it:

> 3. For what the Law could not do, weak as it was through the flesh, God did: sending His own Son in the likeness of sinful flesh and as an offering for sin, He condemned sin in the flesh, 4. so that the requirement of the Law might be fulfilled in us, who do not walk according to the flesh but according to the Spirit. (Rom 8:3-4)

There is also much needed debate today on how our laws should deal with prostitution and drug abuse.

There are, however, three areas where the values of secularism and our Judaeo-Christian heritage strongly conflict:

(i) Defining sexual morality.

(ii) Using the Lord's name.

(iii) Defining the value of human life.

Firstly, then, let us consider what secularism calls sexual liberation and the Law of Moses defines as sexual immorality.

Secularism and Sexual Liberation

Aldous Huxley, considered one of the leading intellectuals of the 20th Century, was quite candid:

> For myself, as, no doubt, for most of my contemporaries, the philosophy of meaningless was essentially an instrument of liberation. The liberation we desired was simultaneously liberation from a certain political and economic system and liberation from a certain system of morality. We objected to the morality because it interfered with our sexual freedom; we objected to the political and economic system because it was unjust. The supporters of these systems claimed that in some way they embodied the meaning (a Christian meaning, they insisted) of the world. There was one admirably simple method of confuting these people and at the same time justifying ourselves in our political and erotic revolt: we could deny that the world had any meaning whatsoever.[300]

He adds:

> No philosophy is completely disinterested... The philosopher who finds meaning in the world is concerned, not only to elucidate that meaning, but also to prove that it is most clearly expressed in some established religion, in some accepted code of morals. The philosopher who finds no meaning in the world is not concerned exclusively with a problem in pure metaphysics. He is also concerned to prove that there is no valid reason why he personally should not do as he wants to do.[301]

In a stunning cultural revolution that began in the mid-1960's, secularism has indeed torn apart the fetters and cast off the

---

300 Aldous Huxley, *Ends and Means*, London; Chatto & Windus, 1941, p. 273, emphasis added.
301 Ibid., p. 272, emphasis added.

cords of our heritage by redefining sexual morality. Before we look at this Sexual Revolution, let us briefly recap what our mainstream society used to consider normal, in line with Moses, Jesus, and Paul.

The Mosaic Law and Sexual Immorality

As we saw in Chapter 6, every time that Jesus spoke on sexual immorality,[302] He was helping 1st Century Jews to better understand the Law of Moses. Accordingly, when He was challenged for not washing His hands ritualistically, He pointed out that was a man-made tradition, not the Law, and that no one is defiled by what they eat but by what they think in their hearts:

> "Out of the heart come evil thoughts, murders, adulteries, fornications [Grk, *porneia* – sexual immorality], thefts, false witness, slanders. These are the things which defile the man..." (Matt 15:19-20)

Every Jew listening would have been in no doubt what He meant by sexual immorality because the Law was quite explicit. It forbade sexual relations before marriage (Ex 22:16) and adultery afterwards (Ex 20:14) as well as Leviticus 18's list:

(i) incest (vv. 6-19)

(ii) adultery (v. 20)

(iii) child sacrifice (v. 21)

(iv) homosexuality (v. 22)

(v) bestiality (v. 23).

The menstrual prohibition (vs 19) and idolatry (v. 21) was in regard to the Egyptian and Canaanite fertility rites which also involved bestiality and sacral prostitution (Deut 23:17). The Law also forbade:

---

302 e.g. Matthew 5:32, 15:19, 19:9, Mark 7:21.

(vi) ordinary prostitution, heterosexual (Lev 19:29) and homosexual (Deut 23:18)

(vii) rape, heterosexual (Deut 22:25) and homosexual (Gen 19:5-7, Jude 1:7).

Leviticus 18:24 summarises:

> "Do not defile yourselves by any of these things; for by all these the nations which I am casting out before you have become defiled."

It is obvious, then, that Jesus' teaching on defiling thoughts and desires was based on the Law's definition of defiling sexual behaviour. He left it to Paul to spell that out to Gentile Christians whose 1st Century cultures still embraced many of the ancient Canaanite practices – the Temple of Aphrodite in Corinth, for example, had 1,000 prostitute priestesses in service.[303] So Paul wrote:

> 9. Or do you not know that the unrighteous will not inherit the kingdom of God? Do not be deceived; neither fornicators, nor idolaters, nor adulterers, nor effeminate, nor homosexuals,
> 10. .. will inherit the kingdom of God.
> 11. Such were some of you; but you were washed, but you were sanctified, but you were justified in the name of the Lord Jesus Christ and in the Spirit of our God. (1 Cor 6:9-11)

Many in the Western world today, especially in the media, consider we are much more enlightened, more liberated, in the 21st Century for casting off these standards of sexual morality.

---

303 Strabo, *Geography*, Book 8, 6:20.

Secular Law and Christians

In 2012, George Weigel[304] published an article, *The Libertine Police State*, in which he describes an INGO[305] meeting just prior to the United Nations debating abortion rights in 1994:

> A... Dutch activist... announced..., "Let's stop fooling around here. What we're talking about is our right to f*** whoever we want, however we want, whenever we want."

Weigel comments:

> The Dutchman's formulation may have lacked elegance, but it certainly didn't lack precision. For that was precisely what was at issue 18 years ago, and it is precisely what is at issue today: will the sexual revolution, which reduced sex to a recreational activity of no moral consequence, be protected, advanced, and indeed mandated by the coercive powers of the modern state?
>
> There is irony... here, of course. What began as a movement to liberate sexuality from the constraints of moral reason, custom, and law has become a movement determined to use the instruments of law to impose its deconstruction of human sexuality and its moral relativism on all of society.[306]

Weigel's question about the modern state was answered almost immediately with the prosecution of a florist, 70-year-old grandmother Baronelle Stutzman of Washington State:

> A longtime gay customer—with whom she had a warm relationship—wanted her to do flower arrangements for his gay wedding. Mrs. Stutzman, a Southern Baptist, explained her Christian belief that marriage is between a

---

304 Distinguished Senior Fellow at the Ethics and Public Policy Center in Washington D.C., where he holds the William E. Simon Chair in Catholic Studies.
305 International Non-Governmental Organisation.
306 https://eppc.org/publications/the-libertine-police-state, published Feb 13, 2012.

man and woman, and thus could not participate in a gay wedding. Washington's attorney general prosecuted her, pursuing not only her business but also Mrs. Stutzman personally. A state judge has ruled against her, and she faces the loss of her life's savings and even her home.[307]

In Colorado, a baker, Jack Phillips of the Masterpiece Cakeshop was similarly prosecuted:

> When he declined two gay men's order to bake a cake celebrating gay marriage (though the men were welcome to buy any of the premade cakes off the shelf), they officially complained that Mr. Phillips violated Colorado's civil-rights law. A court ruled against him, ordering him and his employees to undergo government-approved "tolerance training," and also ordering him to bake cakes celebrating gay marriage for anyone who asks. If he refuses, he can go to jail—put behind bars—for contempt of court.[308]

Since the passing of liberalising laws in the USA, many states have passed Religious Freedom Acts (RFRAs) and, in 2014, the US Supreme Court upheld the case of Hobby Lobby, a corporation owned by a devout Christian family, who asked for religious-liberty rights, but the battle has only just begun for LGBTI[309] rights organisations.

In 2015, the Australian Catholic Bishops' Conference published a defence of traditional marriage in a pamphlet called, *Don't Mess With Marriage*. They began by urging their parishioners to accept anyone 'with deep-seated homosexual tendencies... with respect, compassion, and sensitivity. Every sign of unjust discrimination in their regard should be avoided'. They then presented their case for marriage:

> Some suggest that it is unjustly discriminatory not to

---

307 www.charismanews.com/opinion/49156-you-won-t-believe-how-many-christian-business-owners-are-under-lgbt-fire, 21 Sep, 2016.
308 Ibid.
309 Lesbian, Gay, Bisexual, Transgender, Intersex.

allow people with same-sex attraction to marry someone of the same sex… If [however] marriage is an institution designed to support people of the opposite sex to be faithful to each other and to the children of their union, it is not discrimination to reserve it to them.[310]

The Church was called before Tasmania's Anti-Discrimination Commission on the grounds that the pamphlet was 'offensive, insulting, and humiliating'.[311]

In September 2016, the Mercure Sydney Hotel was forced to cancel a conference booking of Anglicans, Catholics, the Marriage Alliance, and the Australian Christian Lobby, gathering to discuss how to respond to their nation's gay-marriage plebiscite, because of threats to staff.[312]

Our Response

What then should be the Christian response within our secular liberal democracies to the decriminalising and mandating of sexual immorality? Should we be seeking to restore the Mosaic Law, or the Ten Commandments, to our nations as some believe?[313]

Firstly, we must never forget the terrible lessons learned from the religious tyrannies of 16th and 17th Century Europe where Roman Catholic and Protestant rulers murderously persecuted dissenting citizens[314] and other nations. Historian D.J.B. Trim tells us that:

---

310 www.sydneycatholic.org/pdf/dmm-booklet_web.pdf, 24 Oct, 2016.
311 *The Australian*, 24-25 Sept, 2016, Inquirer, p. 19.
312 Ibid.
313 e.g. in movements such as Calvinism from 16th Century Geneva to 20th Century America's Dominion Theology, Christian Reconstructionism, Kingdom Now, and the New Apostolic Reformation, I believe there is often confusion regarding which covenants apply to whom. See details in Appendix A – God's Covenants.
314 Details in *STB*, pp. 60-65, 141-146.

> ...from the 1520s until approximately 1650 the greatest nations in Christendom – France, Spain, Portugal, Austria, Sweden, the Dutch Republic, and Britain – were all caught up in wars that were, either in part or in whole, the result of the divisions engendered by the Reformation.[315]

These internecine wars were not caused by the recovered doctrine of justification by faith but by both sides merging church and state. These powers are always to be kept separate, as God revealed to Moses in the 15th Century BC. If power corrupts, even within Israel as a theocracy, how much more so in our pluralistic Gentile societies?

We are instead, as individuals, to reject coercion and seek to persuade our neighbours and our democratic state:

> 13. "You are the salt of the earth; but if the salt has become tasteless, how can it be made salty again? It is no longer good for anything, except to be thrown out and trampled underfoot by men.
> 14. "You are the light of the world. A city set on a hill cannot be hidden;
> 15. nor does anyone light a lamp and put it under a basket, but on the lampstand, and it gives light to all who are in the house.
> 16. "Let your light shine before men in such a way that they may see your good works, and glorify your Father who is in heaven."
> (Matt 5:13-16)

Walking the talk as loving, moral activists, we are to be a conscience within our society and our nation, as Mother Theresa or William Wilberforce and the early Methodists so wonderfully demonstrated.[316]

Secondly, restoring the Mosaic Law would mean restoring the death penalty for sexual immorality.[317] Restoring even only the Ten Commandments would mean the death penalty

---
315 D.J.B. Trim, *European Warfare, 1350–1750*, New York & Cambridge; Cambridge University Press, 2010, chap 13.
316 *STB*, pp. 148-150.
317 Incest (Lev 20:11-12, 14 and 17); adultery (Lev 20:10); homosexuality (Lev 20:13); bestiality (Lev 20:15-16); rape (Deut 22:25).

for breaking the fourth, i.e. not keeping the Sabbath (Ex 35:2). We are instead to follow Jesus who forgave sexually immoral people: the woman caught in adultery (John 8:3-11); the much-married Samaritan woman (John 4:7ff); the notoriously sinful with whom He often ate (Matt 9:10, 11:19). Historically, Christians such as the Salvation Army have been in the forefront of rescuing women from sexual exploitation.[318]

Tragically, today we are often seen, or portrayed, as overbearing moralists who hate homosexuals or women who have abortions. However, as Rick Warren said regarding relating to Muslims:

> Our culture has accepted two huge lies. The first is that if you disagree with someone's lifestyle, you must fear or hate them. The second is that to love someone means you agree with everything they believe or do. Both are nonsense. You don't have to compromise convictions to be compassionate.[319]

Our culture has also widely accepted the lie that if anything has become legal, it is no longer immoral. As Christians, our first loyalty must always be to God and His definitions of morality, or good and evil. Our second loyalty is to always love our neighbours as ourselves, seeking to win them to God and His kingdom.

So how did we get to this state?

"For What It's Worth…"

In 1967, an American-Canadian rock band called Buffalo Springfield released Stephen Stills' classic, *For What It's Worth*:

> There's something happenin' here

---

318 *Encyclopedia of Prostitution and Sex Work: A-N.* Vol. 1, ed. Melissa Hope Ditmore, Santa Barbara; ABC-Clio Greenwood, 2006, p. 424.
319 Interview with Brandon A. Cox, *The Christian Post*, www.christianpost.com/news/exclusive-rick-warren-flat-out-wrong-that-muslims-christians-view-god-the-same-70767/, 15 Sep, 2016.

What it is ain't exactly clear...
Think it's time we stopped, children, what's that sound?
Everybody look what's goin' down...

What was happening then, I believe, bore a striking resemblance to a vast popular uprising fifty years earlier which transformed Russia; it was then hijacked by the Bolsheviks in October 1917, and channelled into what they promised would be a Workers' Paradise from which no-one was allowed to leave. However, 1967 in the West was not a political sea-change, but an ideological sea-change – we were hijacked by secularism. Here is my view, for what it's worth, and I leave it to the reader to judge for themselves whether the timing of all these events is fulfilling Revelation 11:9-10 or simply coincidental.

The ideas and practices of the 1960's Sexual Revolution were not new – far from it, as we know from the Egyptians and the Canaanites in the time of ancient Israel, and the Greeks and Romans in the time of the Early Church. However, for the first time in Western liberal democracies, the Revolution's mores became mainstream, centre stage. With the globalisation of the media, these were broadcast throughout the world for all to see, hear, and adopt as their own.

In this summation, I have to briefly address issues that are complex and controversial, such as the use of the contraceptive pill, the breakthrough that largely sparked the Revolution. Although condemned by Pope Paul VI in 1968 as a mortal sin,[320] I believe that contraception within marriage is a perfectly acceptable practice to God.[321] Also, I have focussed on both Britain and America: Britain, because most Western democracies inherited their legal system through the British Empire, which had ruled over one quarter of the globe and

---

320   Exception was made to 'cure bodily diseases' and for nuns in danger of rape, as in the Belgian Congo.
321   Onan's sin was not in controlling fertility but in violating Tamar's right to be a mother (Gen 38:9-10, Deut 25:5-6).

one fifth of its peoples, the USA, because it extended the Anglo-cultural influence.

The Sexual Revolution

The Revolution arose from a confluence of many social phenomena in the West. This was particularly so in the USA which, following World War II, quickly became the world's dominant superpower, as well its primary source of television and movies, the new forms of mass communication and entertainment.

Let us consider seven of these phenomena.

1. The Pill

In 1960, the Pill was approved as a contraceptive in the USA. Within three years, over two million American women were using it. Britain released it to single women in 1974 and by then, it was on the World Health Organisation's List of Essential Medicines. Today, it is ubiquitous.

In 1962, American writer Helen Gurley Brown published her *Sex and the Single Girl*, which advised women to have a stable job and casual sexual affairs. The book sold two million copies in three weeks and was soon sold in thirty-five countries. Hugh Hefner's *Playboy* empire flourished.

Freed from the fear of pregnancy, 'free love' became possible for all. The Free Love movement rejected marriage, seeing it as a form of social and financial bondage. This also was not a new idea, but gained unimaginable momentum through a burgeoning youth culture and mass communication. Today, living together before marriage is considered normal.

2. Abortion

Britain legalised abortion in 1967 and the USA in 1973. Between 1950 and 1985, most developed countries liberalised their abortion laws for reasons of human rights and safety and by 2005, the U.N. had declared abortion a universal human right for mothers.

3. Protest movements

Throughout the Sixties, there was a worldwide escalation of social conflicts, some undoubtedly good and necessary. In the USA, the Civil Rights Movement had motivated multitudes to protest segregation, and in 1964, Martin Luther King Jr was awarded the Nobel Peace Prize.

Youth movements and student protests became common throughout the USA and Europe, usually against the Vietnam War. In the USA in 1970, one boycott of classes involved four million students, closing 450 campuses across the nation. Socialist movements likewise grew, and in the May 1968 protests in France, students linked up with wildcat strikes by some ten million workers.

The feminist movement was revitalised in part by the 1963 publication of Betty Friedman's *The Feminine Mystique* and the 1966 founding of NOW (The National Organization for Women).

Illicit drug use, which had mostly been confined to the fringes, the Counter-Culture, or the artistic community, was popularised through music and mass communication. Young and old experimented with marijuana, hashish, cocaine, amphetamines, or heroin. This brought a new attitude towards intoxication – whereas alcoholic intoxication had been widely considered shameful, these drugs aimed for 'highs', or intoxication.

In summary, it became normal to protest, to challenge the status quo in a wide variety of causes.

4. Mass communication

Television was invented in 1925, but World War II had slowed the spread of the technology. By the early 1960's, however, over 90% of American households had sets. By the late 60's, colour television was widespread and in Britain, by 1969, the BBC and ITV were broadcasting in colour.

Popular music was ubiquitous on radio, television, and cinema screens, as well as in most homes on vinyl records. In 1962, Philips Electronics invented cassette tapes, allowing replays anywhere. Bob Dylan's *Blowin' in the Wind* (1963) and *The Times, They Are a-Changin'* (1964) became anthems for the protest movements. On 25 June, 1967, the world's first live global television link broadcast the Beatles' *All You Need is Love* to over 400 million in 25 countries. In 1969, Woodstock, the most famous of music festivals, was attended by 400,000.

Not so public, at 10:30 p.m. on October 29, 1969, was the first computer network link up between the University of California, Los Angeles (UCLA) and the Stanford Research Institute. Five weeks later, the network included the University of Utah and the University of California, Santa Barbara (UCSB) and by 1981, it had grown to 213 hosts. This was the start of the Internet; today, it is ubiquitous.

5. Public modesty

Woodstock was also famous for its 'naked hippies' and skinny-dipping, but public undressing had been slowly progressing in mainstream culture. While bikinis were worn in antiquity, their reintroduction in 1946 was condemned as sinful by Pope Pius XII in 1951 and banned in many countries. Nine years later, Brian Hyland's *Itsy Bitsy Teenie Weenie Yellow Polkadot Bikini* moved it from risqué to okay. In 1962, the Bond move, *Dr No*, featured Ursula Andress emerging from the waves in a white bikini, a scene later described as a 'defining moment in the sixties liberalization of screen eroticism'.[322]

A series of *Beach Party* movies (1963-65) starred Annette Funicello, an ex-Disney Mouseketeer, and her teenage

---

322 Martin Rubin, *Thrillers*, Cambridge; Cambridge University Press, 1999, p. 128

girlfriends all wearing bikinis. By 1967, *Time* was reporting that 65% of the 'young set' were wearing them 'and this seems the season when the more mature will follow suit'.[323]

In 1967 in Britain, two Swedish films, *I Am Curious (Yellow)* and *Inga* were ground-breaking, showing explicit sex and nudity. Both were initially banned in the U.S. but rated X when shown in 1968. British film *If...* was notorious in 1968 for its frontal male nudity (which was censored out), female nudity, sex scenes, violence and homosexuality.

In 1968 in the USA, the Motion Picture Production Code (MPPC) was replaced by a more liberal rating system. The MPMC, often known as the Hays Code, had set strict moral guidelines for movies since 1930. Women began to appear topless in movies and sex scenes became increasingly explicit.

Nudity, explicit sex scenes, and sexual discussions are now mainstream.

6. Pornography

The USA's Golden Age of Porn, or porno chic, followed. This 15-year period (1969-1984) began with Andy Warhol's *Blue* and Bill Osco's *Mona*, the first two movies to depict explicit sex scenes to mainstream American audiences. Moderated in 1973 by the Supreme Court's Miller decision, which pegged obscenity to local 'contemporary community standards', the Age ended with the rise of home videos for pornography in the early 1980's.

In 2015, *Playboy* announced it would do away with naked women in their magazine because, as their chief executive Scott Flanders stated, the Internet has made their focus obsolete:

> That battle has been fought and won. You're now one click away from every sex act imaginable for free. And so it's just passé at this juncture.[324]

---

323 *Time* article, Fashion: Brief, Briefer, Briefest, 2 June, 1967.
324 *New York Times*, 12 Oct, 2015. In Feb, 2017, *Playboy* announced

7. Decriminalising homosexuality

In 1967, Britain passed the Sexual Offences Act which decriminalised homosexuality between consenting adult males (lesbianism has never been a crime). Canada followed suit in 1969; New Zealand in 1986. In the USA, Illinois had legislated in 1962 and over the next decade, a third of the states did likewise. In 2003, the Supreme Court legalised same-sex sexual activity in every state and territory.

This was both just and consistent with the New Covenant and Britain's decriminalising of fornication and adultery over a hundred years earlier, in 1857. However, the New Covenant's decriminalising is not to condone these behaviours but to change how we address them. By 2015, same-sex marriage was legalised in Britain, Canada, New Zealand, and the USA, with accompanying adoption rights.

Using the Lord's Name

As mentioned above, in 1968 the Americans' Motion Picture Production Code (MPMC) was replaced by today's more liberal rating system, a guideline for parental control of children.[325]

---

their decision to remove nudity entirely 'was a mistake… Today we're taking our identity back and reclaiming who we are'. www.bbc.com/news/world-us-canada-3896300, accessed 20 Feb, 2017.
325 G – General Audience. All ages admitted. Nothing that would offend parents for viewing by children.
PG – Parental Guidance Suggested. Some material may not be suitable for children. Parents urged to give "parental guidance". May contain some material parents might not like for their young children.
PG 13 – Parents Strongly Cautioned. Some material may be inappropriate for children under 13. Parents are urged to be cautious. Some material may be inappropriate for pre-teenagers.
R – Restricted. Under 17 requires accompanying parent or adult guardian. Contains some adult material. Parents are urged to learn more about the film before taking their young children with them.
NC-17 – Adults Only. No One 17 and Under Admitted. Clearly adult. Children are not admitted.

One perhaps unintended consequence was that movies began to use the Lord's name profanely because the MPMC's first point had forbidden…:

> 1. Pointed profanity – by either title or lip – this includes the words "God," "Lord," "Jesus," "Christ" (unless they be used reverently in connection with proper religious ceremonies), "hell," "damn," "Gawd," and every other profane and vulgar expression however it may be spelled[326]

The Code had also been called the Hays Code, after William H. Hays, president of the Motion Picture Producers and Distributors of America (MPPDA) from 1922 to 1945, who was also a Presbyterian elder. The Code, however, was written and given to him by Daniel Lord, a Catholic priest, so both Catholics and Protestants had had a say.

Under English law, the last person to be imprisoned for blasphemy was a John Gott in 1921 and blasphemy was decriminalised in 2008. New Zealand had already decriminalised it in 1990, to protect the right to free speech, as did Australia in 1995.

The United Nations' Human Rights Committee declared in 2011 that blasphemy laws are incompatible with the International Covenant on Civil and Political Rights (ICCPR) which is binding on all signatory nations.

However, vain use of the Lord's name was forbidden by the third of the Ten Commandments:

> "You shall not take the name of the LORD your God in vain, for the LORD will not leave him unpunished who takes His name in vain." (Ex 20:7)

While this command was to warn anyone from prophesying or teaching falsely, Jesus taught that we are always to keep the name of God hallowed, or holy (Matt 6:9). Instead, these

---

326 Thomas Streissguth, *The Roaring Twenties*, New York; Infobase Publishing, 2007, p. 364.

names are today used profanely, as expletives everywhere, even in movies for children.

This is particularly horrendous because, as Peter said to all the leaders of Israel[327] in 30 AD:

> "There is salvation in no one else; for there is no other name under heaven that has been given among men by which we must be saved." (Acts 4:12, emphasis added)

Our society's new liberalism is mocking our only means of salvation (Rom 10:13).

Redefining the Value of Life

Secularism has also largely reshaped society's views on abortion and the death penalty.

1. Abortion

As mentioned earlier, Britain legalised abortion in 1967 and the USA in 1973. Between 1950 and 1985, most developed countries liberalised their abortion laws for reasons of human rights and safety.

'Liberal' originally meant 'befitting a free human being'[328] so abortion has been redefined as freeing women from their 'products of conception' in 'reproductive health centres'. Despite incontrovertible evidence that every human being's life begins at conception, by 2005, the U.N. had declared abortion a universal human right for mothers. Babies in utero are no longer considered to be, as Moses wrote, 'created in the image of God' (Gen 1:26-27) or, as David wrote, 'fearfully and wonderfully made':

> 13. For You formed my inward parts; You wove me in my mother's womb.
> 14. I will give thanks to You, for I am fearfully and wonderfully

---

327 Acts 4:5.
328 *Concise Oxford Dictionary*, p. 579.

made; wonderful are Your works, and my soul knows it very well. (Psa 139:13-14)

Today, we can see it all for ourselves in extraordinary detail in medical scans, photos, and videos, but our society is in dogmatic denial.

2. Abolition of the death penalty

In 1965, Britain passed the Murder Act which abolished the death penalty for murder while retaining it for treason, espionage, arson in royal dockyards, and 'piracy with violence'. The USA briefly stopped executions in 1967 and the Supreme Court briefly forbade capital punishment in 1972, but executions recommenced in 1977. Today, the States are divided over capital punishment with the federal government and thirty-two states still retaining it and eighteen not. New Zealand abolished it in 1961, except for treason, likewise Australia in 1967 and Canada in 1976.

I include the death penalty legislation because both the Law of Moses and the Noahide Laws[329] established the death penalty for murder on the grounds that the victim's life is as valuable as the perpetrator's (Gen 9:5-6, Rom 13:4). Ironically, our society now values the lives of convicted murderers above the lives of our innocent unborn. Whether we like it or not, legalising abortion and abolishing capital punishment for murder ignores or rejects the testimony of the Law and the Prophets.

'God is Dead' Theology

In mid-1966, *Time* magazine's cover asked, 'Is God Dead?',[330] bringing into the mainstream a trend among liberal theologians to write God out of theology. Begun three years earlier by Episcopal professor Paul van Buren's *The Secular Meaning of*

---
329 See Appendix A – God's Covenants.
330 *Time*, 8 April, 1966.

the Gospel, it was fuelled in Britain by the Bishop of Woolwich, John Robinson, declaring his lack of faith in *Honest to God*.

Heresy charges brought against the Bishop of California, James Pike, for rejecting central Christian beliefs were dropped in 1967 after the Episcopal Church of America declared that all heresy was 'out of date'.

In 1968, the Lambeth Conference of the Church of England decided that their clergy no longer had to believe their thirty-nine articles of faith.[331]

In 1967 in New Zealand, the principal of the Presbyterian theological seminary, Professor Lloyd Geering, freely acknowledged he did not believe in God, or the resurrection of Jesus, or the Scriptures except as a useful myth. The Presbyterian Assembly decided: 'no doctrinal error has been established, dismisses the charges and declares the case closed'.[332] Still hailed in our media as 'New Zealand's greatest theological thinker',[333] he was awarded the nation's highest honour in 2007.[334]

Peter warned us two thousand years ago:

> 1. ...there will also be false teachers among you, who will secretly introduce destructive heresies, even denying the Master who bought them...
> 18. For speaking out arrogant words of vanity they entice by fleshly desires, by sensuality, those who barely escape from the ones who live in error,
> 19. *promising them freedom while they themselves are slaves of corruption*; for by what a man is overcome, by this he is

---

331 Resolution 43b, www.anglicancommunion.org/media/127743/1968.pdf, 6 May, 2016.
332 www.abc.net.au/religion/stories/s1333339.htm, 20 Aug, 2016.
333 *NZ Listener*, 15 Aug, 2013.
334 In 1988, he was honoured as a Commander of the Order of the British Empire (CBE); in 2001, as Principal Companion of the New Zealand Order of Merit (re-designated in 2009 to Knight Grand Companion of the New Zealand Order of Merit (GNZM)); and in 2007, he was appointed a Member of the Order of New Zealand (ONZ), an honour limited to twenty living recipients.

> enslaved. (2 Pet 2:1, 18-19, emphasis added)

Remember Aldous Huxley's testimony above:

> We objected to the [Christian] morality because it interfered with our sexual freedom.

This theology was just the icing on the secular cake, the Gentiles celebrating the two witnesses lying dead and dishonoured in the street while theologians proclaimed the death of God Himself. The theology derived its name from Friedrich Nietzsche's *Zarathustra* – they should have read on, to his warning addressed to 'you conquerors of the old God' that they would end up on their knees before 'the new idol', the state, the first beast of Revelation 13.[335]

Summary of Revelation 11:9-10

It was not only Israel that killed the two witnesses in 1967 – so too did the Gentiles.

(i) Ironically, this is most obvious in the Western liberal democracies whose very existence as liberal democracies is due to their five essential elements being revealed through Moses, Jesus, and Paul.

(ii) In seeking to be secular, to keep the powers separate, our nations have gone too far and tried instead to overturn some of the values on which they were founded due to the testimony of our Judaeo-Christian heritage.

(iii) We are not called as Christians to recriminalise sexual immorality but to live as examples and activists to influence our society to accept Jesus and His way, which includes the indwelling power of the Holy Spirit to help us.

---

335 *STB*, pp. 180-181.

(iv) In liberalising our nations' laws, secularists do not want a world where murder, theft, rape, kidnapping, or sex trafficking are legalised. Instead, they aim to drive out any vestige of religion, whether good or bad, so in some areas their values are congruent with the Law and the Prophets.

(v) Three areas where these values are in conflict are in defining sexual morality, using the Lord's name profanely, and in defining the value of life.

(vi) The Law defined in plain language sexually immoral, defiling behavior in Israel's contemporaries in ancient Egyptian and Canaanite culture in 1500 BC; Jesus applied this definition to the thought-life and heart-desires of His 1st Century Jewish audience; Paul spelled it out for 1st Century Gentiles, and for all of us ever since.

(vii) In redefining sexual morality for mainstream society, secularists portray their views as liberating, i.e. tearing apart fetters and casting off cords. This can be readily seen in the Sexual Revolution of the 1960's which created today's permissive society.

(viii) Use of the Lord's name as a profanity or expletive has become common-place. This is particularly heinous because calling on His name is our only means of salvation.

(ix) The silencing of the testimony of Law and the Prophets is also seen in the about-face of our laws on abortion and capital punishment for murder.

(x) False teachers and prophets have not only presided over the killing of Moses and Elijah as witnesses but also pronounced the death of God Himself.

(xi) In my view, these events in the mid-60's are not coincidental but fulfill Revelation 11:9-10. You need to judge this for yourself.

15
Israel's Restoration
"Dem Dry Bones…"

It is often taught today that Israel's restoration in the 20th Century is also mere coincidence, that God gave up on the Jews in the 1st Century when the majority rejected Jesus as Messiah. However, as we saw in Revelation 12, although Israel is like a woman who has forgotten her own Son, God has never forgotten or rejected them. Instead, He exiled them from the land into "the wilderness of the nations" until "the times of the Gentiles were fulfilled". These times are apparently now fulfilled: Israel is back in the land.

Some still argue that because the restoration promises of Leviticus 26:40-42 are conditional,[336] He would not and could not restore them until they repented.

It is ironic that we Christians are quick to argue for God's amazing grace for Gentiles while we were yet sinners but abandon the whole idea when it comes to Israel while they are still sinners. The restoration promises of Leviticus 26 are indeed conditional but they are not the only texts we have to consider and, as R.C. Trench observed:

> Another rule of interpretation, as of common sense, …is that we are not to expect in every place the whole circle of [Biblical] truth, and that nothing is proved by the absence of a doctrine from one passage, which is clearly stated in others…[337]

While Leviticus 26 tells Israel what they must do before they can legitimately expect Him to act, that does not rule out God acting graciously before that. He also promised the exile to

---
336 e.g. www.equip.org/articles/modern-israel-in-bible-prophecy-promised-return-or-impending-exile, 9 Jun, 2015.
337 Archbishop R.C. Trench, *Notes on the Parables*, 1890, p. 41.

Babylon would only last seventy years (2 Chron 36:21) and that the exile to all the nations in 70 AD would be only until "the times of the Gentiles" were fulfilled (Luke 21:24). Did Israel deserve to be restored either time? Had they repented enough? Not that we know.

Ezekiel's Predictions

In 585 BC,[338] Ezekiel prophesied that God would restore Israel to their land from Babylon before they repented and that this would cause them to repent. This should not surprise us. We are supposed to know, as Paul wrote:

> ...that the kindness of God *leads* you to repentance (Rom 2:4, emphasis added)

Ezekiel is unequivocal about Israel's sinfulness – they had been exiled for "their ways and their deeds":

> 17. "Son of man, when the house of Israel was living in their own land, they defiled it by *their ways and their deeds*...
> 18. "Therefore I poured out My wrath on them for the blood which they had shed on the land, because they had defiled it with their idols.
> 19. "Also I scattered them among the nations and they were dispersed throughout the lands. According to *their ways and their deeds* I judged them" (Ezek 36:17-19, emphasis added)

However, the Babylonian exile had caused a major problem for God because He had created Israel to be an example to all the nations. Accordingly:

> 20. "When they came to the nations where they went, they profaned My holy name, because it was said of them, 'These are the people of the LORD; yet they have come out of *His land*.'
> 21. "But I had concern for My holy name, which the house of Israel had profaned among the nations where they went". (Ezek 36:20-21, emphasis added)

---

338 *Zondervan Pictorial Encyclopedia of the Bible*, Vol 2, p. 457.

Their coming out of "His land" (v. 20) had undermined the open revelation of God as the provider and protector of Israel. This is why the exile was only to be for seventy years (Jer 29:10); He would then restore them, but He wanted Israel to understand why:

> 22. "Therefore say to the house of Israel, 'Thus says the Lord GOD, "It is not for your sake, O house of Israel, that I am about to act, but for My holy name, which you have profaned among the nations where you went.
> 23. "I will vindicate the holiness of My great name… when I prove Myself holy among you in their sight.
> 24. "For I will take you from the nations, gather you from all the lands and bring you into your own land…
> 32. "I am not doing this for your sake," declares the Lord GOD, "let it be known to you. Be ashamed and confounded for your ways, O house of Israel!" (Ezek 36:22-24, 32)

This restoration would not be because Israel had repented. Like an impenitent prisoner, most of them had merely served their time of punishment;[339] when the 70 years was up, God would vindicate His name as the God of Israel. Then He would cleanse them and offer them a new way, a change of heart:

> 25. "Then I will sprinkle clean water on you, and you will be clean; I will cleanse you from all your filthiness and from all your idols.
> 26. "Moreover, I will give you a new heart and put a new spirit within you; and I will remove the heart of stone from your flesh and give you a heart of flesh.
> 27. "I will put My Spirit within you and cause you to walk in My statutes, and you will be careful to observe My ordinances. (Ezek 36:25-27)

---

[339] The people had sinned for 430 years (Ezek 4:4-6), not keeping the Sabbath and Jubilee years (2 Chron 36:21). The seventy years was to allow the land 'to enjoy its Sabbaths' (2 Chron 36:21).

This, of course, is the New Covenant, as also promised by Jeremiah (Jer 31:31-34). Ezekiel 36 continues, adding promises of prosperity in the Promised Land:

> 28. "You will live in the land that I gave to your forefathers; so you will be My people, and I will be your God"
> 29. "Moreover, I will save you from all your uncleanness; and I will call for the grain and multiply it, and I will not bring a famine on you.
> 30. "I will multiply the fruit of the tree and the produce of the field, so that you will not receive again the disgrace of famine among the nations" (Ezek 36:28-30)

Only then, when back in the land and as a direct result of seeing God's unmerited kindness or grace, would Israel at last repent:

> 31. "Then you will remember your evil ways and your deeds that were not good, and you will loathe yourselves in your own sight for your iniquities and your abominations.
> 32. "I am not doing this for your sake," declares the Lord GOD, "let it be known to you. Be ashamed and confounded for your ways, O house of Israel!" (Ezek 36:31-32)

The land of Israel would be thoroughly restored:

> 33. 'Thus says the Lord GOD, "On the day that I cleanse you from all your iniquities, I will cause the cities to be inhabited, and the waste places will be rebuilt.
> 34. "The desolate land will be cultivated instead of being a desolation in the sight of everyone who passes by.
> 35. "They will say, 'This desolate land has become like the garden of Eden; and the waste, desolate and ruined cities are fortified and inhabited.'
> 36. "Then the nations that are left round about you will know that I, the LORD, have rebuilt the ruined places and planted that which was desolate; I, the LORD, have spoken and will do it" (Ezek 36:33-36)

The ruined cities of Israel were rebuilt over the next four hundred years and Jesus introduced the New Covenant in 30 AD.

Today, the restoration of the people of Israel to the land of Israel testifies to all the nations that the God of Israel is again openly intervening in the affairs of mankind.

The Dry Bones

We see a similar pattern in Ezekiel 37, in the famous vision of the valley of dry bones. As children, many of us may have sung the old Negro spiritual, 'Dem bones, dem bones gonna walk aroun'....' but in our familiarity, we may have overlooked that Ezekiel saw Israel being restored in two stages: first the natural, then the spiritual.

He is placed in the valley full of very dry bones (vv. 1-2). The Lord tells him to prophesy and, as he does, the bones reconnect, the sinews and flesh grow back and skin covers them (vv. 3-8):

> ...but there was no breath in them (Ezek 37:8)

After the first prophecy, the whole valley is full of dead bodies.

The second time he prophesies, it is to the breath of life to come from the four winds to:

> "...breathe on these slain, that they come to life"... and the breath came into them, and they came to life and stood on their feet, an exceedingly great army (Eze 37:9-10)

The Lord explains:

> 11. ..."Son of man, these bones are the whole house of Israel; behold, they say, 'Our bones are dried up and our hope has perished. We are completely cut off.'
> 12. "Therefore prophesy and say to them, 'Thus says the Lord GOD, "Behold, I will open your graves and cause you to come up out of your graves, My people; and I will bring you into the land of Israel.
> 13. "Then you will know that I am the LORD, when I have opened your graves and caused you to come up out of your graves, My people.
> 14. "*I will put My Spirit within you and you will come to life,* and I

will place you on your own land. Then you will know that I, the LORD, have spoken and done it," declares the LORD.'" (Ezek 37:11-14, emphasis added)

This restoration is not only as a people to the land but also to God – "I will put My Spirit within you" is the promise of the New Covenant.

Obviously, these predictions of Ezekiel were fulfilled by Jesus coming with that covenant in the 1st Century, but they also provide a pattern to be repeated[340] in the 20th Century in the land and nation of Israel.

Before…

As covered in Book 1, *Dancing in the Dragon's Jaws*, at the end of the 19th Century, the land of Israel had again become 'a desolation in the sight of everyone who passes by' (Ezek 36:34). In *Innocents Abroad*, Mark Twain described the land as he saw it in 1867, 'under the Ottoman crescent':

> Here [northern Palestine] were evidences of cultivation – a rare sight in this country – an acre or two of rich soil studded with last season's dead corn-stalks… But in such a land it was a thrilling spectacle. Close to it was a stream…[341]

> Miles of desolate country whose soil is rich enough, but is given over wholly to weeds… alas, there is no dew here, nor flowers, nor birds, nor trees. There is a plain and an unshaded lake, and beyond them some barren mountains…[342]

> Jerusalem is mournful, and dreary, and lifeless. I would not like to live here.[343]

---

340 Called a recapitulation by theologians.
341 Mark Twain, *Innocents Abroad*, Hartford, CT; American Publishing Co, 1869, p. 481.
342 Ibid., p. 488.
343 Ibid., p. 560.

As he saw Palestine:

> Such dismal desolation cannot surely exist elsewhere on earth.[344]

> Of all the lands there are for dismal scenery, I think Palestine must be the prince. The hills are barren, they are dull of color, they are unpicturesque in shape. The valleys are unsightly deserts fringed with a feeble vegetation that has an expression about it of being sorrowful and despondent... It is a hopeless, dreary, heart-broken land... Palestine sits in sackcloth and ashes. Over it broods the spell of a curse that has withered its fields and fettered its energies...[345]

He mourned its lost grandeur:

> Nazareth is forlorn... Jericho the accursed, lies a moldering ruin... Bethlehem and Bethany, in their poverty and their humiliation...Renowned Jerusalem itself, the stateliest name in history, has lost all its ancient grandeur, and is become a pauper village... The noted Sea of Galilee... was long ago deserted...and its borders are a silent wilderness; Capernaum is a shapeless ruin; Magdala is the home of beggared Arabs; Bethsaida and Chorazin have vanished from the earth...Palestine is desolate and unlovely. And why should it be otherwise? Can the curse of the Deity beautify a land? Palestine is no more of this work-day world. It is sacred to poetry and tradition – it is dream-land.[346]

In 1913, Sir Frederick Treves published an illustrated 'account of a tour in Palestine'. He too was unrelentingly bleak:

> On nearing Jaffa... what is there to see? Merely a low line of bare coast, treeless and blank... Of this it is possible to say little more than that it is not water.[347]

---

344 Ibid., p. 602.
345 Ibid., p. 606.
346 Ibid., p. 608, emphasis added
347 Sir Frederick Treves, *The Land That is Desolate*, London; Smith,

> ...the vast Plain of Sharon, so far as the eye can reach, is practically treeless. Such hedges as exist are mostly of prickly cactus...[348]

> The first impression of Jerusalem... So harsh, bleached, and colourless is the country round about that the city itself is a shadow of a rock in a weary land... the environs of Jerusalem are a dusty, ungenial limestone waste.[349]

Heading north, he noted that fertile areas were uncultivated:

> Caesarea, the once proud seaport... is now a mere wraith, a formless drift of stones and dust tenanted by slum dwellers, and as Dean Stanley says, the most desolate site in the Holy Land.[350]

> The country around the lake [in Galilee] is characterless, monotonous and bare. It is a treeless country, grey with stone rather than green with grass... Only one town remains out of them all – the half-ruinous and wholly dirty town of Tiberias... The Plain of Gennesaret, still fertile and even luxuriant, but neglected and forsaken like the rest of the land that surrounds the sea.[351]

Prior to 1922, the land was also notorious for malaria:

> 1922 [was] the beginning of probably the first successful national malaria eradication campaign anywhere. Before then, 100 years ago, Palestine had been soaked in malaria, and was either thinly populated or uninhabitable in many areas. Even the British in 1918 considered the malarial position 'almost hopeless'. Yet approx. 45 years later, malaria had been eradicated there.[352]

Elder & Co, 1913, p. 4.
348 Ibid., p. 20.
349 Ibid., p. 40.
350 Ibid., p. 156.
351 Ibid., pp. 192-193.
352 https://malariaworld.org/blog/enthusiasm-alone-was-insufficient-defeat-malaria-palestine-100-years-ago-it-required, 24 Oct, 2016.

...and After

In April, 1960, *Scientific American* described the transformation since Israel's rebirth:

> The 20th Century Israelites did not find their promised land "flowing with milk and honey," as their forebears did 3,300 years ago. They came to a land of encroaching sand dunes along a once-verdant coast, of malarial swamps and naked limestone hills from which an estimated three feet of topsoil had been scoured, sorted and spread as sterile overwash upon the plains or swept out to sea...
>
> Yet [within 10 years] Israel was... an exporter of agricultural produce and had nearly achieved the goal of agricultural self-sufficiency...It had more than doubled its cultivated land, to a million acres. It had drained 44,000 acres of marshland and extended irrigation to 325,000 acres; it had increased many-fold the supply of underground water from wells... diverting and utilizing the scant surface waters. On vast stretches of uncultivable land it had established new range-cover to support a growing livestock industry and planted 37 million trees in new forests and shelter belts.[353]

Today, the Hula swamps are a sanctuary to millions of migrating birds, the desert is blooming because of drip-irrigation,[354] there are over 240 million trees,[355] one fifth of the land is nature reserves, the Biblical animals and birds are being reintroduced and Israel is famous for its exports of fruit, such as Jaffa oranges, vegetables and flowers.[356]

Is this not what Isaiah describes?

---

353 www.scientificamerican.com/article/reclamation-of-man-made-desert/, 9 Jun, 2015.
354 www.israel21c.org/environment/top-10-ways-israel-fights-desertification/, 4 Jun, 2015.
355 www.jnf.org/work-we-do/our-projects/forestry-ecology/, 20 Aug, 2016.
356 www.mfa.gov.il/MFA/MFAArchive/2000-2009/2001/9/Flora%20and%20Fauna%20in%20Israel, 12 Jun, 2010.

> The wilderness and the desert will be glad,
> And the Arabah will rejoice and blossom;
> Like the crocus it will blossom profusely
> And rejoice with rejoicing and shout of joy.
> The glory of Lebanon will be given to it,
> The majesty of Carmel and Sharon (Isa 35:1-2)

'The glory of Lebanon' and 'the majesty of Carmel and Sharon' were trees and myriads of wild-flowers, now to be seen in 'the wilderness and the desert'.[357] Isaiah's prophecy was only metaphorically fulfilled when Israel returned from the Babylonian exile – today it is being literally fulfilled. So too with Ezekiel's prophecy:

> 34. "The desolate land will be cultivated instead of being a desolation in the sight of everyone who passes by.
> 35. "They will say, 'This desolate land has become like the garden of Eden; and the waste, desolate and ruined cities are fortified and inhabited.'
> 36. "Then the nations that are left round about you will know that I, the LORD, have rebuilt the ruined places and planted that which was desolate; I, the LORD, have spoken and will do it" (Ezek 36:34-36)

Israel's Resurrection?

As mentioned earlier, Yad Vashem, Israel's Holocaust Museum in Jerusalem, has inscribed over its entrance a portion of Ezekiel's 6th Century BC promise of national resurrection and restoration:

> "I will put My breath in you and *you shall live again*, and I will set you *upon your own soil*…" (Ezek 37:14, emphasis added)

We also saw earlier Ezekiel's prediction of two stages in this resurrection: first, he saw the skeletons reassemble and become dead bodies, then he saw the dead bodies being raised to life.

---

357 The Arabah is the southern desert of Israel.

This was fulfilled in the 5th Century BC, when Israel was reassembled in the land, and in the 1st Century AD, when Jesus introduced the New Covenant.

Paul then built on this imagery. He argued that the nation of Israel's rejection of Jesus led to their being cut off from God, like olive branches 'broken off for their unbelief' (Rom 11:20), while the riches of Christ were then offered to all the nations (v. 12). He then predicted a resurrection of Israel:

> For if their rejection is the reconciliation of the world, what will their acceptance be but life from the dead? (Rom 11:15)

In 1948, they were restored as a nation to their land, reassembled but still 'dead in their trespasses and sins' (Eph 2:1) – their accepting Jesus will be a spiritual resurrection, as we will see in the next chapter. When is this to happen?

> For I do not want you, brethren, to be uninformed of this mystery – so that you will not be wise in your own estimation – that a partial hardening has happened to Israel *until the fullness of the Gentiles has come in.* (Rom 11:25, emphasis added)

I believe we are living in those days – 'the fullness of the Gentiles has come in', the times of the Gentiles have been fulfilled, and the gospel has been "preached in the whole world" (Matt 24:14).[358]

Christian leaders and teachers today who can see no Biblical significance in Israel's resurrection should remember the Christian leaders and teachers of 30 AD. They did not believe in Jesus' resurrection until they had seen with their own eyes:

> So the other disciple [John] who had first come to the tomb [with Peter] then also entered, and he saw and believed. *For as yet they did not understand the Scripture,* that He must rise again from the dead. (John 20:8-9, emphasis added)

---

358 See details in Book 1, *DDJ*, pp. 173-178.

We too, then, may need to reconsider our understanding of the Scriptures regarding Israel's resurrection, especially the promise of Leviticus 26.

> 44. "Yet in spite of this, when they are in the land of their enemies, I will not reject them, nor will I so abhor them as to destroy them, breaking My covenant with them; for I am the LORD their God.
> 45. "But I will remember for them the covenant with their ancestors, whom I brought out of the land of Egypt in the sight of the nations, that I might be their God. I am the LORD."
> (Lev 26:44-45)

I believe we should be proclaiming to all the nations that God has "rebuilt the ruined places and planted that which was desolate" (Ezek 36:36), as He did after the Babylonian exile, and again after the Roman exile.

Many in Israel today also do not believe God has done it, preferring natural explanations. Nor do they believe Moses and Elijah… but they will.

The Two Witnesses' Resurrection

Returning to Revelation 11, we see another startling resurrection – the two witnesses in Jerusalem. They were to 'prophesy for twelve hundred and sixty days' (Rev 11:3) before being killed by the beast. Their bodies were to be left lying in the street for 'three and a half days' (v. 9):

> 11. But after the three and a half days, *the breath of life from God came into them, and they stood on their feet;* and great fear fell upon those who were watching them. (Rev 11:9-11, emphasis added)

When is this resurrection to take place? As argued throughout this series, the 'twelve hundred and sixty days', or three and a half years, is metaphorical and symbolises the last 2,000 years of Jewish history – so too, the 'three and a half days' are metaphorical, but how are we to calculate them?

We could take an exact approach. With the Jewish year of 360 days, the ratio of one year to a day is 360:1 so, if the three and a half years symbolise 30 AD until 1967, i.e. 1,937 years, the three and a half days could symbolise 5.38 years, or five years, four months and seventeen days.

However, most of Revelation's numbers are inexact, e.g. 'a third' of the earth, the trees, the sea, the fish and aquatic animals, the rivers, the stars, or 'thousands of thousands' of angels, or 'one thousand years'. Accordingly, while these times could be literal and exact periods, I see the 3.5 years as a metaphor and the 3.5 days as simply a correspondingly shorter time within that metaphor.

Either way, it is only a short time before they will be resurrected. As a result:

> 11. ...*great fear* fell upon those who were watching them.
> 12. And they heard a loud voice from heaven saying to them, "Come up here". Then they went up into heaven in the cloud, and their enemies watched them. (Rev 11:11-12, emphasis added)

'Their enemies' (v. 12) will be forced to watch on, unable to hinder 'the breath of life from God' (v. 11a), and the two witnesses will ascend, just like Jesus (Acts 1:9). The 'great fear' (v. 11b) in those watching will be, I suggest, a very healthy fear of God.

As for the summoning, "Come up here", this will be their honouring and vindication. No one could simply wander into the presence of an earthly monarch whenever they chose. Esther told Mordecai:

> "All the king's servants and the people of the king's provinces know that for any man or woman who comes to the king to the inner court who is not summoned, he has but one law, that he be put to death, unless the king holds out to him the golden scepter so that he may live." (Est 4:11)

In Revelation 11:12, the two witnesses are being summoned to the heavenly throne to be rewarded for their faithful service. We also see this honouring, rewarding, and vindication in Daniel's vision of Messiah:

> "I kept looking in the night visions,
> And behold, with the clouds of heaven
> One like a Son of Man was coming,
> And *He came up* to the Ancient of Days
> And was *presented* before Him
> And to Him was given dominion,
> Glory and a kingdom." (Dan 7:13-14, emphasis added)

The resurrection and ascension of the two witnesses is a metaphor meaning that Moses and Elijah will once again be honoured and restored to their former glory, vindicated as God's faithful witnesses to Israel – the Hebrew Bible will be seen as perfectly fulfilled in Jesus as Messiah.

When is this to happen? Just before a great revival in Israel and the Lord Jesus returns.

Before we look at that, however, let us summarise this chapter.

Summary of Israel's Restoration (Rev 11:11-12)

God has never given up on Israel:

(i) In Leviticus 26, He promises to never forget His covenants with Israel – to punish them when they stray and to restore them when they repent. Both their Babylonian exile and their exile into all the nations had a time limit; into Babylon for seventy years and into all the nations for the last 2,000 years.

(ii) In Ezekiel 36, God promised to restore Israel from Babylon for two reasons: firstly, so that everyone, Jews and Gentiles, would know He keeps His covenants; secondly, so that Israel would see His kindness and repent.

(iii) In Ezekiel 37, this restoration is in two stages: first, the dry bones are reassembled and the flesh restored into dead bodies; second, they come to life as the Spirit comes into them.

(iv) After Babylon, the first stage was Nehemiah and Ezra leading Israel back to the Promised Land; the second stage was Jesus introducing the covenant of the Spirit. After Rome and all the nations, the first stage was in 1948 but as 'dead bodies' still – there was 'no breath', i.e. Holy Spirit, within them. As I see it, we can expect the second stage to be fulfilled by a spiritual revival when Israel turns to Jesus as their Messiah.

(v) Israel was restored in 1948 but, for the first time in their 3,500 year history, chose to be a secular nation rather than to renew the Mosaic Covenant. Thus the two witnesses are dead and dishonoured in the street of Jerusalem while unbelieving Gentiles who reject our Judaeo-Christian heritage rejoice and celebrate.

(vi) 'Three and a half days' is a metaphor based on the 'three and a half years', being a correspondingly shorter period of time before the two witnesses will be raised up and vindicated when the Lord returns.

16
The Late Rain
Israel's Revival

We now come to the last verse in this study and while it may seem terrible to us, Jewish disciples in the 1st Century would have been delighted:

> And in that hour there was a great earthquake, and a tenth of the city fell; seven thousand people were killed in the earthquake, and the rest were terrified and gave glory to the God of heaven. (Rev 11:13)

How can this be good? It means that Elijah has returned!

Elijah's Coming

To this day, every practising Jewish family is looking for the return of Elijah, to fulfill Malachi 4:5-6 and to announce the coming of Messiah. At the annual Passover meal, they set aside a special cup for Elijah; to conclude the weekly Sabbath ceremony, they often sing their prayer that he will come in the following week:

> Elijah the Prophet, Elijah the Tishbite.
> Let him come quickly, in our day with the Messiah, the son of David!

In Book 1, I showed that the two metaphorical comings of Elijah are based on his literal 'three years and six months' drought (Luke 4:25, Jas 5:17).[359] Like bookends, they mark the beginning and end of the mysterious period, 'a time, times and half a time' (Rev 12:14), when Israel was to remain in exile in all the nations. This period is also called "the times of the

---

359 *DDJ*, pp. 127-147.

Gentiles" because, as in the days of Elijah, God was ignoring the needs of Israel to instead help the Gentiles (Luke 4:26).

Most know Jesus said that John the Baptist fulfilled the first metaphorical coming in the 1st Century (Matt 17:12-13). Coming "in the spirit and power of Elijah" (Luke 1:17), he prepared the way for Jesus but also marked the beginning of a spiritual drought on all in Israel who rejected and crucified Him.

Not so well known is Jesus' saying that Elijah will come again to "restore all things" (Matt 17:11). Jesus will Himself restore the whole of Creation when He returns (Acts 3:21) but before then, Elijah is to restore all things to Israel by ending their spiritual drought, i.e. there will be an amazing outpouring of the Holy Spirit on the people of Israel.[360]

James gave us another rain-based metaphor for the Second Coming from the rainy seasons in Israel – there was an 'early rain' (i.e. autumn) outpouring in 30 AD and there is to be a 'late rain' (i.e. spring) outpouring, just prior to summer harvest which is the Second Coming:

> 7. Therefore be patient, brethren, until the coming of the Lord. The farmer waits for the precious produce of the soil, being patient about it, until it gets the *early and late rains*.
> 8. You too be patient; strengthen your hearts, for the coming of the Lord is near....
> 17. Elijah was a man with a nature like ours, and he prayed earnestly that it would not rain, and it did not rain on the earth for three years and six months.
> 18. Then he prayed again, and the sky poured rain and *the earth produced its fruit*. (Jas 5:17-18, emphasis added)

'The earth' here is not only the whole earth being harvested,

---

[360] In the last one hundred years, the land has been restored, as above, Hebrew has been revived as a living language, Israel reborn as a sovereign state, Jerusalem recaptured, and the Jewish population has blossomed from 50,000 to 6.1 million. *DDJ*, p. 126.

as we saw in Book 3's study of 'first-fruits',[361] but in particular, the land of Israel.

Both of these beautiful metaphors are full of hope – Elijah breaks the drought of the ages! Israel will yet bear fruit for Jesus before He returns!

'A Great Earthquake...'

In Revelation 11, we have been looking at this same time period from another metaphorical perspective. In verses 1 to 12, the two witnesses, i.e. the Law and the Prophets, have been testifying to the Jewish people (Rev 11:3). Now, in verse 13, we have reached the end of that time. What then will be the effect on them? A great earthquake, and Elijah will at last see the fruit.

Is this earthquake literal or metaphorical? In keeping with the tenor of the text, I believe it is, or rather will be, metaphorical. If 'the city' is 'the present Jerusalem' (Gal 4:25), Israel according to the flesh and still under the covenant from Sinai (Gal 4:24), this great earthquake will not be a natural disaster but a great shaking of everything they believe, specifically what they believe about Jesus as their Messiah.

The two olive trees and two lampstands will be finally seen in their rightful place, standing alongside the Lord of the whole earth; He is the living Stone with seven eyes, the rejected Cornerstone, and the Top Stone of the 'spiritual house', the temple not made by human hands.

'A tenth of the city' falling does not refer to the stone and wooden buildings of old Jerusalem but to a tenth of the people of the Mosaic Covenant (Gal 4:25) who will 'fall', i.e. still not believe Jesus. Simeon prophesied to Mary:

> "Behold, this Child is appointed for *the fall and rise* of many in Israel..." (Luke 2:34, emphasis added)

---

361 *GSS*, pp. 169-171.

All in Israel who refused to believe in Him in the 1st Century 'fell' (Heb 4:11, 1 Cor 10:12) but how did Jesus cause many to 'rise'? By speaking to them:

> 24. "Truly, truly, I say to you, he who hears My word, and believes Him who sent Me, has eternal life, and does not come into judgment, but has passed out of death into life.
> 25. "Truly, truly, I say to you, an hour is coming and now is, when the dead will hear the voice of the Son of God, and *those who hear will live.*" (John 5:24-25, emphasis added)

This spiritual resurrection, which we who believe have experienced today, will ultimately be followed by everyone being physically resurrected by Him on the Last Day (John 5:28-29). Paul uses the same metaphor of us being raised up spiritually:

> 5. even when we were dead in our transgressions, [God] made us alive together with Christ (by grace you have been saved),
> 6. and *raised us up* with Him, and seated us with Him in the heavenly places in Christ Jesus. (Eph 2:5-6, emphasis added)[362]

'A Tenth of the City Fell'

N.T. Wright comments:

> We should not mistake the powerful impact of the symbolism in verse 13. When God judged Sodom and Gomorrah, he might have spared it if ten righteous persons were found there (Genesis 18.32). Now, however, only one-tenth of the wicked city is to fall, and nine-tenths is to be saved.[363]

This will be a massive revival! And we are not given this ratio due to God's predetermining and coercing anyone – He does not do that – but from His foreknowledge of how many will freely choose Him.

---

362 See also Romans 6:4 and Colossians 2:12.
363 *Revelation for Everyone*, p. 101.

Compare this with Amos's time, when Israel was facing the Assyrian armies:

> For thus says the Lord GOD,
> "The city which goes forth a thousand strong
> Will have a hundred left,
> And the one which goes forth a hundred strong
> Will have ten left to the house of Israel." (Amos 5:3)

Only a tenth of the army would survive. Similarly in Isaiah's time, facing the Babylonians:

> 11. Then I said, "Lord, how long?"
> And He answered, "Until cities are devastated and without inhabitant,
> Houses are without people
> And the land is utterly desolate,
> 12. "The LORD has removed men far away,
> And the forsaken places are many in the midst of the land.
> 13. "Yet there will be a *tenth portion* in it,
> And it will again be subject to burning,
> Like a terebinth or an oak
> Whose stump remains when it is felled.
> The holy seed is its stump." (Isa 6:11-13, emphasis added)

Israel's fortunes will be completely turned around.

Elijah's 7000

We see this turnaround also in the 7,000 deaths. This metaphorical number comes from the earlier earthly ministry of Elijah, as Paul also highlights (Rom 11:1-5). Remember how Elijah had complained to God:

> "I have been very zealous for the LORD, the God of hosts; for the sons of Israel have forsaken Your covenant, torn down Your altars and killed Your prophets with the sword. And I alone am left; and they seek my life, to take it away". (1 Kin 19:14)

The Lord assured Elijah that He would indeed judge the nation:

> 18. "Yet I will leave *7,000 in Israel*, all the knees that have not bowed to Baal and every mouth that has not kissed him". (1 Kin 19:17-18, emphasis added)

At that time, only 7,000 were faithful in Israel, the godly remnant; John sees the situation completely reversed – only 7,000 will be unfaithful to God. This time, Elijah's ministry will be wonderfully effective as he again fulfils Malachi's prophecy:

> "Behold, I am going to send you Elijah the prophet before the coming of the great and terrible day of the LORD". (Mal 4:5)

And, as Gabriel told Zacharias, quoting and explaining Malachi 4:6:

> "…TO TURN THE HEARTS OF THE FATHERS BACK TO THE CHILDREN, and the disobedient to the attitude of the righteous, so as to make ready a people prepared for the Lord". (Luke 1:17)

The numbers 'one tenth' and '7,000' are metaphorical[364] and refer to the small minority of the nation of Israel according to the flesh who will refuse to accept Jesus as Messiah, just prior to His return. As for the rest, they will repent and turn, just in time:

> …and the rest were terrified and gave glory to the God of heaven. (Rev 11:13)

This fear, translated here as 'terrified', is the healthy fear engendered when the supernatural becomes apparent in the natural realm. The same word (Grk, *emphobos*) is used when the women at the tomb see the angels (Luke 24:5), the disciples see Jesus resurrected (Luke 24:37), and when Cornelius encounters the angel (Acts 10:4).

---

[364] As partially explained in *STB*, pp.36-39, and *GSS*, pp. 148-149, and will be fully in Book 5, *Kingdom Come*.

21st Century Israel

In 2012, the Israel Democracy Institute released *A Portrait of Israeli Jews*, a detailed analysis of an earlier survey.[365] They conclude that about 80% believe that God exists:

> A vast majority... believe [that they] will be rewarded for good deeds and punished for misdeeds, as well as in the power of prayer. Most (about two-thirds) also reported a strong belief in the uniqueness of the Jewish people and the Torah. Smaller percentages (about half) indicated a belief in the World to Come and the Messiah; about a third reported a strong belief that a Jew who does not observe the precepts endangers the entire Jewish people.[366]

While only half believe in a future 'World to Come' and a future Messiah, 90% celebrate Passover,[367] a ritual which perfectly illustrates why Jesus *had* to die as an innocent sacrifice.

Now compare the 80% of Jews in Israel who believe God exists with those in the USA.[368] According to the Pew Landscape Survey:

> Where the percentage of mainline Protestants and Catholics who were absolutely certain about the existence of God was between 72% and 73%, only 41% of Jews had such firm convictions. Based on their analysis... Robert Putnam and David Campbell, authors of an expansive study of religious attitudes and practices in the United States[369], have concluded that "half of all self-identified Jews are not so sure they believe in God".[370]

---

365 *Beliefs, Observance, and Values among Israeli Jews*, 2009.
366 http://en.idi.org.il/media/164429/guttmanavichaireport2012_engfinal.pdf, p. 15.
367 Ibid., p. 14.
368 In 2014, 6,103,200 living in Israel; 5,700,000 in USA. www.jewishvirtuallibrary.org/jsource/Judaism/jewpop.html, 9 Jun, 2015.
369 *American Grace: How Religion Divides and Unites Us,* New York; Simon & Shuster, 2012.
370 www.jewishjournal.com/judaismandscience/item/jewish_atheism_

Regarding the place of the Law and the Prophets in Israel today:

> Most Israeli Jews (61%) believe that public life in the State of Israel should be conducted according to the Jewish religious tradition; a majority are "interested" or "very interested" in the place of religion in the State of Israel (65%) and in the meaning of a "Jewish state" (70%). About half of Israeli Jews believe that public life in the country should continue to be conducted as it is today; about a quarter believe that Israel should be more religious than it is today, and about a quarter believe that it should be less religious.[371]

Unfortunately, the survey does not distinguish between the Hebrew Bible and 'tradition', i.e. the rabbinic teachings based on the Oral Law. To get another perspective on this, we could ask how would Protestants view Roman Catholic traditions being injected into the laws of our own nation?

As for Messianic Jews, or Jewish followers of Jesus, Michael L. Brown, author of *The Real Kosher Jesus*, wrote in 2012:

> By the mid 1970s, *Time* magazine placed the number of Messianic Jews in the U.S. at over 50,000; by 1993 [they] had grown to 160,000 in the U.S. and about 350,000 worldwide (1989 estimate)... There are currently over 400 Messianic synagogues worldwide, with at least 150 in the U.S.[372]

Given that in 2014 there are 13,897,200 Jews worldwide, of whom 6,103,200 live in Israel,[373] there is still a long way to go.

Or is there?

---

and_jewish_theism_in_america, 9 Jun, 2015.
371 http://en.idi.org.il/media/164429/guttmanavichaireport2012_engfinal.pdf, p. 14.
372 Michael L. Brown, *The Real Kosher Jesus: Revealing the Mysteries of the Hidden Messiah*, Lake Mary, Florida; FrontLine, 2012.
373 www.jewishvirtuallibrary.org/jsource/Judaism/jewpop.html, 9 Jun, 2015.

"Home for Christmas"?

On 24th December, 2015, *Israel Today* had a startling headline, 'Orthodox Rabbis Bring Jesus Home for Christmas'. David Lazarus, a Messianic Jewish leader in Israel, was commenting on a statement[374] issued three weeks earlier in Israel by twenty-five Orthodox rabbis from around the world:

> "*Jesus brought a double goodness to the world,*" declare the group of well-known rabbis. "*On the one hand he strengthened the Torah of Moses majestically... and not one of our Sages spoke out more emphatically concerning the immutability of the Torah. On the other hand, he removed idols from the nations.*" Saying that Jesus, even more than any other Jewish Sage, honored, strengthened and protected the "immutability of the Torah," is an extraordinary acknowledgement. These leading rabbis are turning the tides of history by removing one of the main stumbling blocks in the path of a major Jewish reclamation of Jesus![375]

Many Jewish leaders in the 1st Century claimed Jesus did not obey the Torah, so He could not be the long-awaited Messiah. However, these rabbis are saying 'not one of our Sages spoke out more emphatically concerning the immutability of the Torah'. David Lazarus comments:

> What we are now witnessing is the undoing of 2,000 years of Jewish rejection and animosity towards Jesus, a miracle by any estimation. For the out-and-out refusal by Jews to accept Jesus is slowly, but surely, coming to an end, as

---

374 The statement, *To Do the Will of Our Father in Heaven: Toward a Partnership between Jews and Christians,* was published by the Center for Jewish-Christian Understanding and Cooperation in Efrat, Israel, on 3rd Dec, 2015. See http://cjcuc.com/site/2015/12/03/orthodox-rabbinic-statement-on-christianity, 4 Jan, 2016.
375 www.israeltoday.co.il/NewsItem/tabid/178/nid/28027/Default.aspx, 2 Jan, 2016, emphasis in original.

growing numbers of prestigious Orthodox rabbis welcome Jesus back.[376]

By New Year, twenty-nine more Orthodox rabbis had added their names.[377]

In their statement, the rabbis cite an authoritative 18th Century rabbi, Jacob Emden,[378] who had argued that Jesus brought this 'double goodness' to the world by upholding the Mosaic and the Noahic Covenants:

> …he removed idols from the nations and obligated them in the *seven commandments of Noah* so that they would not behave like animals of the field, and instilled them firmly with moral traits…[379]

Orthodox Jews rightly believe that all Jews who do not yet believe in Jesus as Messiah are still under the Law of Moses. What may be new to many Gentile Christians is that they also rightly believe that all Gentiles, Christian and non, are still under the 'seven commandments of Noah': six prohibit idolatry, blasphemy, murder, sexual immorality, theft, and eating flesh or blood from a living animal, while the seventh is to maintain a system of justice.[380]

These rabbis are recognising Jesus as fully Jewish, faithful to the Scriptures, and speaking to us all, both Jews and Gentiles. They further clarify that this…:

> …in no way minimizes the ongoing differences between the two communities and two religions. We believe that G-d employs many messengers to reveal His truth, while we affirm the fundamental ethical obligations that all

---

376 Ibid.
377 http://cjcuc.com/site/2015/12/03/orthodox-rabbinic-statement-on-christianity, 4 Jan, 2016.
378 Rabbi Jacob Emden (1697-1776) is seen by Orthodox Jews as one of their leading Torah authorities.
379 http://cjcuc.com/site/2015/12/03/orthodox-rabbinic-statement-on-christianity/, 4 Jan, 2016, emphasis added.
380 For details, see Noah's everlasting covenant in Appendix A – God's Covenants.

people have before G-d that Judaism has always taught through the universal Noahide covenant.[381]

They also cite two other major authorities:

> As did Maimonides[382] and Yehudah Halevi,[383] we acknowledge that Christianity is neither an accident nor an error, but the willed divine outcome and gift to the nations. In separating Judaism and Christianity, G-d[384] willed a separation between partners with significant theological differences, not a separation between enemies.[385]

David Lazarus comments:

> These so-called *"significant theological differences"* between Christianity and Judaism are really about Jesus. He is the stumbling block. Jesus may be Messiah, Son of the Living God for the Gentiles, but my Jewish people are still not quite sure just who he is for them. So while these rabbis are making major and unprecedented strides in bringing my people closer to Jesus, they are still far from the truth. For if Jesus is the Messiah for the Gentiles, how much more must he be for the Jews?

He concludes:

> Perhaps Jesus will not quite be at home this Christmas in Israel, or Jewish homes around the world, but he is certainly knocking on the door.[386]

---

381 http://cjcuc.com/site/2015/12/03/orthodox-rabbinic-statement-on-christianity/, 4 Jan, 2016.
382 As noted in Chapter 1, Moses Maimonides was a 12th Century rabbi, also known as Rambam. Perhaps most well-known of all Jewish commentators, he is considered by many to be the Second Moses.
383 Yehudah Halevi was a 12th Century philosopher and is considered one of the greatest of Hebrew poets. Reference in the article: Mishneh Torah, Laws of Kings 11:4 (uncensored edition); *Kuzari*, section 4:22.
384 Orthodox Jews do not refer to God as such, often using HaShem (Heb. The Name) instead.
385 http://cjcuc.com/site/2015/12/03/orthodox-rabbinic-statement-on-christianity/, 4 Jan, 2016.
386 www.israeltoday.co.il/NewsItem/tabid/178/nid/28027/Default.aspx, 2 Jan, 2016.

What Triggered The Change?

This fundamental shift in the rabbis' perception of Jesus is largely in response to the Roman Catholic Church's repenting of anti-Semitism and belated recognition of the Mosaic Covenant's endurance:

> We recognize that since the Second Vatican Council[387] the official teachings of the Catholic Church about Judaism have changed fundamentally and irrevocably. The promulgation of Nostra Aetate[388] fifty years ago started the process of reconciliation between our two communities. Nostra Aetate and the later official Church documents it inspired unequivocally reject any form of anti-Semitism, affirm the eternal Covenant between G-d and the Jewish people, reject deicide and stress the unique relationship between Christians and Jews, who were called "our elder brothers" by Pope John Paul II and "our fathers in faith" by Pope Benedict XVI.... Now that the Catholic Church has acknowledged the eternal Covenant between G-d and Israel, we Jews can acknowledge the ongoing constructive validity of Christianity as our partner in world redemption, without any fear that this will be exploited for missionary purposes.[389]

Accordingly, the rabbis report that since 1965, there has been 'many dialogue initiatives, meetings and conferences around the world'[390] with Catholic leaders and Protestant groups such as the International Christian Embassy in Jerusalem (ICEJ).[391]

---

387   Held from 11 October 1962 to 8 December 1965..
388   *Nostra Aetate* (Latin: *In Our Time*) is the Second Vatican Council's Declaration on the Relation of the Church with Non-Christian Religions. It was passed by a vote of 2,221 to 88 of the assembled bishops and promulgated by Pope Paul VI on 28 Oct, 1965.
389   http://cjcuc.com/site/2015/12/03/orthodox-rabbinic-statement-on-christianity, 4 Jan, 2016.
390   Ibid., emphasis added.
391   '...in the summer of 1980, the Israeli Parliament declared the city of Jerusalem to be the undivided, eternal capital of the State of Israel, established as such by King David almost 3,000 years earlier. Protest resounded across the international political spectrum, resulting

How official is the rabbis' position? As official as the Chief Rabbinate of Israel:

> We are no longer enemies, but unequivocal partners in articulating the essential moral values for the survival and welfare of humanity.[392]

What an astonishing effect we can have as Christians when we stop pointing the finger and instead repent of our own sins! The rabbis summarise:

> After nearly two millennia of mutual hostility and alienation, we Orthodox Rabbis who lead communities, institutions and seminaries in Israel, the United States and Europe recognize the historic opportunity now before us. We seek to do the will of our Father in Heaven by accepting the hand offered to us by our Christian brothers and sisters. Jews and Christians must work together as partners to address the moral challenges of our era.[393]

Dr. Eugene Korn is an Orthodox Rabbi and the Academic Director of the Center for Jewish-Christian Understanding & Cooperation, based in Efrat, Israel. He notes:

> This proclamation's breakthrough is that influential Orthodox rabbis across all centers of Jewish life have finally acknowledged that… Christianity and Judaism have much in common spiritually and practically. Given

---

in the closure of thirteen national embassies in Jerusalem. A number of Christians living in Israel… sensed Israel's deep hurt over the withdrawal of the foreign embassies and felt the call of the Lord to open a Christian Embassy in this, the City of the Great King. They called it the International Christian Embassy Jerusalem and it represents Christians from around the world, speaking words of comfort and support to Israel.' http://int.icej.org/history, 10 Jan, 2016.
392 Fourth meeting of the Bilateral Commission of the Chief Rabbinate of Israel and the Holy See's Commission for Religious Relations with Jewry, Grottaferrata, Italy, on 19 Oct, 2004.
393 http://cjcuc.com/site/2015/12/03/orthodox-rabbinic-statement-on-christianity/, 23 Aug, 2016.

our toxic history, this is unprecedented in Orthodoxy.[394]

As a Messianic Jew, David Lazarus finds this miraculous:

> Two thousand years of Christian Anti-Semitism, Crusades, Inquisitions, and a Holocaust cannot keep the Star of Bethlehem from rising again in Israel. This call by these distinguished rabbis to embrace Christians as "brothers and sisters" is no less a miracle. For Jews to accept Christians with such endearment, after so much misunderstanding and anti-Semitic ugliness, can only be understood as a divine work of heavenly grace, the likes of which I find unfathomable.
>
> For, as this group of Orthodox rabbis points out, it is their "Father in Heaven" who is calling the Jewish people to lay down the past, put aside the enmity, and willingly embrace Christians and their faith in Jesus. That, my friends, is the deeper work of the Holy Spirit as spoken about throughout Scripture.[395]

As wonderful as may be the growing reconciliation between Jews and Gentile Christians, tragically, the same cannot be said for the relationship between Israel and all the Gentile nations.

Zechariah 12

I suggested earlier the great earthquake of Revelation 11:13 will not be literal but metaphorical, i.e. a great shaking of everything they believe and, in particular, what they believe about the testimony of Moses and Elijah in revealing Jesus as the Messiah.

What exactly will that shaking be, or what will cause it?

I believe it will be the realisation that 'all the nations' have turned against them yet again, just as they have throughout the

---

394 www.israeltoday.co.il/NewsItem/tabid/178/nid/28027/Default.aspx, 2 Jan, 2016, emphasis in original.
395 www.israeltoday.co.il/NewsItem/tabid/178/nid/28027/Default.aspx, 2 Jan, 2016, emphasis in original.

last 4,000 years, and that in the next great battle for Jerusalem, only God can save them. We Christians should not be surprised because this was predicted of the seventh and last head of the dragon and of the beast.[396] And if we are indeed living in the time of the seventh head, this will be the last great battle for Jerusalem, as I will establish in Book 5, *Kingdom Come*.

For now, let us focus on the shattering of Jewish thinking that results from the battle predicted in Zechariah 12.

Zechariah begins his prophecy with Israel in terrible strife again, Jerusalem under siege by "all the nations of the earth":

> 1. The burden of the word of the LORD concerning Israel. Thus declares the LORD who stretches out the heavens, lays the foundation of the earth, and forms the spirit of man within him, 2. "Behold, I am going to make Jerusalem a cup of reeling to all the peoples around; and when the siege is against Jerusalem, it will also be against Judah.
> 3. "It will come about in that day that I will make Jerusalem a heavy stone for all the peoples; all who lift it will be severely injured. And *all the nations of the earth* will be gathered against it". (Zech 12:1-3, emphasis added)

Some believe this was fulfilled in 70 AD but the Roman legion were not "all the nations".[397] Also, that siege ended in the destruction of Jerusalem and the Temple but this siege will not:

> 8. "In that day the LORD will defend the inhabitants of Jerusalem, and the one who is feeble among them in that day will be like David, and the house of David will be like God, like the angel of the LORD before them.
> 9. "And in that day I will set about to destroy all the nations that come against Jerusalem. (Zech 12:8-9)

---

396   *DDJ*, pp. 22-33; *STB*, pp. 27-27-33.
397   Nigel Pollard, archaeologist and historian, estimates that the Roman legions who sacked Jerusalem were only 20-25% Italians, the rest being recruits from Syria, Asia Minor and the Arab nations, as recorded by Tacitus and Josephus. *Soldiers, Cities, and Civilians in Roman Syria*, University of Michigan Press, 2000, pp. 114-115.

Jerusalem has therefore not yet been besieged by "all the nations of the earth" (v. 3) and God has not yet destroyed those nations (v. 9), but, it seems obvious this will happen just before the Second Coming. As mentioned above, we will look at this great battle, the Battle of Har-Magedon,[398] when we come to Revelation 16:13-16.

When the people of Israel realise that "all the nations" have turned against them yet again, they will begin to call on the God of Israel. And His response?

> 10. "I will pour out on the house of David and on the inhabitants of Jerusalem, the Spirit of grace and of supplication, so that they will look on Me whom they have pierced…" (Zech 12:10)

Our heavenly Father will "pour out… the Spirit of grace and of supplication" to help them pray properly; the Holy Spirit 'helps our weakness; for we do not know how to pray as we should, but the Spirit Himself intercedes for us with groanings too deep for words' (Rom 8:26). When they then begin to pray in this way, they will see Jesus, the crucified One:

> "…and they will mourn for Him, as one mourns for an only son, and they will weep bitterly over Him like the bitter weeping over a firstborn". (Zech 12:10)

This will be the great earthquake that shakes apart everything they have believed about Him and, turning to their Hebrew Bibles, they will see that Moses and Elijah have always been testifying about Him, as established in Chapter 4.

Now let us consider the role of Jerusalem as also portrayed in Zechariah 12.

---

398 Often referred to as Armageddon.

"A Cup of Reeling"

At a specific time, "when the siege is against Jerusalem [and] Judah" (v. 2) and "all the nations of the earth will be gathered against it" (v. 3), God promises to intervene:

> "Behold, I am going to make Jerusalem a cup of reeling to all the peoples around… (Zech 12:2)

Notice, this effect will not be on Jews but on Gentiles who drink from it. For the last 2,000 years, the Gentiles have been allowed to "tread underfoot the holy city" (Rev 11:2. Also Luke 21:24) but no longer: God has re-sanctified the holy city for Judah, i.e. the Jewish people.[399]

There are two outcomes from Jerusalem being "a cup of reeling", or staggering: firstly, any Gentile who drinks from it will get drunk; secondly, any Gentile who drinks from it will incur His judgement.

1. Drunkenness

Isaiah denounces the pride of northern Israel's leaders in blunt terms:

> And these also reel with wine and stagger from strong drink:
> The priest and the prophet reel with strong drink,
> They are confused by wine, they stagger from strong drink;
> They reel while having visions,
> They totter when rendering judgement. (Isa 28:7)

---

[399] When Israel was divided in the time of Rehoboam (1 Kings 12), the ten tribes who left him took the name of their leading tribe, Ephraim, who also bore the name Israel (Gen 48:16) so the northern kingdom was called Israel; those who stayed with Rehoboam as David's heir kept the name of their leading tribe, Judah, for the southern kingdom. However, while in Babylon, the two kingdoms became one again (Ezek 37:15-28) so by the time Jesus came, the names Jew and Israelite had become interchangeable (1 Cor 9:20, Rom 11:1). Accordingly, as the Son of David (Ezek 37:24), He was the King of the Jews (Matt 2:2, 27:11) and of Israel (Matt 27:42).

Intoxication, as opposed to merely drinking alcohol, is thoroughly condemned throughout the Scriptures because it destroys discernment and reasoning. Accordingly, the priests were forbidden to drink at all when on duty (Lev 10:8-11, Eze 44:21); kings likewise when judging (Prov 31:4-5). Intoxication can also bring out the worst in us, especially aggression in word and deed:

> Wine is a mocker, strong drink a brawler,
> And whoever is intoxicated by it is not wise. (Prov 20:1)

This is vivid imagery for me; as a young man, I worked as a barman and often saw up close the insulting and brawling of drunkenness.

Jerusalem becoming "a cup of reeling to all the peoples around", therefore, means that the holy 'city of the great King' (Psa 48:2) will bring out the worst in Israel's neighbours; they will lose their discernment and ability to reason, becoming scornful and aggressive. Isaiah again:

> Thus the multitude of all the nations will be
> Who wage war against Mount Zion...
> They become drunk, but not with wine,
> They stagger, but not with strong drink. (Isa 29:8-9)

Is this not what we already see and hear in our daily news in the rhetoric of Israel's Middle Eastern neighbours? Unable to discern the hand of God in the miraculous rebirth of Israel in 1948, they instead redefine it as the *Nakbar*, Arabic for the Catastrophe. Ignoring the will of God for the Jewish people, and not content with twenty-two Arab states,[400] they belligerently claim Jerusalem and the land of Israel as well. Their calls for Islamic jihad to destroy the Jewish state, demonised as 'the Zionist entity', have been unrelenting, despite all the peace-talks.

Even here in New Zealand, at the uttermost parts of the

---

400   www.arableagueonline.org/hello-world/#more-1, 23 Aug, 2016.

earth from Jerusalem, I find that casual conversations about Israel, even its right to exist, can quickly turn into irrational and belligerent denunciations of Zionism. These are usually based on our news media's often truncated perspective and superficial coverage of the Palestinians' horrendous plight.[401]

2. God's judgement

"A cup of reeling" is also a metaphor for the judgement of God. David gives its meaning as 'hardship' when he prays:

> You have made Your people *experience hardship*;
> You have given us *wine* to drink that *makes us stagger*.
> (Psa 60:3, emphasis added)

Isaiah refers to it as the wrath or anger of God:

> Rouse yourself! Rouse yourself!
> Arise, O Jerusalem,
> You who have drunk from the LORD'S hand the *cup of His anger*;
> The *chalice of reeling* you have drained to the dregs.
> (Isa 51:17, emphasis added)

And again:

> Thus says your Lord, the LORD, even your God
> Who contends for His people,
> "Behold, I have taken out of your hand the *cup of reeling*,
> The *chalice of My anger*;
> You will never drink it again". (Isa 51:22, emphasis added)

'To the dregs' (v. 17) – Israel drained every drop in this cup, receiving seventy years of punishment in Babylon.[402]

Six hundred years later, it was this cup that Jesus earnestly prayed three times would be removed from Him in the Garden of Gethsemane (Matt 26:39-44) before He chose to accept it as the Father's will that He be crucified for our sins (1 Pet 2:24).

---

401   These issues are addressed in Book 1, *DDJ*, pp. 196-216.
402   Each generation, however, can experience the wrath of God. The generation that came out of Egypt died during the forty years in the wilderness; their children were allowed to enter the land.

John warns us that if anyone worships the beast and its image and receives its mark...:

> ...he also will drink of the wine of the wrath of God, which is mixed in full strength in the cup of His anger. (Rev 14:10)

Over the last 2,000 years, Israel has again drained the cup of reeling to the last drop but, punishment over, they have been restored to the land and to Jerusalem. Now Jews can rejoice in Jerusalem, but it has become "a cup of reeling for the nations". If any Gentile nation drinks from it, they will be drinking judgement on themselves, as Zechariah continues:

> 8. "In that day the LORD will defend the inhabitants of Jerusalem, and the one who is feeble among them in that day will be like David, and the house of David will be like God, like the angel of the LORD before them.
> 9. "And in that day I will set about to destroy all the nations that come against Jerusalem". (Zech 12:8-9)

"A Heavy Stone"

Lastly, Jerusalem also becomes a self-inflicted punishment for the wrong-doers:

> 3. "It will come about in that day that I will make Jerusalem *a heavy stone* for all the peoples; all who lift it will be severely injured [Heb, *sarat*, gashed or lacerated]. And all the nations of the earth will be gathered against it". (Zech 12:3, emphasis added)

Another graphic image – failing to lift a heavy stone, the lifter is gashed or lacerated by its falling on him. As long as Gentiles leave Jerusalem to the Jews, no one will get hurt but ignoring God's purpose will bring inevitable and unavoidable pain to the perpetrator.

Attempts to lift the stone may not always be obvious. In December 2016, my own nation of New Zealand foolishly co-sponsored Resolution 2334 in the Security Council of the United Nations. The resolution's seemingly laudable aim was to condemn Jewish settlements[403] in the disputed West Bank as a hindrance to peace-talks but it reaffirmed the UN's prejudgment that East Jerusalem, which includes the holiest sites in Judaism – the Old City with its Jewish Quarter, the Temple Mount, and the Western Wall – is wholly Palestinian territory and not Jewish.[404]

As Gentiles, we can underestimate not only the Jewish attachment to Jerusalem but also God's. It is His city: the devil's tempting of Jesus was in "the holy city" (Matt 4:5); the resurrection was in 'the holy city' (Matt 27:53); Jesus referred to Jerusalem as "the city of the great King" (Matt 5:35). He was quoting Psalm 48:

> 1. Great is the LORD, and greatly to be praised,
> In *the city of our God*, His holy mountain.
> 2. Beautiful in elevation, the joy of the whole earth,
> Is Mount Zion in the far north,
> *The city of the great King*. (Psa 48:1-2, emphasis added)

Accordingly, in 95/96 AD, John is still being told:

> "Leave out the court which is outside the temple and do not measure it, for it has been given to the nations; and they will tread under foot *the holy city* for forty-two months". (Rev 11:2, emphasis added)

Twenty five years after the total destruction of Jerusalem by Titus and the Romans, Jerusalem is still "the holy city".

---

403 Israel has to trade land for peace to establish a Palestinian state because absorbing all the Palestinians into Israel would result in a non-Jewish state. As of 2014, Israel has 1.7 million Arab citizens so, with Gaza's 1.7 million and the West Bank's 2.8 million, these 6.2 million Arabs would have an edge over Israel's 6.1 million Jewish citizens, with another 5.8 million Palestinians apparently wanting to return from Jordan, Syria, Chile, Lebanon, Saudi Arabia, Egypt, and the Americas. The only question then is how to keep the new state from being able to attack Israel.
404 www.un.org/press/en/2016/sc12657.doc.htm, 12 Mar, 2017.

Remember, this is a parallel prophecy to the words of Jesus regarding that event:

> ...and they [Israel] will fall by the edge of the sword, and will be led captive into all the nations; and Jerusalem will be trampled under foot by the Gentiles until the times of the Gentiles are fulfilled. (Luke 21:24)

Throughout the last 2,000 years, while the nations have been treating Jerusalem with disdain, God's attitude to them has been gracious – He gave it to the Gentiles for this time – but no more.

He has now re-sanctified Jerusalem as the holy city. His city.

Summary of the Revival (Rev 11:13)

Given that this is yet to occur, we have to rely on foreshadowing as a guide and watch events as they unfold:

(i) The second return of Elijah is to "restore all things" (Matt 17:11), not just the language, the land, the people of Israel, their sovereignty as a nation, and their rule over Jerusalem, but also, and especially, the 'rain', after a spiritual drought that has lasted 2,000 years. The 'partial hardening' of Israel (Rom 11:25) is almost over.

(ii) Before the harvest of the earth by the Lord at His second coming, James 5:7 tells us, we are to watch for the 'the late rain' (i.e. spring rain) which gives a final boost to the crops. James also reminds us it was Elijah's prayer that ended Israel's original drought; after 'three years and six months… the sky poured rain and the earth produced its fruit' (Jas 5:17-18).

(iii) The great earthquake when the two witnesses are resurrected is, in keeping with the metaphor, not literal but a great shaking of everything the people of Israel believe about Jesus as their Messiah. Nine tenths will turn to Jesus. The tenth of the city falling is a metaphor for only a small proportion that still will not believe.

(iv) The 7,000 who are killed in this earthquake are in dramatic contrast to Elijah's time: then, only 7,000 in Israel would not 'bow the knee to Baal'; now in this metaphor, only 7,000 will not bow the knee to Jesus.

(v) Israel in the 21st Century is showing clear evidence of spiritual growth, but not at the level John's prophecy indicates. It seems to me that will not happen until the events of Zechariah 12.

(vi) Zechariah 12 predicts a time to come when Jerusalem will be again under siege, not just by the Romans and their mercenaries but by "all the nations". It is then that God will demonstrate that Jerusalem is indeed the holy city, His city.

(vii) When Israel look around and see they really are on their own because every nation is against them, they will look up and call for Divine help. It is at this point they will at last see Him whom they pierced and turn to Him.

(viii) Jerusalem being "a cup of reeling to all the peoples" means that all Gentiles who drink from it will be as if staggering from drunkenness, becoming aggressive and irrational.

(ix) Jerusalem being "a heavy stone for all the peoples" means all Gentiles who try to lift it will hurt themselves rather than succeed.

Conclusions

What should we learn from Revelation 11:1-13 and the two witnesses symbolising the Law and the Prophets?

1. There is a new temple, a new altar and new worshippers

John's measuring is a prophetic drama to illustrate Jesus' revelation that we are no longer to worship in the Jerusalem Temple but 'in spirit and in truth' (John 4:23), as royal priests in a new temple made of living stones, both Jews and Gentiles, who have come to Jesus as the Corner Stone (1 Pet 2:4-6).

2. Jerusalem has been re-sanctified as the earthly city of God

God did not give up on Israel in 70 AD but had a continuing plan for Jerusalem, both as a literal city to be re-sanctified when "the times of the Gentiles are fulfilled" (Luke 21:24), and as a metaphor for Israel 'according to the flesh' (Rom 9:3) who have rejected Jesus and are still under the Law (Gal 4:25-26). In Revelation 11, the two metaphorical witnesses, the Law and the Prophets, are prophesying in metaphorical Jerusalem, i.e. to unbelieving Jews. Those 'times' seem to have been fulfilled in literal Jerusalem in 1967.

3. The Mosaic Covenant will endure as long as 'the present heavens and earth'

Jesus meant what He said:

> 17. "Do not think that I came to abolish the Law or the Prophets; I did not come to abolish but to fulfill.
> 18. "For truly I say to you, until heaven and earth pass away, not the smallest letter or stroke shall pass from the Law until all is accomplished." (Matt 5:17-18)

Jesus fulfilled the Law, making atonement for all who trust

in Him, without abolishing the Law, so it still applies to all Jews who reject Him and the New Covenant. With the loss of the Temple and its sacrifices, the Law can no longer make any atonement for sin – it can only testify to sin and condemn all who fall short of it.

How then do Jewish people escape from the Law's curse to its blessing? Not by perfect behaviour, because no one is perfect, but by being forgiven. As David prayed:

> How blessed is he whose transgression is forgiven,
> Whose sin is covered! (Psa 32:1)

The only way the people of Israel can escape the curse of the Law is by dying to themselves, turning to Jesus, and being born again in Him. As Paul carefully explained:

> 1. Or do you not know, brethren (for I am speaking to those who know the Law), that the Law has jurisdiction over a person as long as he lives?
> 2. For the married woman is bound by law to her husband while he is living; but if her husband dies, she is released from the law concerning the husband.
> 3. So then, if while her husband is living she is joined to another man, she shall be called an adulteress; but if her husband dies, she is free from the law, so that she is not an adulteress though she is joined to another man.
> 4. Therefore, my brethren, you also were *made to die to the Law* through the body of Christ, *so that you might be joined to another, to Him who was raised from the dead*, in order that we might bear fruit for God. (Rom 7:1-4, emphasis added)

Otherwise, when 'the present heavens and earth'[405] do finally pass away (2 Pet 3:7) on the Last Day:

> ...all who have sinned under the Law will be judged by the Law... (Rom 2:12)

---

[405] We will look at the 'new heavens and a new earth' (2 Pet 3:13) in Book 5, *Kingdom Come*.

4. There is 'vengeance for the covenant' (Lev 26:25)

It is the enduring curse of the Law of Moses, described in both Leviticus 26 and Deuteronomy 28, which the Jewish people have been suffering. For over a thousand years before the destruction of the Second Temple in 70 AD, this cause and effect was recognised and openly confessed by Samuel, David, Amos, Isaiah, Josiah, Huldah, Jeremiah, Daniel, Nehemiah, Ezra, Malachi, and the returnees from Babylon. In other words, throughout the whole Hebrew Bible.

Jesus taught in 30 AD that it would fall on Jerusalem, as it did in 70 AD:

> "But when you see Jerusalem surrounded by armies, then recognize that her desolation is near… because these are *days of vengeance*, so that all things which are written will be fulfilled. (Luke 21:20 & 22, emphasis added)

Tragically, ever since then, Israel's leaders and teachers have signally failed to recognise either the curse or its cause, denying any connection with their sinfulness and their on-going rejection of Jesus as their atoning sacrifice and resurrected Messiah.

5. Vengeance comes to an end

Moses prophesied Israel's punishment would eventually end:

> 43. "For the land will be abandoned by them, and will make up for its sabbaths while it is made desolate without them. They, meanwhile, will be *making amends for their iniquity*, because they rejected My ordinances and their soul abhorred My statutes.
> 44. "Yet in spite of this, when they are in the land of their enemies, I will not reject them, nor will I so abhor them as to destroy them, breaking My covenant with them; for I am the LORD their God.
> 45. "But I will remember for them the covenant with their ancestors, whom I brought out of the land of Egypt in the sight of the nations, that I might be their God. I am the LORD." (Lev 26:43-45, emphasis added)

Having served their time of punishment, the people of Israel once again formed a sovereign state on May 14, 1948, and regained Jerusalem in the Six Day War of June, 1967.

6. The two witnesses are silenced, but not for long

When the two witnesses 'have finished their testimony' (Rev 11:7), seemingly in 1967, they were to be killed and dishonoured by the nation of Israel. Despite its own miraculous restoration, Israel did not recommit to the covenant for the first time in its history as a nation. The two witnesses, however, will be silenced for a much shorter time than they testified.

7. Gentiles are no better than Jews

The Gentiles' celebration of the witnesses' demise, if that also began in 1967, seems to me to have been fulfilled by secularism rising up in the midst of the vast social upheaval in the Western world at that time. This confluence of many liberation movements, with technological and communication breakthroughs, led to the abandonment of our Judaeo-Christian values in at least three areas: the redefining of sexual morality, the profane use of the Lord's name, and the redefining of the value of life, as seen in the legalising of abortion and the abolition of capital punishment for murder.

8. The two wtnesses will be resurrected

On the Last Day, when God judges all under the Law according to the Law, the Law and the Prophets will be honoured and vindicated as having been His word all along.

9. There is yet to be a massive revival in Israel

Happily, by the time the Lord returns, the vast majority in Israel will believe – only a symbolic 'one tenth of the city' will fall; only 7,000 will have not bowed the knee to Jesus (Rev 11:13). This is also predicted in Zechariah 12 as occurring when

Israel is surrounded on all sides by all the nations trying to capture Jerusalem. We will be considering this event in more detail in Book 5, *Kingdom Come*.

10. David's legacy

His most obvious legacy to us all is Jesus of Nazareth, who sits on the throne of David forever. David has also left us all his inspired psalms, prayers, prophecies, and personal example in faith, creativity, repentance, and restoration.

Not so obvious is that God used him to reveal the Messianic priesthood, 'according to the order of Melchizedek' (Psa 110), of which Jesus is the High Priest and to which all of us who trust in Him belong. In capturing Jerusalem, he also created a type, a foreshadowing, of the new, heavenly Jerusalem to which we belong today (Heb 12:22).

Finally, to the earthly descendants of Abraham, Isaac, and Jacob, Israel 'according to the flesh', he bequeathed the earthly city of Jerusalem, which is today back in their possession after a 2,000 year hiatus.

11. Israel's regaining Jerusalem is a sign of the times

If I am correct in this exegesis of Revelation 11, John's vision will not be literally fulfilled at some time in the future but has already been metaphorically fulfilled throughout the last two millennia. Its metaphorical time period of 'forty two months' and '1,260 days' signifies "the times of the Gentiles" which, in real time, lasted until 1967 when the Jews regained Jerusalem, when the 'holy city' was no longer being 'trampled underfoot' by the Gentiles.

Throughout these 2,000 years, the Lord's 'two witnesses', i.e. the Law and the Prophets personified as Moses and Elijah, prophesied to every Jew who would not accept Jesus as Messiah. They testified every time the Law was broken, warning of the consequences but also revealing the forgiveness available through Him.

By the time Jerusalem was regained in 1967, Israel had been re-established as a sovereign nation but, for the first time in 3,500 years, not under the Mosaic Covenant. The beast from the abyss, i.e. the feral state, had overcome and silenced the witnesses by installing secularism instead, leaving the Law and the Prophets lying dead and dishonoured 'in the street' of Jerusalem.

The only events in this vision yet to be fulfilled are the witnesses' resurrection, when the Law and the Prophets will be vindicated, and the 'great earthquake', when most in Israel will turn to Jesus. Paul wrote of this time:

> For if their rejection is the reconciliation of the world, what will their acceptance be but life from the dead? (Rom 11:15)

It seems to me that we are very close to both events now.

> 1. The Pharisees and Sadducees came up, and testing Jesus, they asked Him to show them a sign from heaven.
> 2. But He replied to them, "When it is evening, you say, 'It will be fair weather, for the sky is red.'
> 3. "And in the morning, 'There will be a storm today, for the sky is red and threatening.' Do you know how to discern the appearance of the sky, but cannot discern the signs of the times?" (Matt 16:1-3)
>
> "…so, you too, when you see all these things, recognize that He is near, right at the door." (Matt 24:32-33)

Epilogue

Where Next?

The next book in this series, Book 5, *Kingdom Come*, will be my last in such detail. Having laid a careful foundation in the first four books by establishing a new hermeneutical approach, we will finally consider the end of the dragon (Rev 20:10) and his beasts (Rev 19:20), as identified in Books 1, 2, and 3.

We will examine their final attack on the earth, and correct a common myth regarding the Battle of Armageddon:

> 13. And I saw coming out of the mouth of the dragon and out of the mouth of the beast and out of the mouth of the false prophet, three unclean spirits like frogs;
> 14. for they are spirits of demons, performing signs, which go out to the kings of the whole world, to gather them together for *the war of the great day of God, the Almighty*...
> 16. And they gathered them together to the place which in Hebrew is called *Har-Magedon*. (Rev 16:13-16, emphasis added)

We will establish the true identity of Babylon the Great. It is not the Roman Catholic Church,[406] which is both too young and too small, although it must have seemed enormous to the Euro-centric leaders of the Reformation. For the same reason, it is not the USA, as some think today.

> 3. And he carried me away in the Spirit into a wilderness; and I saw a woman sitting on a scarlet beast, full of blasphemous names, having seven heads and ten horns.
> 4. The woman was clothed in purple and scarlet, and adorned with gold and precious stones and pearls, having in her hand a gold cup full of abominations and of the unclean things of her immorality,

---

[406] As taught in 1520 by Martin Luther in *On the Babylonian Captivity of the Church*.

> 5. and on her forehead a name was written, a mystery, "BABYLON THE GREAT, THE MOTHER OF HARLOTS AND OF THE ABOMINATIONS OF THE EARTH."
> 6. And I saw the woman drunk with the blood of the saints, and with the blood of the witnesses of Jesus. When I saw her, I wondered greatly.
> 7. And the angel said to me, "Why do you wonder? *I will tell you the mystery* of the woman and of the beast that carries her, which has the seven heads and the ten horns."
> (Rev 17:3-7, emphasis added)

We will delight in the bride of Christ, new Jerusalem, as revealed in Revelation 21:

> 1. Then I saw a new heaven and a new earth; for the first heaven and the first earth passed away, and there is no longer any sea.
> 2. And I saw the holy city, *new Jerusalem*, coming down out of heaven from God, made ready as *a bride adorned for her husband*. (Rev 21:1-2, emphasis added)

We will resolve the controversy of Revelation 20, the Millennium, the thousand year reign of Jesus and the saints that precedes Judgement Day:

> 1. Then I saw an angel coming down from heaven, holding the key of the abyss and a great chain in his hand.
> 2. And he laid hold of the dragon, the serpent of old, who is the devil and Satan, and bound him for *a thousand years*;
> 3. and he threw him into the abyss, and shut it and sealed it over him, so that he would not deceive the nations any longer, until the thousand years were completed; after these things he must be released for a short time.
> 4. Then I saw thrones, and they sat on them, and judgement was given to them. And I saw the souls of those who had been beheaded because of their testimony of Jesus and because of the word of God, and those who had not worshiped the beast or his image, and had not received the mark on their forehead and on their hand; and they came to life and reigned with Christ for *a thousand years*. (Rev 20:1-4, emphasis added)

Best of all, we will study the return of the King of kings and

Lord of lords, Jesus of Nazareth (Rev 19:6), Messiah of Israel, bridegroom to the bride and judge of all the earth, when He will establish justice for all:

> 11. Then I saw a great white throne and Him who sat upon it, from whose presence earth and heaven fled away, and no place was found for them.
> 12. And I saw the dead, the great and the small, standing before the throne, and books were opened; and another book was opened, which is the book of life; and the dead were judged from the things which were written in the books, according to their deeds. (Rev 20:11-12)

Justice for all, at last, and a new beginning for all of Creation:

> 13. …according to His promise we are looking for *new heavens and a new earth*, in which righteousness dwells.
> 14. Therefore, beloved, since you look for these things, be diligent to be found by Him in peace, spotless and blameless,
> 15. and regard the patience of our Lord [in not coming sooner] as salvation… (2 Pet 3:13-15, emphasis added)

> 3. There will no longer be any curse; and the throne of God and of the Lamb will be in it, and His bond-servants will serve Him;
> 4. they will see His face… (Rev 22:3-4)

Appendix A – God's Covenants

All of God's covenants are still in force for those under them, all being referred to as Eternal or Everlasting (Heb *olam*, Grk, *aionios*). Here they are in chronological order.

Adam's Covenant – 'In the Beginning…'

Genesis is not explicit about God making a covenant with Adam but it is implicit and the essential elements of covenant-making are there.[407] He therefore reproved Israel through Hosea:

> "What shall I do with you, O Ephraim? What shall I do with you, O Judah?
> For your loyalty is like a morning cloud
> And like the dew which goes away early…
> …*like Adam they have transgressed the covenant*;
> There they have dealt treacherously against Me". (Hos 6:7, emphasis added)

Israel was as disloyal as Adam was to the covenant.

So too with all of us who are Gentiles. Our mortality is a direct result of our father Adam breaking this covenant and its curse of death and decay will remain in force until the Resurrection and the New Heavens and Earth (1 Cor 15:22-26, Rev 22:3). We each, therefore, have to seek eternal life with Him. As Paul told the Athenians, thankfully death has a redemptive purpose:

> 26. "[God] made from one man every nation of mankind to live on all the face of the earth, having determined their appointed times and the boundaries of their habitation,
> 27. that they would seek God, if perhaps they might grope for Him and find Him, though He is not far from each one of us;
> 28. for in Him we live and move and exist…" (Acts 17:26-28)

---

[407] e.g. conditions, commitment, consequences, clothing, sacrifice, naming.

God has set boundaries and limited times for us so that, as we recognise our mortality and the ultimate futility of our best endeavours, we will "seek God, ...grope for Him and find Him" (v. 27), who alone can give us immortality and our soul's satisfaction. As Blaise Pascal said:

> There is a God-shaped vacuum in the heart of every man which cannot be filled by any created thing, but only by God, the Creator, made known through Jesus.

Every single one of us in "every nation of mankind" (vs. 26) will be held accountable for choosing, like Adam, to decide for ourselves what is good and evil (Gen 2:17), for doing what is right in our own eyes, instead of in His.[408] We have all broken the covenant:

> 4. The earth mourns and withers, the world fades and withers, the exalted of the people of the earth fade away.
> 5. The earth is also polluted by its inhabitants, for they transgressed laws, violated statutes, *broke the everlasting covenant.*
> 6. Therefore, a curse devours the earth, and those who live in it are held guilty... (Isa 24:4-6, emphasis added)

Like Paul, Isaiah was not speaking to Israel alone but to all mankind. The curse of the 'everlasting' Adamic Covenant still applies to us all, whether Jew or Gentile, believer or unbeliever.

However, there was also a promise in the Adamic Covenant that God would provide a way out: the virgin-born Seed of the woman (Gen 3:15, Jer 31:22, Matt 1:18-25). The Seed, Jesus of Nazareth, was unfailingly faithful to do all our Father's will:

> ...tempted in all things as we are, yet without sin (Heb 4:15)

---

408 It is a common misconception that God forbade us 'knowing' good and evil – the Hebrew idiom actually forbids us 'knowing' both good and evil *through intimacy and deciding for ourselves.* We are instead to discern and trust His decisions as to good and evil (Heb 5:12), as Jesus did: "I can do nothing on My own initiative. As I hear, I judge; and My judgement is just, because I do not seek My own will, but the will of Him who sent Me" (John 5:30).

Jesus perfectly fulfilled the Adamic Covenant. Paul therefore describes what He will do for us in Adamic terms from Genesis:

> 45. So also it is written, "The first MAN, Adam, BECAME A LIVING SOUL." *The last Adam* became a life-giving spirit…
> 47. The first man is from the earth, earthy; *the second man* is from heaven…
> 49. Just as we have borne the image of the earthy, we will also bear the image of the heavenly. (1 Cor 15:45-49, emphasis added

As 'the last Adam' and 'the second man', Jesus not only resolves all the issues of the first Adam but He also begins the new Creation as the new Man, and the saints are His Eve, His bride. "In the resurrection on the Last Day" (John 11:24) of the old Creation, all who believe in Jesus will finally be freed from the Adamic curse:

> 4. and He will wipe away every tear from their eyes; and there will *no longer be any death*; there will no longer be any mourning, or crying, or pain; the first things have passed away."
> 5. And He who sits on the throne said, "Behold, I am making all things new." And He said, "Write, for these words are faithful and true." (Rev 21:4-5, emphasis added)
>
> There will *no longer be any curse*. (Rev 22:3, emphasis added)

Those who do not trust in Jesus, however, will remain under the curse but, after the Judgement, it is called the Second Death (Rev 21:8). In other words, Heaven and Hell are outcomes of the everlasting Adamic Covenant; we either return to Paradise by being forgiven or we forever remain outside (Rev 22:14-15).

The Marriage Covenant – 'From the Beginning'

This covenant is different in that it is not an 'everlasting covenant' made by God for us; designed for mortal men and women, it is a lifelong, temporal covenant (Mal 2:14, Rom 7:2-3). It is a 'covenant of God' (Prov 2:17) and He will hold every one of us accountable for it:

> Marriage is to be held in honor *among all*, and the marriage bed is to be undefiled; for fornicators and adulterers God will judge. (Heb 13:4, emphasis added)

It is the marriage covenant that defines these terms: fornication is having sexual intercourse without or before making a marriage covenant; adultery is having sexual intercourse with anyone other than the covenant partner. Since this was God's design for all of mankind, also providing an enduring environment for our children, He will judge us all by this standard (1 Cor 6:9):

> For this reason a man shall leave his father and his mother, and be joined to his wife; and they shall become one flesh. (Gen 2:24)

Again, Genesis is not explicit about Adam and Eve making a marriage covenant, but it is implicit. Being the very first couple, they portray God's ideal for every marriage. When Jesus refers to this ideal, He attributes this phrase to the very mouth of God:

> 3. Some Pharisees came to Jesus, testing Him and asking, "Is it lawful for a man to divorce his wife for any reason at all?"
> 4. And He answered and said, "Have you not read that He who created them from the beginning MADE THEM MALE AND FEMALE,
> 5. and said, 'FOR THIS REASON A MAN SHALL LEAVE HIS FATHER AND MOTHER AND BE JOINED TO HIS WIFE, AND THE TWO SHALL BECOME ONE FLESH'?
> 6. "So they are no longer two, but one flesh. What therefore God has joined together, let no man separate." (Matt 19:3-6)

Notice, the subject of v. 4, "He who created them", is also the subject of v. 5, "and said". According to Jesus, it was God who "said".

This covenant is not everlasting, being broken by the death of either partner (Rom 7:1-3) and will not be renewed at the

Resurrection (Matt 22:30). Divorce for due cause also breaks it (Matt 5:32, 1 Cor 7:15). However, it provides a living illustration of one of the great mysteries of the Scriptures:

> 28. So husbands ought also to love their own wives…
> 29. …just as Christ also does the church…
> 31. FOR THIS REASON A MAN SHALL LEAVE HIS FATHER AND MOTHER AND SHALL BE JOINED TO HIS WIFE, AND THE TWO SHALL BECOME ONE FLESH.
> 32. This mystery is great; but I am speaking with reference to Christ and the church. (Eph 5:28-32)

God describes Himself as being a husband to the people of Israel (Jer 31:32), remaining faithful even when devastated by their adulteries (Hos 1:2, 2:18-20). Jesus likewise is called the Bridegroom, with the saints, both Jews and Gentiles, as His bride (John 3:29, Rev 19:7-8).

Noah's Covenant – In Antiquity

Obviously, we are all safe today from a repeat of the Flood because of this covenant:

> 9. "Now behold, I Myself do establish My covenant with you, and with your descendants after you…
> 11. "I establish My covenant with you; and all flesh shall never again be cut off by the water of the flood, neither shall there again be a flood to destroy the earth.
> 12. …the covenant which I am making between Me and you and every living creature that is with you, *for all successive generations*"… (Gen 9:9-12, emphasis added)

It is therefore described as an "everlasting covenant":

> 16. "When the bow is in the cloud, then I will look upon it, to remember *the everlasting covenant* between God and every living creature of all flesh that is on the earth." (Gen 9:16, emphasis added)

However, it is often overlooked by Gentile Christians today that in this covenant, God commissioned Noah and "all successive generations" (v. 12) to address the injustice of murder:

> 5. "Surely I will require your lifeblood; from every beast I will require it.
> And from every man, from every man's brother I will require the life of man.
> 6. "Whoever sheds man's blood,
> By man his blood shall be shed,
> For in the image of God He made man". (Genesis 9:5-6)

Capital punishment is too complex an issue to address here but when God spoke to Noah, He was answering Cain's arrogant question after he had killed Abel (Gen 4:9) – "Yes, Cain, you are your brother's keeper". He will hold 'every man' accountable for 'every man's brother' because we are all made 'in the image of God'. We are required as communities to bring every murderer to justice. This is why Paul says of all governing authorities:

> … it is a minister of God to you for good. But if you do what is evil, be afraid; for it does not bear the sword for nothing; for it is a minister of God, an avenger who brings wrath on the one who practices evil. (Rom 13:4)

God has given 'the sword', i.e. the power of lethal force, to every government to enforce justice (Rom 13:1-7, 1 Tim 2:1-3). In New Zealand, our police do not carry guns but they have them available if necessary and our Armed Offenders Squad and Armed Forces deal with any armed threat to our society and nation. We may not have realised it but this is fulfilling the Noahic Covenant.

This covenant also sanctifies "every living creature… on the earth" (v. 16):

> 3. "Every moving thing that is alive shall be food for you; I give all to you, as I gave the green plant.
> 4. "Only you shall not eat flesh with its life, that is, its blood."
> (Gen 9:3-4)

To this day, our Judaeo-Christian heritage has our abattoirs bleed our meat. Even if we personally do not pour out that blood as an offering to the God who created every creature we eat, we are still to offer thanks:

> 4. For everything created by God is good, and nothing is to be rejected if it is received with gratitude;
> 5. for it is sanctified by means of the word of God and prayer. (1 Tim 4:4-5)

This includes dealing humanely with all animal life:

> A righteous man has regard for the life of his animal,
> But even the compassion of the wicked is cruel. (Prov 12:10)

Accordingly, William Wilberforce not only championed the abolition of slavery within the British Empire but he also co-founded the RSPCA (Royal Society for the Prevention of Cruelty to Animals).[409]

Noah's covenant provided the basis for what the Early Church's Jewish leaders said to the Gentile disciples:

> "For it seemed good to the Holy Spirit and to us to lay upon you no greater burden than these essentials: that you abstain from things sacrificed to idols and from blood and from things strangled and from fornication; if you keep yourselves free from such things, you will do well." (Acts 15:28-29)

These four "essentials" forbid idolatry, murder,[410] un-bled meat, and immorality and correspond to the Jewish teaching of the seven Noahide Laws, which they believe were given to all non-Jews as 'sons of the covenant of Noah'.[411]

---

409 Philip Johnson & Gus diZerega, *Beyond the Burning Times: A Pagan and Christian in Dialogue*, Oxford; Lion Books, 2008, p. 82.
410 'Blood' is a common Jewish idiom for bloodshed, as in Matthew 23:30, 23:35, 27:6, 27:25, Luke 11:50-51, Acts 5:28. 'Things strangled' refers to un-bled meat.
411 Six prohibit idolatry, blasphemy, murder, sexual immorality, theft, and eating flesh or blood from a living animal while the seventh is to maintain a system of justice. David van Drunen, *Divine Covenants and*

The everlasting Noahic Covenant still applies to us all, whether Jew or Gentile, believer or unbeliever.

Abraham's Covenant – c. 2050 BC

God made this covenant not only with Abraham but also with Abraham's son, Isaac, and his grandson, Jacob:

> God remembered His covenant with Abraham, Isaac, and Jacob. (Exo 2:24)

The writer of Hebrews therefore speaks of Abraham as 'dwelling in tents with Isaac and Jacob, fellow heirs of the same promise' (Heb 11:9)

It is an everlasting covenant for the Jewish people and Paul assures us that the Law, or the Mosaic Covenant, did not nullify it:

> 15. Brethren, I speak in terms of human relations: even though it is only a man's covenant, yet when it has been ratified, *no one sets it aside* or adds conditions to it.
> 16. Now the promises were spoken to Abraham and to his seed. He does not say, "And to seeds," as referring to many, but rather to one, "And to your seed," that is, Christ.
> 17. What I am saying is this: *the Law*, which came four hundred and thirty years later, *does not invalidate a covenant previously ratified by God*, so as to nullify the promise.
> (Gal 3:15-17, emphasis added)

Writing to the Romans, he explains that all Gentiles who believe in Jesus are now included in the Abrahamic Covenant:

> 16. ...it is by faith... that the promise will be guaranteed to all the descendants, not only to those who are of the Law, but also to those who are of the faith of Abraham, who is the father of us all,

---

Moral Order: A Biblical Theology of Natural Law, Cambridge; Wm B. Eerdmans Publishing, 2014, Appendix 5 – Noahic Natural Law and the Noahide Laws in Jewish Ethics. Also www.jewishvirtuallibrary.org/jsource/Judaism/The_Seven_Noahide_Laws.html, 16 Jun, 2015.

17. (as it is written, 'A FATHER OF MANY NATIONS HAVE I MADE YOU')... (Rom 4:16-17)

'Those who are of the Law' (v. 16) are the believing Jews of the Mosaic Covenant; those of 'many nations' (v. 17) who have 'the faith of Abraham' (v. 16) are also fulfilling this particular promise made to Abraham (Gen 17:5).

However, it is easy to misread Galatians 3:16.

Some think that since the promises were not spoken 'to many, but rather to one,... that is, Christ', Jesus alone can fulfil them[412] and that Israel's rebirth as a nation is therefore simply coincidental rather than God fulfilling His promises to them. This is sometimes referred to as Fulfilment Theology, which has a slightly different emphasis to Supercessionism or Replacement Theology,[413] but the same outcome: Israel is no longer relevant to God.

In believing this, they are merging two distinct promises. In Galatians 3:16, Paul refers to Genesis 22:18 which was made to 'seed' singular, as he says, but in Romans 4:17, Paul quotes the promise that Abraham will be 'a father' not of 'seed' singular but of "many nations" (Gen 17:5).

These two distinct promises are also readily distinguishable in the context of Genesis 22:18. Just look at v. 17 as well:

> 17. "...I will greatly bless you, and I will greatly *multiply your seed* as the stars of the heavens and as the sand which is on the seashore; and your seed shall possess the gate of their enemies. 18. "In *your seed* all the nations of the earth shall be blessed, because you have obeyed My voice" (Gen 22:17-18, emphasis added)

In v. 17, "seed" is unmistakably plural, being like the innumerable stars and grains of sand; it is v. 18 which Paul

---

412 Also inferred from 2 Corinthians 1:20.
413 This was the official doctrine of Roman Catholicism from Augustine until 1965. See Paul VI's *Nostra Aetate*, www.vatican.va/archive/hist_councils/ii_vatican_council/documents/vat-ii_decl_19651028_nostra-aetate_en.html.

quotes in Galatians 3:16 as being "seed" singular.

It is through the second promise, through the 'one' seed, that all the earlier promises that Abraham would bless all the families (Gen 12:3) and nations (Gen 17:4-5) of the earth would be fulfilled. It is undoubtedly in Jesus that believers from "all the nations of the earth" receive every spiritual blessing now:

> Blessed be the God and Father of our Lord Jesus Christ, who has blessed us with *every spiritual blessing* in the heavenly places *in Christ*… (Eph 1:3, emphasis added)

Ultimately, this will include the whole earth (Matt 5:5, Rom 4:13).

However, in the meantime, before the Lord returns to receive His inheritance of the whole earth, Abraham's other 'seed' were to receive the land of Israel. It is these multiplied descendants 'according to the flesh' (Rom 9:3) of Abraham, Isaac, and Jacob (or Israel) who were to receive the land of Israel, promised to Abraham (Gen 12:1-3; 12:7; 13:14-17; 15:7, 15:18-21; 17:8), to Isaac (Gen 26:2-4), and to Jacob (Gen 28:4, 13-15; 35:12). The writer of Hebrews summarises:

> 8. By faith Abraham, when he was called, obeyed by going out to a place which he was to receive for an inheritance; and he went out, not knowing where he was going.
> 9. By faith he lived as an alien in *the land of promise*, as in a foreign land, dwelling in tents with Isaac and Jacob, *fellow heirs of the same promise*… (Heb 11:8-9, emphasis addded)

This covenanted promise of the land therefore remains to this day; it is an 'everlasting covenant' with Abraham (Gen 17:7), Isaac (Gen 17:19-21), and Jacob (1 Chron 16:17, Psa 105:10). Their descendants 'according to the flesh' will be "a nation… forever":

> 35. Thus says the LORD,
> Who gives the sun for light by day
> And the fixed order of the moon and the stars for light by night,
> Who stirs up the sea so that its waves roar;

> The LORD of hosts is His name:
> 36. "If this fixed order departs
> From before Me," declares the LORD,
> "Then the offspring of Israel also will cease
> From being a nation before Me forever."
> 37. Thus says the LORD, "If the heavens above can be measured
> And the foundations of the earth searched out below,
> Then I will also cast off all the offspring of Israel
> For all that they have done," declares the LORD. (Jer 31:35-37)

Despite "all that they have done" (v. 37), God will not give up on them as "a nation" (v. 36).

Moses' Covenant – 1446 BC

If all of this was to be achieved through the Abrahamic Covenant, why was there a need for Moses' covenant, the Law, 430 years later (Gal 3:17)? Paul explains:

> Why the Law then? It was added because of transgressions, having been ordained through angels by the agency of a mediator, *until the seed* would come to whom the promise had been made. (Gal 3:19, emphasis added)

The Law was to spell out God's unique requirements of the people of Israel, to keep them a distinct people 'according to the flesh' until Messiah came to be born of the flesh, as Paul puts it in Romans 9:3-5. They were to be "a holy nation" (Ex 19:6), for example, by maintaining strict dietary laws so that they could not even eat with people from other nations (Gal 2:12, Acts 10:28). This is why the food laws became irrelevant after Jesus (Acts 10:13-16).

The Law also contained extraordinary prophetic dramas in the sacrifices, rituals, Sabbaths, and festivals that all foreshadowed what Messiah would do (Col 2:16-17), and how we should respond (1 Cor 5:7-8). It also created the Tabernacle, which demonstrated the Incarnation of God in human form:

> And the Word became flesh, and dwelt [lit. tabernacled] among us, and we saw His glory, glory as of the only begotten from the Father, full of grace and truth. (John 1:14)

Tabernacles, or tents, were temporary dwelling places that could be dismantled and moved as required, providing a graphic illustration of our mortal bodies:

> 1. For we know that if the earthly tent which is our house is torn down, we have a building from God, a house not made with hands, eternal in the heavens...
> 4. ...while we are in this tent, we groan, being burdened, because we do not want to be unclothed but to be clothed, so that what is mortal will be swallowed up by life. (2 Cor 5:1-4)

The Law's Tabernacle was therefore set up in midst of Israel's tents whenever they stopped in the wilderness to reveal God's desire to come and live among us in human form.

As for the land, as we saw earlier in Leviticus 26, that was promised to the flesh and blood descendants of Abraham, Isaac, and Jacob, whether they believe or not. This is perfectly fair because we Gentiles have our own lands (Acts 17:26), e.g. China for the Chinese, Arabia for the Arabs, Nigeria for the Nigerians, whether we believe or not. The only difference is that when the Israelites were consistently unfaithful, God sent them into exile, as in Babylon for seventy years, and into "all the nations" for the last 2,000 years.

Leviticus 26 is emphatic, however, that no exile will be forever – God will always bring them back:

> 42. ...I will remember My covenant with Jacob, and I will remember also My covenant with Isaac, and My covenant with Abraham as well, and *I will remember the land* (Lev 26:42, emphasis added)

Leviticus 26 explains that this will not only be because of their forefathers of 2000 BC but also those of the Exodus, five hundred years later:

> 44. "Yet in spite of this, when they are in the land of their enemies, I will not reject them, nor will I so abhor them as to destroy them, breaking My covenant with them; for I am the LORD their God.
> 45. "But I will remember for them t*he covenant with their ancestors, whom I brought out of the land of Egypt* in the sight of the nations, that I might be their God. I am the LORD."
> 46. These are the statutes and ordinances and laws which the LORD established between Himself and the sons of Israel through Moses at Mount Sinai. (Lev 26:44-46, emphasis added)

He simply will not break the Mosaic Covenant which created the nation of Israel (Ex 19:5-6).

Jeremiah reminded them of this a thousand years later again, during the Babylonian exile, as we saw in the series of rhetorical questions regarding the longevity of the sun, moon, stars, and sea quoted earlier:

> 36. "If this fixed order departs
> From before Me," declares the LORD,
> "Then the offspring of Israel also will cease
> From *being a nation before Me forever."*
> 37. Thus says the LORD, "If the heavens above can be measured
> And the foundations of the earth searched out below,
> Then I will also cast off all the offspring of Israel
> For all that they have done," declares the LORD.
> (Jer 31:36-37, emphasis added)

Despite "all that they have done" (v. 37), Israel will *never* cease from "being a nation" forever (v. 36), and that includes them always being restored to the land of Israel.

This provides the context for Jesus' teaching about the Mosaic Covenant:

> 17. "Do not think that I came to abolish the Law or the Prophets; I did not come to abolish but to fulfill.
> 18. "For truly I say to you, until heaven and earth pass away, not the smallest letter or stroke shall pass from the Law until all is accomplished." (Matt 5:17-18)

This is not semantics – there is a huge difference between "fulfil" and "abolish" which Fulfilment Theology overlooks. The Greek verb translated here as abolish, *kataluo*, is elsewhere translated as to 'destroy' and 'tear down', as in destroying and tearing down the Temple (Matt 24:2, 26:61, 27:40).

While Jesus perfectly fulfilled every foreshadowed detail of the Law, He did not abolish, destroy, or tear it down. The Mosaic Covenant remains in force for all who remain under it, i.e. every Jewish man, woman, and child who does not yet accept Him as Messiah, "until heaven and earth pass away" on the Last Day.

And here is the relevance of Revelation 11 – it shows the on-going ministry of Moses and Elijah through the Book of the Covenant, also known as the Tanakh or the Hebrew Bible.

Levi's Covenant – 1446 BC

In 587 BC,[414] Jeremiah used similar imagery to reassure Israel of the longevity of God's covenants with Levi, made in 1446 BC,[415]) and David, made in 1003 BC[416]:

> 20. 'If you can break My covenant for the day and My covenant for the night, so that day and night will not be at their appointed time,
> 21. then *My covenant* may also be broken with David My servant so that he will not have a son to reign on his throne, and *with the Levitical priests, My ministers.*
> 22. 'As the host of heaven cannot be counted and the sand of the sea cannot be measured, so I will multiply the descendants of David My servant and *the Levites who minister to Me.'"*
> (Jer 33:20-22, emphasis added)

---

414 *Zondervan Pictorial Encyclopedia of the Bible*, Vol 3, p. 435.
415 According to 1 Kings 6:1, the Exodus took place 480 years before 'the fourth year of Solomon's reign', i.e. 966 BC. See too David Rohl, *Exodus: Myth or History?* St Louis Park, MN; Thinking Man Media, 2015, p. 162.
416 *Zondervan Pictorial Encyclopedia of the Bible*, Vol 2, p. 43.

These two covenants are referenced to validate the promises just made through Jeremiah:

> 17. "For thus says the LORD, 'David shall never lack a man to sit on the throne of the house of Israel;
> 18. and the Levitical priests shall never lack a man before Me to offer burnt offerings, to burn grain offerings and to prepare sacrifices continually'." (Jer 33:17-18)

We will look at the Davidic Covenant next; let us look now at the promise made regarding the Levites:

> 18. and the Levitical priests shall never lack a man before Me to offer burnt offerings, to burn grain offerings and to prepare sacrifices continually'." (Jer 33:17-18)

The Levitical covenant is often overlooked, but it was made because they remained faithful to the Mosaic Covenant during the golden calf apostasy (Ex 32:26-29), as Moses prayed in his last words:

> 8. Of Levi he said, "Let Your Thummim and Your Urim[417] belong to Your godly man,
> Whom You proved at Massah,
> With whom You contended at the waters of Meribah;
> 9. Who said of his father and his mother,
> 'I did not consider them";
> And he did not acknowledge his brothers,
> Nor did he regard his own sons,
> For they observed Your word,
> And *kept Your covenant.*
> 10. "They shall teach Your ordinances to Jacob,
> And Your law to Israel.
> They shall put incense before You,
> And whole burnt offerings on Your altar."
> (Deut 33:8-10, emphasis added)

Their own keeping of the Law qualified them to teach it to the

---

[417] Lit. Lights and Perfections, the *Urim* and *Thummim* were the sacred lots kept in the breast-piece of the High Priest (Ex 28:30) and their 'every decision' was 'from the LORD' (Prov 16:33).

others who had not, and earned the tribe of Levi their own covenant as the priests.[418] This covenant is also referred to as an "everlasting covenant":

> "All the offerings of the holy gifts, which the sons of Israel offer to the LORD, I have given to you and your sons and your daughters with you, as a perpetual allotment. It is an *everlasting covenant* of salt before the LORD to you and your descendants with you" (Num 18:19, emphasis added)

There are two points to consider here.

1. Superseded by Melchizedek?

Many Christians today assume that the Levitical priesthood was superseded by Melchizedek's priesthood, but it was not. The writer of Hebrews argues that the two priesthoods co-existed in Abraham's time to prove that Melchizedek's is superior (Heb 7:7-10), and they still co-exist today. While the Levitical priesthood cannot make or offer any atonement – that only comes through Jesus – they still have a role within Israel to teach the Law.

Consider this. Jesus, our "high priest forever of the order of Melchizedek" (Heb 6:20), introduced the New Covenant but, as we have seen, the Old Covenant is still in force. So too is the covenant with Levi, until day and night cease:

> 20. 'If you can break My covenant for the day and My covenant for the night, so that day and night will not be at their appointed time,
> 21. then *My covenant* may also be broken... *with the Levitical priests, My ministers.* (Jer 33:20-21, emphasis added)

Jeremiah had predicted:

> '...the Levitical priests *shall never* lack a man before Me to offer

---

418 Originally, all in Israel were to be priests "if you keep My covenant" (Ex 19:5-6), with Aaron and his descendants providing the high priest. However, only the tribe of Levi kept it. Peter restates God's original intention in calling every follower of Jesus to now be a priest, but of the order of Melchizedek, the royal priesthood (1 Pet 2:9).

burnt offerings, to burn grain offerings and to prepare sacrifices continually'. (Jer 33:18, emphasis added)

However, Daniel had also prophesied of Messiah:

> "And He will make a firm covenant with the many for one week, but in the middle of the week *He will put a stop to sacrifice and grain offering*; and on the wing of abominations will come one who makes desolate, even until a complete destruction, one that is decreed, is poured out on the one who makes desolate." (Dan 9:27, emphasis added)

This prophecy is often mistakenly thought to refer to the Antichrist, but, as we established in Book 1, the 70th Week of Daniel belongs to Messiah the Prince.[419] He made this "firm covenant with the many" in 30 AD, i.e. the New Covenant, for all mankind, whom He also called the "many" (Matt 22:14). Tragically, only a "few" respond. He did this through His atoning death "in the midst of the week", i.e. after He had ministered for three and a half years, which rendered all literal "sacrifice and grain offering" obsolete to God.

We established in Book 2[420] that His crucifixion is this particular "abomination of desolation" in Daniel 9:27 and actually the fourth in Jewish history. This led to the "complete destruction, one that is decreed" of Jerusalem, because Israel had made everything "desolate" when they crucified Jesus, the real Tabernacle (John 1:14) and Temple of God (John 2:19-22).[421]

The prediction that "the people of the prince who is to come will destroy the city and the sanctuary" (Dan 9:26), i.e. Jerusalem and the Second Temple, was fulfilled by the Romans in 70 AD, led by their general Titus who later became Emperor of Rome. The Romans then set up the fifth "abomination of desolation", worshipping the *imago imperatoris*, the image of

---

419 *DDJ*, pp. 95-106.
420 *STB*, pp. 265-280.
421 *STB*, pp. 273-278.

the emperor, on the Temple Mount.

The promise of Jeremiah was not that the sacrifices and grain offering would continue forever but that the "Levitical priests would never lack a man" (33:18), and, to this day, they have not.

2. "Cohen, Levi or Israel?"

In most Jewish synagogues today, the identity of all participants is carefully established as to whether they belong to Cohen (the Hebrew word for priest), Levi, or Israel:[422]

> The Holy Temple was destroyed millennia ago, but Conservative and Orthodox Jews still acknowledge the three-fold division of ancient Israel into Kohanim, Leviim and Yisraelim. Reform Jews do not believe any congregant should have a different status than another, and therefore do not acknowledge these divisions…
> Today, Leviim are believed to be the direct patrilineal descendants of Levi, while Kohanim are Leviim who descend directly, through their fathers, from Aaron. Other Jews are assumed to come from one of the other tribes and are called, simply, Yisraelim. A convert to Judaism takes the status as a Yisrael.
> The only valid method of being a Levite (or Kohen) is to have an unbroken tradition, passed from generation to generation, stretching back to the time of Moses. In many Jewish communities, meticulous records were kept throughout the generations to ensure that ancestral lines remained clear. If one has no clear evidence, such as a family tradition, of descending from Levi or Aaron one should assume he/she is a Yisrael.[423]

Replying to a young man's question as to why his application form to join a synagogue asked him which one he was, Rabbi David Sedley explains:

---

422 These names have a variety of transliterations.
423 www.jewishvirtuallibrary.org/jsource/Judaism/tribes1.html, 30 Jun, 2015.

> The Jewish nation is divided up into 12 tribes (the children of each of Jacob's 12 sons). One of these sons is Levi, and a subgroup of Levi is Cohen. Levi and Cohen were singled out to be the ones to work in the Temple. There are special laws relating to them, which are different than to everyone else.
> The main difference nowadays in Synagogue is that the first person called to the Torah reading is always a Cohen and the second a Levi (unless there are none in the Synagogue, in which case anyone may be called up).[424]

While there are no animal sacrifices or grain offerings to be offered, and therefore no atonement, the priests were also to teach the Law (Ezek 44:23, Mal 2:7). Accordingly, those from Levi and Aaron's descendants, now called Cohens or Kohanim, are still carefully identified today and set apart to read aloud the Scriptures to Israel.

David's Covenant – 1003 BC

Rather than revisit Chapter 12 – David's Legacy, let us consider what Jeremiah prophesied four hundred years after David, during the 6th Century BC Babylonian exile. Humiliated and full of despair, the people of Israel were losing their sense of national identity:

> 23. And the word of the LORD came to Jeremiah, saying,
> 24. "Have you not observed what this people have spoken, saying, 'The two families which the LORD chose, He has rejected them'? Thus they despise My people, no longer are they as a nation in their sight."(Jer 33:23-24)

As we saw above in Jeremiah 33:17-18 and 21-22, 'the two families' were those of David and Levi. In believing that God had rejected these families, the children of Israel were forgetting God's everlasting covenants with all of them:

---

[424] www.jewishanswers.org/ask-the-rabbi-1586/cohen-levi-and-yisroel/?p=1586, 1 Jul, 2015.

> 25. "Thus says the LORD, 'If My covenant for day and night stand not, and the fixed patterns of heaven and earth I have not established,
> 26. then I would reject the descendants of Jacob and David My servant, not taking from his descendants rulers over the descendants of Abraham, Isaac and Jacob. But I will restore their fortunes and will have mercy on them.'" (Jer 33:23-26)

Jeremiah therefore reminds Israel of three covenants, the Abrahamic, the Levitical, and the Davidic, which are to last as long as "day and night" and "the fixed patterns of heaven and earth" (v. 25). David's covenant ensures that his descendants will always be "rulers over the descendants of Abraham, Isaac and Jacob" (v. 26) because God had promised:

> 3. "I have made a *covenant* with My chosen;
> I have sworn to David My servant,
> 4. I will establish your seed *forever*
> And build up your throne to all generations…" (Psa 89:3-4, emphasis added)

It is to endure as long as the sun and moon:

> 36. "His seed shall endure forever
> And his throne as the sun before Me.
> 37. "It shall be established forever like the moon,
> And the witness in the sky is faithful." (Psa 89:36-37)

Accordingly, anyone today who believes in David's "seed", Jesus of Nazareth, is receiving the benefit of the Davidic Covenant.

The New Covenant – 30 AD

Most reading this study will already be well familiar with the New Covenant so I will keep this brief.

In the 6th Century BC, Jeremiah prophesied:

> 31. "Behold, days are coming," declares the LORD, "when I will make *a new covenant* with the house of Israel and with the

> house of Judah,
> 32. *not like the covenant* which I made with their fathers in the day I took them by the hand to bring them out of the land of Egypt, My covenant which they broke, although I was a husband to them," declares the LORD. (Jer 31:31-32, emphasis added)

This covenant is therefore not a renewal of the Mosaic. It is "not like" it because it has a very different means of fulfilment:

> 33. "But this is the covenant which I will make with the house of Israel after those days," declares the LORD, "I will put *My law within them* and *on their heart I will write it*; and I will be their God, and they shall be My people". (Jer 31:33, emphasis added)

Whereas the Law was written on tablets of stone, the will of God is now to be written on our hearts and minds, giving us new desires and understanding (2 Cor 3:3). This new covenant also provides a unique intimacy with God for all who will partake:

> 34. "They will not teach again, each man his neighbor and each man his brother, saying, 'Know the LORD,' for t*hey will all know Me*, from the least of them to the greatest of them," declares the LORD, "for I will forgive their iniquity, and their sin I will remember no more." (Jer 31:34, emphasis added)

It is, of course, Jesus of Nazareth who made and still offers this covenant of a personal, first-hand knowledge of God to any who will trust in Him:

> ...He took the cup after they had eaten [the Last Supper], saying, "This cup which is poured out for you is the new covenant in My blood". (Luke 22:20)

No longer is there any need for animal or grain sacrifice or libations of wine because Jesus offered Himself instead, once for all time (Heb 10:14). We also are changed internally, not only as we receive new desires but as the Holy Spirit Himself comes to dwell within us. This extraordinary intimacy was also prophesied by Ezekiel in the 6th Century BC:

> 26. "Moreover, I will give you a new heart and put a new spirit within you; and I will remove the heart of stone from your flesh and give you a heart of flesh.
> 27. "I will put My Spirit within you and cause you to walk in My statutes, and you will be careful to observe My ordinances." (Ezek 36:26-27)

This wonderful promise of God changing even our motivations – He will "cause" us, motivate us, to walk in His ways – transformed my life when I first heard it in 1974, and it has sustained and refreshed me ever since. Whenever I find my heart going cold, hard, or dead, like a "heart of stone", and I begin to despair, I call on the Lord according to this promise that He will give me "a heart of flesh", one that is warm, sensitive, motivated, and alive to Him; He has always done it.

I have also clung to two promises of Jesus:

> "...the Helper, the Holy Spirit, whom the Father will send in My name, *He will teach you all things*, and bring to your remembrance all that I said to you". (John 14:26, emphasis added)

> "...when He, the Spirit of truth, comes, He will *guide you into all the truth*; for He will not speak on His own initiative, but whatever He hears, He will speak; and He will disclose to you what is to come". (John 16:13, emphasis added)

The New Covenant is also an everlasting covenant because it guarantees us eternal life:

> "For God so loved the world, that He gave His only begotten Son, that whoever believes in Him shall not perish, but have *eternal life*". (John 3:16, emphasis added)

Who cannot say, "Hallelujah!"?

The Eternal or Everlasting Covenant – Before Creation

The New Covenant is also described as eternal:

> Now the God of peace, who brought up from the dead the great Shepherd of the sheep through the blood of the eternal covenant, even Jesus our Lord... (Heb 13:20)

Notice, it is not 'an' everlasting or eternal covenant but 'the' eternal covenant. Here we come to the heart of all the Biblical covenants of God. When Jesus came, He did not abolish any of them – He fulfilled them all and gained us eternal life as promised before Creation:

> 2. in the hope of eternal life, which God, who cannot lie, *promised long ages ago*,
> 3. but at the proper time manifested, even His word, in the proclamation with which I was entrusted according to the commandment of God our Savior. (Titus 1:2-3, emphasis added)

Dr Derek Prince points out that the Greek phrase translated as 'long ages ago' is πρὸ χρόνων αἰωνίων, literally 'before ages eternal',[425] and asks rhetorically, "Promised to whom?" He reasons that since this occurred before Creation, the promise can only have been made within the Godhead – the Father promised the Son. This is consistent with John's use of the expression 'from the foundation of the world':

> All who dwell on the earth will worship him, everyone whose name has not been written in the book of life of the Lamb who has been slain from the foundation of the world. (Rev 13:8, NASB alternative reading)

Translators often provide two alternatives, the other being that the phrase 'from the foundation of the world' refers

---

425 See also Marvin R. Vincent: 'before time began to be reckoned by aeons', *Vincent's Word Studies*, http://biblehub.com/commentaries/titus/1-2.htm, 23 Jul, 2015.

to names written or not written 'in the book of life'.[426] However, Peter also refers to the death of Christ as known 'before the foundation of the world', reminding us that we are redeemed…:

> 19. …with precious blood, as of a lamb unblemished and spotless, the blood of Christ.
> 20. For He was foreknown *before the foundation of the world*, but has appeared in these last times for your sake,
> 21. who through Him are believers in God… (1 Pet 1:19-21, emphasis added)

Unsurprisingly then, the eternal covenant was created before the foundation of the world. In our heavenly Father's foreknowledge of our sinfulness, He provided redemption for us through the death of Christ for everyone who will believe in Him. This gains us the 'eternal life… promised before times eternal' (Tit 1:2) to Jesus, just as He prayed at the Last Supper:

> 1. …"Father, the hour has come; glorify Your Son, that the Son may glorify You,
> 2. even as You gave Him authority over all flesh, that to all whom You have given Him, He may give eternal life.
> 3. "This is eternal life, that they may know You, the only true God, and Jesus Christ whom You have sent". (John 17:1-3)

We all receive eternal life when we know intimately the Father and the Son through the Holy Spirit (John 16:12-15).

---

426 Also Revelation 17:8. The phrase refers to all who will and all who will not believe in the Lamb, thus demonstrating God's wonderful foreknowledge of every individual.

Summary of God's Covenants

The Scriptures describe nine[427] covenants initiated by God, eight of which are described as everlasting or eternal. Only the marriage covenant is not everlasting since it is until death parts us (Rom 7:1-3). The rest still apply today to those with whom they were made and the heirs of these promises:

1. Adam's covenant required letting God decide what is good and what is evil.

Their unwillingness to trust Him in this way led not only to their separation from Him and subsequent death but to our mortality as well. We are and will remain under the Adamic curse of death and decay until the Resurrection.

Our sinfulness, however, does not come from the Fall but from our each choosing to follow Adam in breaking this everlasting covenant. Only Jesus of Nazareth, 'the last Adam' and 'the second Man' (1 Cor 15:45-47), has been unfailingly faithful to our heavenly Father's will, thereby fulfilling the Adamic Covenant, removing its curse and gaining eternal life for all who trust in Him.

2. The marriage covenant.

Lasting only until death, it nevertheless provides a wonderful illustration of the degree of intimacy God longs to have with us (Eph 5:31-32).

3. Noah's everlasting covenant.

It guarantees there will never again be a flood and provides the basis of all government today, requiring all in authority to uphold the value of every individual as made in the image and likeness of God. It also requires us to value all animal life.

---

427 One other, made with Phinehas, Aaron's grandson, was within the Aaronic priesthood (Num 25:11-13).

4. Abraham's everlasting covenant was to redeem all of mankind from the Fall.

It was to create a 'holy nation' in the midst of 'all the nations' through whom Messiah would come 'in the flesh' (Rom 9:5).

Passed on through Isaac and Jacob to Jacob's twelve sons, who became the twelve tribes of Israel, the Abrahamic Covenant contained two distinct promises: one made to the 'Seed' who would redeem from 'all the nations' all who trust in Him; the other made to multiplied 'seed' who were to possess the Land of Promise. Israel's existence as a nation in that land today is a testimony to the Abrahamic Covenant.

5. Moses mediated an everlasting covenant at the birth of the nation.

This spelled out God's requirements, the Law, to keep them a distinct people until Messiah came. It confirmed their everlasting title to the land, despite their twice being exiled because of their unfaithfulness to God – 'if we are faithless, He remains faithful, for He cannot deny Himself' (2 Tim 2:13).

The Mosaic Covenant also created prophetic dramas in festivals, rituals, and sacrifices in the Tabernacle and the Temple, to foreshadow how God would come to live amongst us and how we should respond. Jesus, perfectly fulfilling the Law, freed all who trust in Him from its requirements (Rom 7:1-6). However, the Law still applies to everyone in Israel 'according to the flesh' who is not yet trusting in Him.

6. Levi's everlasting covenant.

It guarantees his sons will be the priests of the Law for as long as the Law exists, i.e. "until heaven and earth pass away" (Matt 5:18).

They were to offer the sacrifices on behalf of Israel but, with no Temple, altar, or legitimate sacrifices possible today, they can offer no atonement for sin. The only role left for them is to teach the Law. With forgiveness no longer available through the Law, there is only condemnation for the Jews, as there is for all Gentiles, until they turn to Jesus to be forgiven.

7. David's covenant.

It sanctified the city of Jerusalem for all time, guaranteeing Israel's restoration to it, as we see today. It also provided rulers for Israel until Messiah came to be both a king and a high priest 'according to the order of Melchizedek', able to mediate a new covenant for both Jews and Gentiles.

8. The New Covenant.

Jesus of Nazareth is the promised Messiah and made the New Covenant for us by offering Himself as the ultimate sacrifice, i.e. God Himself died in our place so that we might live forever. In cleansing us, He has made us fit to receive the Holy Spirit into our hearts to write there the will of the Father and change our desires, ideas and motivations to do His will.

9. The Eternal Covenant.

All of these covenants outwork the Eternal Covenant which the Father made with the Son 'before time began to be reckoned by aeons'.

Appendix B – Grown from 'Missionary Roots'

Robert D. Woodberry is Associate Professor of Political Science at the National University of Singapore. After twelve years of research, with at times up to fifty research associates at the University of Texas, his article, *The Missionary Roots of Liberal Democracy*, was published by the *American Political Science Review*,[428] and won eight academic research awards. He found that:

> Christianity profoundly shaped both the development and global spread of stable liberal democracy. Some of these religious influences were direct, shaping the ideas and institutions that made stable liberal democracy more likely; some influences were indirect, shaping mass education, mass printing, voluntary associations, nonviolent social movement tactics, and particular types of reform which dispersed power beyond traditional elites and allowed a broader segment of the population to influence politics.[429]

He demonstrates historically and statistically that:

> ...the historic prevalence of Protestant missionaries explains about half the variation in democracy in Africa, Asia, Latin America, and Oceania.[430]

One of the great enigmas of modern history is why some nations become stable liberal democracies, where their citizens can vote, speak, and assemble freely, while neighboring countries become unstable and authoritarian. Why are there such dramatic differences in public health and economic

---

428 *American Political Science Review*, Vol. 106, No. 2, 2012. He provided 192 pages of supporting material.
429 http://kellogg.nd.edu/vfellowships/woodberry.shtml, 4 May, 2016.
430 Ibid.

growth between one country and another, when they share similar geography, cultural background, and natural resources?

One answer Woodberry found in Togo and Ghana in 2001:

> During the colonial era, British missionaries in Ghana had established a whole system of schools and printing presses. But France, the colonial power in Togo, severely restricted missionaries. The French authorities took interest in educating only a small intellectual elite. More than 100 years later, education was still limited in Togo. In Ghana, it was flourishing.[431]

Similarly, in French and Belgian Congo:

> While studying the Congo, Woodberry made one of his most dramatic early discoveries. Congo's colonial-era exploitation was well known: Colonists in both French and Belgian Congo had forced villagers to extract rubber from the jungle. As punishment for not complying, they burned down villages, castrated men, and cut off children's limbs. In French Congo, the atrocities passed without comment or protest, aside from one report in a Marxist newspaper in France. But in Belgian Congo, the abuses aroused the largest international protest movement since the abolition of slavery.
>
> Why the difference? Working on a hunch, Woodberry charted mission stations all across the Congo. Protestant missionaries, it turned out, were allowed only in the Belgian Congo. Among those missionaries were two British Baptists named John and Alice Harris who took photographs of the atrocities—including a now-famous picture of a father gazing at his daughter's remains—and then smuggled the photographs out of the country. With evidence in hand, they traveled through the United States and Britain to stir up public pressure and, along with other missionaries, helped raise an outcry against the abuses.[432]

---

431 *Christianity Today*, Jan/Feb, 2014.
432 Ibid.

I described in Book 2[433] the work of these other missionaries, Briton A.E. Scrivener and Americans William Sheppard and William Morrison, as well as the subsequent parts played by Mark Twain and Joseph Conrad.

By 2012, Woodberry and his fifty research assistants at the University of Texas could conclude:

> Areas where Protestant missionaries had a significant presence in the past are on average more economically developed today, with comparatively better health, lower infant mortality, lower corruption, greater literacy, higher educational attainment (especially for women), and more robust membership in nongovernmental associations.[434]

'Conversionary Protestants'

This effect was not evident everywhere however. Woodberry found:

> The positive effect of missionaries on democracy applies only to "conversionary Protestants". Protestant clergy financed by the state, as well as Catholic missionaries prior to the 1960s, had no comparable effect in the areas where they worked. Independence from state control made a big difference. "One of the main stereotypes about missions is that they were closely connected to colonialism," says Woodberry. "But Protestant missionaries not funded by the state were regularly very critical of colonialism."[435]

He defines Conversionary Protestants (CPs) as 'not necessarily orthodox or conservative' but those who:

> (i) actively attempt to persuade others of their beliefs
> (ii) emphasise lay vernacular Bible reading
> (iii) believe that grace/faith/choice saves people, not group membership or sacraments.[436]

---

433 *STB*, pp. 146-148.
434 *Christianity Today*, Jan/Feb, 2014.
435 Ibid.
436 *American Political Science Review*, Vol. 106, No. 2, p. 244.

Their focus on individual responsibility in relating to God and the Scriptures valued every individual as made in His image and every individual's conscience, thereby discouraging tribalism, prejudice, and corruption. Woodberry even found this effect when many did not convert to Protestantism[437] – the salt and light had a disproportionate impact.

We saw this here in 19th Century New Zealand, as also explained in Book 2.[438]

• • •

---

[437] Ibid., p. 245.
[438] *STB*, pp. 148-150.

Bibliography

Books

Aikman, David. 2003. *Jesus in Beijing: How Christianity is Transforming China and Changing the Global Balance of Power*. Washington D.C.: Regnery Publishing.

Arendt, Hannah. 2005. *Eichmann and the Holocaust*. London: Penguin Books.

Baldwin, Joyce C. 1978. *Daniel* (Tyndale Old Testament Commentaries). Leicester: InterVarsity Press.

Barclay, William. 1969. *The New Testament*, Vol. II. London: Collins.

Boda, Mark J. 2016. *The Book of Zechariah: The New International Commentary of the Old Testament*. Grand Rapids, MI: William B. Eerdmans.

Brown, Michael L. 2012. *The Real Kosher Jesus: Revealing the Mysteries of the Hidden Messiah*. Lake Mary, FL: FrontLine.

Calvin, John, trans. Henry Beveridge. 1962. *Institutes of the Christian Religion*. Cambridge: James Clark & Co.

Carlé, Graeme. 1998. *Because of the Angels (Unveiling 1 Corinthians 11:2-16)*. Auckland: Emmaus Road Publishing

- 2001. *The Red Heifer's Ashes (Mysteries of Ancient Israel)*. Auckland: Emmaus Road Publishing.

- 2011. *Dancing in the Dragon's Jaws (The Mystery of Israel's Survival)*. Auckland: Emmaus Road Publishing.

- 2012. *Slouching Towards Bethlehem (The Rise of the Antichrists)*. Auckland: Emmaus Road Publishing.

- 2014. *Gotta Serve Somebody (The Mystery of the Marks & 666)*. Auckland: Emmaus Road Publishing.

- 2015. *Eating Sacred Cows (A Closer Look at Tithing)* Revised ed. Auckland: Emmaus Road Publishing.

Cline, Eric. 2004. *Jerusalem Besieged: From Ancient Canaan to Modern Israel*. Anne Arbor, MI; University of Michigan Press.

Cross, Frank Moore. 1998. *From Epic to Canon: History and Literature in Ancient Israel.* Baltimore, MD; John Hopkins University Press.

diZerega, Gus, with Philip Johnson. 2008. *Beyond the Burning Times: A Pagan and Christian in Dialogue.* Oxford: Lion Books.

Drunen, David van. 2014. *Divine Covenants and Moral Order: A Biblical Theology of Natural Law.* Cambridge: Wm B. Eerdmans Publishing.

Fackenheim, Emil L. 1970. *God's Presence in History: Jewish Affirmations and Philosophical Reflections.* New York: Harper & Row.

Fee, Gordon D. with Douglas Stuart. 2002. *How to Read the Bible for All Its Worth.* Grand Rapids, MI: Zondervan.

Fensham, F. Charles. 1982. *The Books of Ezra and Nehemiah: The New International Commentary of the Old Testament.* Grand Rapids, MI: William B Eerdmans.

Flannery, Edward H. 1985. *The Anguish of the Jews: Twenty-Three Centuries of Antisemitism.* Mahweh, NJ: Paulist Press.

Glatzer, Nahum N. 1961. *Franz Rosenzweig: His Life and Thought.* New York: Schocken Books.

Greenberg, Irving. 1977. *Auschwitz: Beginning of a New Era? Reflections on the Holocaust,* ed. Eva Fleischner. New York: KTAV Publishing House, Inc.

Guy, Laurie. 2009. *Making Sense of the Book of Revelation.* Oxford: Regent's Park College.

Habermas, Jürgen. 2006. *Time of Transitions.* Cambridge: Polity Press.

Hendriksen, William. 1986. *More than Conquerors: An Interpretation of the Book of Revelation.* Grand Rapids, MI: Baker Book House.

Herman, Geoffrey. 2012. *A Prince Without a Kingdom: The Exilarch in the Sassanian Era.* Tubingen: Moir Sieback.

House, Paul R. 1995. *The New American Commentary, 1-2 Kings,* Vol 8. Nashville, TN: B & H Publishing Group.

Hubbard, David Allan. 1989. *Joel and Amos* (Tyndale Old Testament Commentary). Leicester: InterVarsity Press.

Hunt, Dave. 1993. *How Close Are We?* Eugene, OR: Harvest House Publishers.

Huxley, Aldous. 1941. *Ends and Means*. London: Chatto & Windus.

Jenkins, Jerry B., with Tim LaHaye. 1999. *Are We Living in the End Times?* Wheaton, IL: Tyndale House Publishers, Inc.

Jenkins, Jerry B., with Tim Lahaye. 1999. *Assassins (Assignment: Jerusalem, Target: Antichrist)*. Wheaton, IL: Tyndale.

-        1999. *Apollyon (The Destroyer is Unleashed)*. Wheaton, IL: Tyndale.

Johnson, Philip, with Gus diZerega. 2008. *Beyond the Burning Times: A Pagan and Christian in Dialogue*. Oxford: Lion Books.

Katz, Arthur. 2001. *Holocaust: Where was God?* 4th Edition. Singapore: Genesis One Media Pte Ltd.

Koester, Craig R. 2001. *Revelation and the End of All Things*. Grand Rapids, MI: Wm B. Eerdmans Publishing Co.

LaHaye, Tim, with Jerry B. Jenkins. 1999. *Are We Living in the End Times?* Wheaton, IL: Tyndale.

LaHaye, Tim, with Jerry B. Jenkins, 1999. *Assassins (Assignment: Jerusalem, Target: Antichrist)*. Wheaton, IL: Tyndale.

-        1999. Apollyon (The Destroyer is Unleashed). Wheaton, IL: Tyndale.

Landau, David, with Shimon Peres. 1998. *Ben-Gurion: A Political Life*. New York: Nextbook Press.

Long, V. Phillips, with Iain Provan & Tremper Longman III. 2003. *A Biblical History of Israel*. Louisville, KY: Westminster John Knox Press.

Longman, Tremper III, with V. Phillips Long & Iain Provan. 2003. *A Biblical History of Israel*. Louisville, KY: Westminster John Knox Press.

Maimonides, Moses, trans. Michael Friedlander. 2007. *The Guide for the Perplexed*. New York: Cosimo, Inc.

Peres, Shimon, with David Landau. 1998. *Ben-Gurion: A Political Life*. New York: Nextbook Press.

Pollard, Nigel. 2000. *Soldiers, Cities, and Civilians in Roman Syria*. Ann Arbor, MI: University of Michigan Press.

Provan, Iain, with V. Phillips Long & Tremper Longman III. 2003. *A Biblical History of Israel*. Louisville, KY: Westminster John Knox Press.

Robinson, Ian. 2016. *If Anyone Thirsts: Biblical Spirituality from the Desert*. Eugene, OR: Wipf and Stock Publishers.

Rohl, David. 2015. *Exodus: Myth or History?* St Louis Park, MN: Thinking Man Media.

Rubin, Martin. 1999. *Thrillers*. Cambridge: Cambridge University Press.

Sheiman, Bruce. 2009. *An Atheist Defends Religion: Why Humanity is Better Off with Religion than Without It*. Royersford, PA: Alpha Publishing.

Sophia Institute for Teachers. 2014. *The Seven Sacraments: The Foundation of Christian Living*, High School Edition. Bedford, NH: Sophia Institute Press.

Streissguth, Thomas. 2007. *The Roaring Twenties*. New York: Infobase Publishing.

Stuart, Douglas, with Gordon D. Fee. 2002. *How to Read the Bible for All Its Worth*. Grand Rapids, MI: Zondervan.

Luther, Martin. 1969. *Luther's Works*. Minneapolis; Fortress Press

Tenney, Merrill C. 1958. *Interpreting Revelation*. London: Pickering & Inglis Ltd.

Trench, R.C. 1890. *Notes on the Parables*. London: Kegan Paul, Trench, Trübner & Co.

Treves, Sir Frederick. 1913. *The Land Most Desolate*. London: Smith, Elder & Co.

Trim, D.J.B. 2010. *European Warfare, 1350–1750*. New York & Cambridge: Cambridge University Press.

Twain, Mark. 1869. *Innocents Abroad*. Hartford, CT: American Publishing Co.

van Drunen, David. 2014. *Divine Covenants and Moral Order: A Biblical Theology of Natural Law*. Cambridge: Wm B. Eerdmans Publishing.

Wiesel, Eliezer. 1968. *Legends of Our Time*. New York: Avon.

- 1982. *The Testament.* New York: Bantam Books
- 2006 *Night.* New York: Hill & Wang.

Wilcock, Michael. 1975. *The Message of Revelation.* Leicester, England: InterVarsity Press.

Wright, N.T. 1997. *Jesus and the Victory of God (Christian Origins and the Question of God*, Vol. 2). Minneapolis: Fortress Press.

- 2011. *Revelation for Everyone.* London: SPCK.

Zerega, Gus di, with Philip Johnson. 2008. *Beyond the Burning Times: A Pagan and Christian in Dialogue.* Oxford: Lion Books.

Zertal, Idith. 2005. *Israel's Holocaust and the Politics of Nationhood.* Cambridge: Cambridge University Press.

Books online

Aquinas, Thomas (1225 - 1274). *Summa Theologica.* www.ccel.org/ccel/aquinas/summa.html

Eusebius (c. 260 - c. 340 AD). *Church History.* www.ccel.org/ccel/schaff/npnf201.toc.html

Josephus, Flavius (37 - c. 100 AD). *Antiquities.* www.ccel.org/j/josephus/works/JOSEPHUS.HTM

Strabo (64 BC - c. 24 AD). *Geography.* http://penelope.uchicago.edu/Thayer/E/Roman/Texts/Strabo/home.html

The Jewish Encyclopedia, 1906. www.jewishencyclopedia.com

Twain, Mark. 1869. *Innocents Abroad.* www.gutenberg.org/files/3176/3176-h/3176-h.htm

Articles online

Ben Gurion, David - www.jta.org/1958/07/03/archive/ben-gurion-gives-his-own-definition-of-who-is-a-jew-draws-on-psalms

Book of Malachi - www.jewishencyclopedia.com/articles/10321-malachi-book-of

Exilarch - www.jewishencyclopedia.com/articles/5937-exilarch

Geering, Lloyd – www.abc.net.au/religion/stories/s1333339.htm

Habermas, Jürgen - http://plato.stanford.edu/entries/habermas/

Halachic State - www.jpost.com/Features/Religious-Affairs-

Whos-afraid-of-a-halachic-state
Libertine Police State - https://eppc.org/publications/the-libertine-police-state
Malaria - https://malariaworld.org/blog/enthusiasm-alone-was-insufficient-defeat-malaria-palestine-100-years-ago-it-required
Melchizedek - www.chabad.org/library/bible_cdo/aid/16331/jewish/Chapter-110.htm#showrashi=true&v=4
Melchizedek - www.cgg.org/index.cfm/fuseaction/Library.sr/CT/HWA/k/745/Mystery-Melchizedek-Solved.htm
Noahide Laws - www.jewishvirtuallibrary.org/jsource/Judaism/The_Seven_Noahide_Laws.html
Rabbis' statement re Jesus, 2015 –To Do the Will of Our Father in Heaven: Toward a Partnership between Jews and Christians. http://cjcuc.com/site/2015/12/03/orthodox-rabbinic-statement-on-christianity
Sheiman, Bruce - www.thechurchofnopeople.com/2010/02/atheist-interview-bruce-sheiman
Warren, Rick - www.christianpost.com/news/exclusive-rick-warren-flat-out-wrong-that-muslims-christians-view-god-the-same-70767/

Bible Translations

New American Standard (NASB), 1970. La Habra, CA: The Lockman Foundation.

New International Version (NIV), 1978. Grand Rapids, MI: Zondervan Bible Publishers.

New King James Version (NKJV), 1992. Nashville, TN: Thomas Nelson Publishers.

New Oxford Annotated Bible (New Revised Standard Version with the Apocrypha), Augmented 3rd Edition, 2001. New York: Oxford University Press.

New Revised Standard Version (NRSV), 1989. New York: American Bible Society.

The Hebrew Study Bible, 2003. Oxford & New York: Oxford University Press.

The Jewish Study Bible, feat. *The Jewish Publication Society's Tanakh Translation*. 2004. Oxford & New York: Oxford University Press.
The Message, 2004. Eugene H. Peterson. Colorado Springs, CO: NavPress.
The New Testament, 1969. William Barclay. London: Collins
Zondervan (NASB) Study Bible, 1999. Grand Rapids, MI: Zondervan.

Dictionaries & Encyclopaedia
Concise Oxford Dictionary. 1985. Oxford University Press.
NAS Exhaustive Concordance of the Bible. 1981. Nashville, TN: Holman.
The New Oxford Annotated Bible, Augmented Third Edition. 2001. New York: Oxford University Press.
Theological Dictionary of the New Testament, Kittel & Friedrich, abridged by Geoffrey Bromley, 1990. Grand Rapids, MI: William B. Eerdmans Publishing Co.
The Zondervan Pictorial Encyclopedia of the Bible, ed. Merrill C. Tenney. 1977. Grand Rapids, MI: Zondervan.
New Bible Commentary, Third Edition, ed. D Guthrie and J.A. Motyer. 1970. Leicester: Inter-Varsity Press.
Strong's Hebrew Dictionary of the Bible. 1890. New York: Abingdon Press.
The Expositor's Bible, ed. W. Robertson Nicoll. 1906. London: Hodder & Stoughton.
The Jewish Encyclopedia. 1906. New York: Funk & Wagnalls.

Newspapers & Magazines
American Political Science Review, Washington, D.C.
Christianity Today, Carol Stream, Illinois.
Houston Chronicle, Houston.
Jewish Telegraphic Agency, Jerusalem.
National Geographic, Washington, D.C.
New York Times, New York.
NZ Listener, Auclkand.

Playboy, Chicago.
The Australian, Surry Hills, NSW.
Time, New York.

Articles & Pamphlets
Herzl, Theodor. 1896. *Der Judenstaat* (The Jewish State).
Luther, Martin. 1520. *On the Babylonian Captivity of the Church*.
Wiesel, Eliezer. 1977. *Freedom of Conscience – A Jewish Commentary*, Journal of Ecumenical Studies 14 (Autumn): 643.
Israel Democracy Institute. 2009. *A Portrait of Israeli Jews - Beliefs, Observance, and Values*.

Miscellaneous
Anglican Resolution 43b, www.anglicancommunion.org/media/127743/1968.pdf
Catholic booklet on marriage - www.sydneycatholic.org/pdf/dmm-booklet_web.pdf
CBS *60-Minutes* interview by Mike Wallace, broadcast February 6, 1983.
Encyclopedia of Prostitution and Sex Work: A-N. Vol. 1, ed. Melissa Hope Ditmore. 2006. Santa Barbara, CA: ABC-Clio Greenwood.
Nostra Aetate (Latin, *In Our Time*), 1965. Second Vatican Council's Declaration on the Relation of the Church with Non-Christian Religions. www.vatican.va/archive/hist_councils/ii_vatican_council/documents/vat-ii_decl_19651028_nostra-aetate_en.html
The Way, movie produced and directed by Emilio Estevez. 2010, Filmax Entertainment, Icon Entertainment International, and Elixir Films, Spain and USA.
The Westminster Confession of Faith. 1981. Glasgow: F.P. Publications.

Websites accessed
www.kolhamevaser.com/2014/04/the-meaning-of-next-year-in-jerusalem
www.timesofisrael.com/netanyahu-jerusalem-only-ever-the-capital-of-the-jewish-people/
www.islamicparty.com/alaqsa/enter.htm
www.islamic-awareness.org/Quran/Contrad/MusTrad/sacrifice.html
www.jewishencyclopedia.com/articles/11124-moses-ben-maimon
www.ou.org/torah/parsha/rabbi-fox-on-parsha/parshat_vayikra_2/
www.torah.org/learning/mlife/LoRch1--3.html?print=1
www.jewishvirtuallibrary.org/jsource/Judaism/vegsacrifices.html
www.dailycatholic.org/issue/10Mar/030407sm.htm
www.lamblion.com/articles/articles_revelation11
www.apocalypsesoon.org/xfile-11.html
www.spiritandtruth.org/teaching/Book_of_Revelation/commentary/htm/03110301.htm
http://w2.vatican.va/content/pius-xii/en/encyclicals/documents/hf_p-xii_enc_11101954_ad-caeli-reginam.html
http://jabalallawz.weebly.com/uploads/2/1/0/4/21048306/chuck_whittaker_jabal_al_lawz.pdf
www.jewfaq.org/holidayc.htm
http://johnmarkhicks.com/2012/02/09/zechariah-41-14-two-olive-trees-and-the-oil-of-god/
http://cojs.org/was-there-a-seven-branched-lampstand-in-solomons-temple/
www.ccjr.us/dialogika-resources/documents-and-statements/roman-catholic/pope-john-paul-ii/297-jp2-80nov17
www.yadvashem.org/yv/en/remembrance/childrens_memorial.asp
www.pbs.org/newshour/bb/religion-jan-june00-apology_3-13/
www.adventist.org/fileadmin/adventist.org/files/articles/official-statements/28Beliefs-Web.pdf
https://rcg.org/articles/acfftoc.html
www.nytimes.com/2014/07/05/opinion/the-persecution-of-witches-21st-century-style.html?_r=0

www.dailymaverick.co.za/article/2012-05-30-witch-hunts-the-darkness-that-wont-go-away/#.WLOeG_mGN1t
www.cob-net.org/anabaptism.htm
www.banneroftruth.org/pages/articles/article_detail.php?457
www.merriam-webster.com/dictionary/moral%20law
www.un.org/en/members/growth.shtml
www.cgg.org/index.cfm/fuseaction/Library.sr/CT/HWA/k/745/Mystery-Melchizedek-Solved.htm
http://tabletmag.com/jewish-news-and-politics/81660/raw-deal
www.jta.org/1958/07/03/archive/ben-gurion-gives-his-own-definition-of-who-is-a-jew-draws-on-psalms
www.saveisrael.com/segal/segalmount.htm
http://dictionary.cambridge.org/dictionary/british/be-dancing-in-the-streets
http://dictionary.cambridge.org/dictionary/british/the-man-woman-person-in-on-the-street
http://plato.stanford.edu/entries/habermas/
http://kellogg.nd.edu/vfellowships/woodberry.shtml
https://eppc.org/publications/the-libertine-police-state
www.charismanews.com/opinion/49156-you-won-t-believe-how-many-christian-business-owners-are-under-lgbt-fir
www.sydneycatholic.org/pdf/dmm-booklet_web.pdf
www.bbc.com/news/world-us-canada-3896300
www.equip.org/articles/modern-israel-in-bible-prophecy-promised-return-or-impending-exile
www.scientificamerican.com/article/reclamation-of-man-made-desert/
www.israel21c.org/environment/top-10-ways-israel-fights-desertification/
www.jnf.org/work-we-do/our-projects/forestry-ecology/
www.mfa.gov.il/MFA/MFAArchive/2000-2009/2001/9/Flora%20and%20Fauna%20in%20Israel
http://en.idi.org.il/media/164429/guttmanavichaireport2012_engfinal.pdf
www.jewishvirtuallibrary.org/jsource/Judaism/jewpop.html
www.jewishjournal.com/judaismandscience/item/jewish_

atheism_and_jewish_theism_in_america
http://en.idi.org.il/media/164429/guttmanavichaireport2012_engfinal.pdf
http://cjcuc.com/site/2015/12/03/orthodox-rabbinic-statement-on-christianity
www.israeltoday.co.il/NewsItem/tabid/178/nid/28027/Default.aspx, 2 Jan, 2016
http://int.icej.org/history
www.arableagueonline.org/hello-world/#more-1
www.jewishvirtuallibrary.org/jsource/Judaism/The_Seven_Noahide_Laws.html
www.jewishvirtuallibrary.org/jsource/Judaism/tribes1.html, 30 Jun, 2015
www.jewishanswers.org/ask-the-rabbi-1586/cohen-levi-and-yisroel/?p=1586
http://biblehub.com/commentaries/titus/1-2.htm

Index

Numbers

7 significance of 59, 149
   being struck seven times 149
   seven eyes on stone 59, 63
   seven horns on the Lamb 63
   seven lamps 62
   seven Spirits of God 62-63, 77, 149
1,260 days (aka 42 months, 3½ years, "a time, times and half a time") 8, 11, 45, 84, 190, 192, 228, 307. See also 'times of the Gentiles'
7,000 89, 284-285, 302, 306

A

"A time, times and half a time" 8-10, 17, 73, 93, 221, 280 See also 'partial hardening of Israel' and 'times of the Gentiles'
Aaron 36, 88-89, 109, 213-214, 327-330, 336
Abdi-Heba, King of Uru-shalim 1
'Abomination of desolation',
   definition of 138
   first 153, 164
   fourth 177, 187, 328
   fifth 16, 328-330
   sixth 229
Abortion 106-107, 252, 254, 260-261, 264, 306
   U.N. debate 248, 254-255
Abraham 1, 6, 44, 66, 69, 72, 83, 93, 207
   and Melchizedek 211-215, 327
   and rich man 80, 86
   covenant of 91, 103, 142-143, 159, 171, 319-323, 331, 337
   descendants of 126, 131-132, 135, 193, 216, 307, 331
   land promise 323
   wives symbolising covenants 186, 221
Abyss, symbolic meaning of 219, 223
   the beast from 11, 217, 219-220, 223, 308
Adoni-Zedek 1, 213
Adultery 122-124, 139, 246, 251-252
   David's 154, 201
   decriminalising of 258
   definition of 315
Ahab, King of Israel 38, 41, 73-74, 78, 230
Ahaziah, King of Israel 74-75, 89-90
Aikman, David 242-243
Akhenaten, Pharaoh 1
Al-Aqsa Mosque 6
al-Buraq, Muhammad's steed 6
Alcohol 108-109, 127, 193
   intoxication 111-113, 255, 296-297
   symbolic meaning 296-298
"All the nations" 10, 64, 83, 92, 182, 224
   betraying Israel 293-297, 307
   blessed through Abraham 69, 320-321, 337
   blessed through Israel 64, 266, 269
   forgiven through Jesus 83,

195, 234, 275-276
Israel's captivity in 17, 34, 78, 144, 172, 177, 233-234, 265-266, 278, 280, 323
Israel's restoration from 266-269, 274-276
judging of 299-300, 302
American Political Science Review 243, 339-341
Amos, the prophet 140, 154-155, 172, 183, 194, 204, 206, 284, 305
Anabaptists 117
Antichrist, the man 8-9, 16, 34, 217, 223, 235, 328
Daniel's 70th Week 328-329
Islamic belief 6
Antichrist, the spirit of 36, 73, 220
1st Century 220, 223
20th Century 220-221, 223
21st Century 224
Catholicism 223-224, 250-251
Islam 224
Protestant nations 223-224, 250-251
Antiochus IV Epiphanes 161, 232
Anti-Semitism 8, 177-178, 180, 291, 293
Aphrodite, Corinthian Temple of 247
Aquinas, Thomas 26, 118, 121
Arendt, Hannah 168, 180
Ark of the Covenant 20, 67-68, 135, 145, 206, 210
Israel's misuse of 153-154
Assyrian Empire 130, 140, 151, 155, 172, 203-205, 231, 236, 284
Atonement, concept of 22-23, 101-102, 110, 193-196
Day of 4, 20-21, 115, 136

Maimonides on 21-24
means of 22-23, 89, 101-102, 125, 128, 133-137, 141, 145, 184, 190, 193-196, 303-304, 327, 330, 337
Augustus Caesar 220, 223
Augustine of Hippo 26, 320

B

Babylonian Empire 4, 156, 179, 205, 220, 235, 284
destruction of the First Temple 15, 24, 145, 191,
exile in 14-15, 92-93, 131, 139-146, 149, 151-152, 163, 172, 196, 204, 233, 266, 274, 296, 298, 323-324, 330
metaphorical Babylon the Great 309-310
return from 49, 54, 56, 60, 142, 232, 266, 276, 278-279, 296, 305
Bathsheba 154, 201
Baldwin, Joyce C. 95
'Banality of evil' 168
Bar Kokhba Revolt 227
Beast 10-11, 217-219, 235-237, 294, 309-310. See also Antichrist.
first (Rev 13:1) 10-11, 38-39, 219-221, 263
from the abyss 11-12, 39, 217-221, 308
image of 328-329
killing the witnesses 223-228, 234, 237, 276
living image of 220, 223, 236, 299, 310
mark of 10, 299
second (Rev 13:11) 38, 220

Beatles, the 256
Bede, the Venerable 26
Ben Gurion, David 224-227
Benedict XVI, Pope 291
Benvenisti, Meron 3, 6
Bestiality 123, 244, 246, 251
Bethel 141
Bethlehem 201, 271, 293
Brown, Helen Gurley 254
Brown, Michael L. 287

C

Caesar 220
Caesarea Maritima 220, 272
Caesarea Philippi 220
Canaanites in Jerusalem 1-2, 212
    sexual mores of 123, 246-247, 253, 264
Calvin, John 118, 121, 173
Calvinism 250
Carmino de Santiago 114
Center for Jewish-Christian Understanding and Cooperation 288, 292
Chinese Academy of Social Sciences 242
Christianity Today 243, 340-341
Chronicles, Book of 35-36, 40, 75, 148, 157, 194
Circumcision 98, 108, 142
Civil Rights Movement 255
Cline, Eric H. 2-3, 6
Cohen, Leonard 201
Cohen, significance of 329-330
Conscience 113, 117, 120-121, 134, 182, 225, 342
    calling to be 251
    value in liberal democracy 240-241, 342

Constantine, Emperor 42,
Corinthian Temple of Aphrodite 247
Counter-Culture, the 255
Covenants
    Abrahamic 91-92, 103, 142-143, 319-322, 331, 337
    Adamic 312-314, 336
    breaking of 89-98, 148-165, 312-314
    Davidic 11, 198, 201-202, 207, 210, 212, 216, 307, 325-326, 330-331, 338
    Dual Covenant Theology 100-104
    enforcers of 72-75, 85, 90-91, 151
    'everlasting' 155, 198, 210, 216, 291, 312-335, 338
    Israel as a nation 130-132, 143-145, 147-165, 265-276, 278-285, 288-289, 303-306
    Jacob and Laban's 67
    Levitical 325-331, 337-338
    Marriage 314-316, 336
    Mosaic 21, 24, 42, 66, 72, 77, 85, 91-92, 99-100, 109-165, 186-188, 193-198, 214-215, 221-222, 241, 291, 303-305, 319-320, 322-325, 337
    New 24, 79, 98-99, 105-106, 109-141, 146, 186-188, 193-198, 209, 214-215, 221-222, 241-242, 258, 267-270, 274-275, 304, 328, 331-333, 338
    Noahic/Noahide 289-290, 316-319, 336
    prophets as enforcers 72-75, 90-91, 151
    renewing the Mosaic 231-232,

236
'suspending the Law' 166-178, 306, 308
'vengeance for…' 90-98, 103, 178-179
wrongly renewing the Mosaic 250-252, 258
Crown of Joshua 54-56
of Messiah 204-205
of twelve stars 33
triregnum Papal 224
Crusaders 234
death toll 5
'Cup of reeling' 294, 296-299
Curse, Adamic 311-314, 336
Curse of the Law 37, 72-73, 97-98, 115, 142, 144, 147-159, 163-165, 194-195, 197, 304-305
escaping 98-100, 303-304
Holocaust 175-177
Kellogg's recognition 160-163
Malachi's 159-160
Modern denial of 166-170, 180, 194
Twain's recognition 271
Cursing 38

D

Daniel, the Book
Chap 1 141
Chap 2 96, 220
Chap 7 8-9, 36, 96, 219-220, 235, 278
Chap 9 3, 8-9, 95-97, 141, 150-152, 183, 194, 328
Chap 12 8-9, 34
defence of 96
Jesus' citing 94-97
Daniel, the prophet 44, 96-97, 139, 148, 150-152, 159, 164,

183, 197, 236, 305
70th Week of 8-10, 17, 192, 328
David, king, psalmist, and prophet 1, 54, 148, 154, 198-216, 260-261, 304-305
branch of 51-52
capture of Zion 1, 198, 208-210, 215-216, 291, 307, 338
confirmed by fire 36
covenant of 11, 198, 201-210, 294, 330-331, 338
dynastic endurance 202-205, 294-296, 299, 307, 325
historicity of 198-201
Messianic prophecies of 18-19, 68, 83, 198-199, 211-212, 215-216, 238-239
recognising the curse 154, 164, 197
Son of 18-19, 56, 140, 194, 205-207, 211-212, 216, 238-239, 280, 296, 307, 325-326
tabernacle of 11, 140, 206-207
Day of Atonement 4, 20-21, 115, 136
Dayan, Moshe 17, 227-228
'Days of vengeance' 94-97, 103, 305
Dea Roma et Augustus, worship of 220, 223
Death penalty, purpose of 118 today 251-252, 260-261
Death toll of Crusades 5
of emperor-worship 178
Decriminalising immorality 250-252, 258
Deuteronomy, Book of 169-170
curse of the Law 72, 148, 150, 156, 164, 178, 195, 305

occult practices 116
tithing 160
Devil, the 300, 310. See also
 Dragon and Satan.
Dinur, Yehiel 167
Diocletian, Emperor 223
Divorce 99, 121, 315-316
 God's, of Israel 131
 Rabbis control of 224-225
Dome of the Rock 6
Dragon 8, 33, 38, 309-310. See also
 Devil and Satan
 attacks on Israel 8, 93, 168-169, 176, 294
 manifesting in Gentile empires 34, 176, 293-294
Drought, as covenant curse 150, 164, 197
 Elijah's as type 9, 37-38, 73, 228, 280-282, 301
 Elijah's literal 41, 73-75, 228, 280, 301
Drunkenness 125, 127
 as metaphor 296-298
 Noah's 121
Dual Covenant Theology 100-103
Dylan, Bob 256

E

Edom, copper mines of 200-201
Egypt 1, 42, 72, 92-93, 179, 230, 298
 as metaphor 29-30, 185, 188-190, 195
 plagues of 38, 41
 sexual mores of 123, 246, 253, 264
Eichmann, Adolf 167-168
Eli, the High Priest 152-154
Elijah, the man 8, 26-28, 52, 185, 192, 217, 235, 325
 confirmed with fire 88-90, 103
 covenant enforcer 72-75, 78, 94
 links with Moses 36-46, 84-86, 160
 literal drought of 9, 73-74, 181, 228, 280, 301
 metaphorical drought of 9, 181, 228, 280-282, 301
 mystery of 8-9, 17, 35, 75, 93, 160, 280-285
 restorer of Israel 74-75, 78, 93, 280-285, 301-302
 vindication of 276-278, 280-285, 295, 301-302, 308
Elisha 38, 41, 44
Emden, Rabbi Jacob 289
Emmaus Bible-study 81-82
Emperor-worship 178, 328
Enoch 26-27, 35-36, 39-40, 66
Esther, Queen 277
Exilarch, the 56, 205
Exodus, the 34, 68, 72, 131, 323
 date of 74, 325
 Jesus' exodus 44-45
Ezekiel, the prophet 14-15, 183
 prophecies of 93, 171-172, 204-205, 210, 266-270, 274-275, 332
 the Temple of 14-16, 24, 191
Ezra, the scribe 21, 56-57, 113, 148, 157, 164, 183, 194, 305
 Book of 35, 53
 renewing the covenant 232

F

Fackenheim, Emil L. 169, 173, 175-176
Fee, Gordon 72
Feminism 255
Festivals 83, 108-110, 114-115, 127, 193, 322, 337
   Atonement 4, 20-21, 115, 136
   First Fruits 42
   Giving of the Torah 42
   Passover 4, 31, 42, 83, 189, 280, 286
   Pentecost (or Weeks) 36, 42-43, 62, 68, 74, 115
   Tabernacles 115, 160
Finkelstein, Israel 199-200
Fire 12, 26, 39, 41-43, 84-85, 88-90, 103, 117, 177, 192
   counterfeit spirit 36, 74
   lampstand 62-63, 77-79
   symbol of judgment 12, 36-38, 45, 74-75, 84, 88-90, 103, 125, 192
   symbol of the Holy Spirit 36, 41-43, 45, 62-63, 74-75, 84-85
   symbol of the Word of God 78-79, 192
Flannery, Edward H. 5
Food laws 110, 124, 225, 322
Foreshadowing, by twelve stones 43
   of Elijah's mystery 73, 301
   of Messiah 55, 133, 214
   of New Jerusalem 216
   of Israel's revival 293, 301
Fornication 124, 246
   decriminalising of 258
   definition of 124, 315
'Forty-two months' 8, 11-12, 17, 25, 191, 300. See also 1,260 days.
   metaphorical meaning of 17, 191, 300-301
Fraud 125, 127
Free Love Movement 254
Friedman, Betty 255

G

Gabriel, the archangel 95-97, 285
Garfinkel, Yosef 200
Geering, Sir Lloyd 262
Gentiles 5, 60, 69, 93-94, 100, 105, 110-111, 148, 178, 206-207, 213, 219, 224, 265, 289-290, 299-301, 306
   Abrahamic Covenant 319-323, 337
   Adamic Covenant 312-314, 336
   anti-Semitism 8, 177-178, 180, 291, 293
   circumcising of 102, 140, 206-207
   conscience of 120, 182
   Court of the 16, 296
   Davidic Covenant 330-331, 338
   'fullness of...' 233-234, 275
   in Israel's land 162, 172, 214-215, 221, 230, 296, 301-302
   Noahic Covenant 289, 316-318, 336
   proselytes 105, 131
   rejection of Mosaic revelation 238-264, 279
   ruling Jerusalem 16-17
   'times of the...' 8-11, 17, 25, 34, 45, 93, 144-145, 172, 181,

190-191, 228, 237, 265-266, 281, 303, 307
Germany 5, 220, 223
Gilgal 141
Giving 108, 115-116
God-emperors of 20th Century 178-179
   Hirohito 94, 178-179, 220, 223
   Hitler 94, 178-179, 220, 223, 234
   Mussolini 94, 178-179, 220, 223
   Stalin 94, 178-179, 220, 223
Gomorrah 37, 125, 155, 189, 283
   as metaphor 185, 188
Greed 125, 242
Greenberg, Irving 170
Gregory the Great 26
Glatzer, Nahum N. 100
Gurley Brown, Helen 254
Guy, Laurie 30, 186, 218

H

Habermas, Jürgen 241
Hadiths regarding Jerusalem 6
Hadrian, Emperor 176, 227
Hagar, Sarah's maid 186, 221
   symbolising the Mosaic Covenant 186, 221-222
Haggai, the prophet 49, 56-57, 63, 65
Hardening, partial, of Israel 8, 35, 233-234, 275, 301
Halevi, Yehudah 290
Harvest, as metaphor 281-282, 301
HaShem, Heb. 'The Name' 290
Hays, William H. 259
Hays Code 257, 259
Hebrew Bible, composition 35-36,
40, 71
Hefner, Hugh 254
Helena, mother of Constantine 42
Hendriksen, William 218-219
Hermeneutics 30-32, 265
Herod's Temple 15, 21, 138
Herzl, Theodor 224
Hezekiah, King of Judah 131, 183, 231
Hezekiah ben David, the Exilarch 205
Hicks, John Mark 58
Hippolytus 26
Hirohito, Emperor of Japan 94, 178-179, 220, 223
Hitler, Adolf 94, 178-179, 220, 223, 234
Holocaust, the 101, 163, 166-172, 175-180, 293
Holocaust Museum 100, 274
Holy, definition of 3-4. See Sanctification.
'Holy of holies' 20-21, 133-136
Homosexuality 123, 246, 251, 257
   decriminalising of 258
Hosea, the prophet 194, 203
   prophecies of 140-141, 172, 205, 312
Huldah 148, 155-156, 164, 194, 305
Huxley, Aldous 245, 263

I

'Image of the beast', definition of 236
Incest 123, 125, 244, 246, 251
International Christian Embassy in Jerusalem (ICEJ) 291-292
Internet, birth of 256
   effect on pornography 257

Intoxication, forbidding of 107,
111-113, 297
  normalising of 255
Inquisition, the 117, 293
Irenaeus 26
Isaiah, the prophet 44, 148, 154-155, 183, 194, 305
  Messianic prophecies of 51-53, 62, 83, 141, 205-206
  other prophecies 60, 95, 101, 172, 179, 185, 188, 210, 273-274, 284, 296-298, 313
Israel Democracy Institute 286

J

Jacob, the patriarch 9, 123, 183, 330, 337
  covenant with God 91, 103, 143, 171, 319-321, 323
  covenant with Laban 66-67
  descendants of 43, 72, 103, 126, 131-132, 135, 216, 307, 323, 331
  nation of 202, 204, 206, 326
James, the Lord's brother 98, 174-175, 281
  Elijah's drought 9, 301
  Jerusalem council 70, 102, 108, 140, 196, 206-207
Jeconiah, King of Judah 56
Jehoiachin, King of Judah 204-205
Jehoiada, the High Priest 231
Jenkins, Jerry 27, 217
Jeroboam, King of Israel 73, 203
Jerusalem
  'above' 186, 209, 221-222
  Christian claims to 5
  'cup of reeling' 294, 296-299, 302
  emperor-worship in 328-329

  'heavy stone' 299-302
  meaning of name 1, 212
  Melchizedek, King of 19, 198, 212-215
  metaphor for 'heathen nations' 28-30, 185-186
  metaphor for Jews against Jesus 186-188, 195, 221-222
  metaphorical names for 185-190, 195
  Muslim claims to 4-6
  New 214, 221, 307, 310
  'present Jerusalem' 186-190, 195, 209, 221-222, 229, 282
  refs in Hebrew Bible 4
  refs in New Testament 5
  refs in Qur'an 6
  sanctified by David 198, 203, 208-210, 216, 300-301, 307, 338
  status as key to times 17, 25, 93-96, 144-145, 171-172, 191, 228-229, 234, 237-238, 276-277, 294-303, 305-308
Jezebel 38, 41, 73-74, 78, 230
Job, the patriarch 13, 54, 175
John Paul II, Pope 100, 291
John the Baptist 37
  fulfilling Elijah's coming 41, 281
  Nazarite 112
Jonah's resurrection 83
Joseph, son of Jacob 183, 230
Josephus 174, 177, 294
Joshua, son of Nun 66, 130, 158, 213
Joshua, the High Priest 49-51, 54-56, 63-64
Josiah, King of Judah 148, 155-156, 194, 197, 231

K

Katz, Arthur 166-169, 180
Kellogg, Samuel H. 160-165
Kim Il Sung 179, 220, 223
King, Martin Luther Jr. 255
Kingdom of God 77, 79, 96, 119-120, 124-125, 130-131, 133, 148, 208, 234, 247
    liberal democracy 240-243, 338-342
Koester, Craig 29-30, 185
Korn, Rabbi Eugene 292-293
Kremlin, the 208

L

LaHaye, Tim 27, 217
Lambeth Conference (1968) 262
Lamech 120-121
Lament of Jesus 187-188
Lamentations of Jeremiah 156
Lampstand, shape of 57-59
    symbol of church 28, 59-60, 76-78
    symbol of Israel 60-61, 64, 76-78
    symbol of witness 26, 47-49, 78-79
Lazarus 79-80, 86
Lazarus, David 288-293
Left Behind series 27
Levitical priesthood 15, 21-23, 48-55, 60, 89, 109, 112, 122, 127, 133, 139-142, 152, 159, 212-216, 224, 297, 325-330, 337-338
Leviticus, Book of 73, 98, 123-124, 169-170

'curse of the Law' 73, 91, 97-98, 148-165, 169, 178, 195-197, 278, 305
    Daniel citing 95-97, 150-152, 328
    Jeremiah citing 324, 327-329
    Jesus citing 94-95, 122-124, 187, 246-247, 305
    Kellogg's commentary 160-163
    'making desolate' 90-91, 96, 143, 150, 171, 305
    restoration promises 73, 91, 93, 143-145, 171-172, 265-266, 276, 278, 305-306, 323-324
    sexual immorality 123-124, 246-247
    Treve's citing 162, 271-272
    Twain's citing 162, 270-271
    vengeance 90-97, 103, 178-179, 305
    Zechariah citing 233
Levy, Thomas 200
LGBTI activism 249
Liberal democracy 253, 263
    Christian role in 240-241, 250-252, 339-342
    definition of 240
    essential elements of 240-241
Long, V. Phillips 78
Longman, Tremper, III 78
Los Angeles, original name of 33
Lubavitcher Rebbe 227
Luther, Martin 31, 309
Lying 125, 127, 193

M

Maccabee, Judas 232
Maccabees, Book of 57, 232

Mahdi, the 6
Maimon, Rabbi Judah L. 225
Maimonides, Moses 22-24, 290
Malachi, the prophet 148, 164, 194, 197, 305
  Book of 28, 36, 40, 75, 280, 285
  curse of 159-160
Mao Zedong 94, 179, 220, 223
Martyr, definition of 66
Mary, mother of Jesus 8, 33
Mazar, Eilat 200
Mass, the 31
Melchizedek, King 1, 211-216
  priesthood of 11, 19, 110, 198, 211-216, 307, 327, 338
Menorah, the 57-61
Mercy seat, the 136
'Messiah the Prince' 9, 328
Mordecai 183, 277
Moriah, Mt 1, 6
Moses, the Law-giver 67-70, 72, 91-92, 102, 161, 217, 231, 322-325
  death of 39-40, 43-44, 65, 76
  defining sexual immorality 244-247
  defining value of life 260-261
  founder of liberal democracy 240-243, 250-252
  Jerusalem 209, 215
  links with Elijah 36-46, 84-86, 160
  miracles of 36-40, 75, 189
  opponents of 88-89
  Pentecost, Day of 74
  personification of the Law 70-71, 76, 78-80, 102-103, 186, 191-192, 222, 307
  predicting the Holocaust 169-172, 175-178
  returning from the dead 27-28, 185, 235
  Tabernacle of 57, 59-60, 68, 85, 113, 133-135, 137-139, 141, 194, 322-323, 337
  testifying to Jesus as Messiah 81-84, 192, 232, 293, 295
  Transfiguration 44-45, 52, 76
  vindication of 276-278
Moses Maimonides 22-24, 290
Mother Theresa 251
Motion Picture Production Code (MPMC) 257-259
Mt Horeb 40, 42, 45, 75, 85, 160
Mt Moriah 1, 6
Mt Nebo 44
Mt Sinai 42, 45, 78, 92, 231, 282, 324
  location of 42
  symbolism of 186-187, 221-222
Mt Zion 208-209
Muhammad 5-6, 114
Muslim claim on Temple Mount 4-6, 197, 230
Mussolini, Benito 178-179, 194, 220, 223
Mystery, definition of 8
  of "a time, times and half a time" 9-10
  of 'Babylon the Great' 310
  of 'Christ and the church' 316
  of Elijah 9, 37, 228
  of 'the partial hardening of Israel' 233-234, 275,
  of "the times of the Gentiles" 9, 228

N

Nakbar, the 297
Narcotics 109, 111
Nazirite vow 112
Nebuchadnezzar 149, 152, 161
Nehemiah, the governor 16, 35, 147-148, 157-158, 183, 194, 197, 232, 279, 305
Netanyahu, Benjamin 5
New Zealand 172, 261-262, 297-300, 317, 342
Noah, the patriarch 66, 121
  covenant of 261, 289-290, 316-319, 336

O

Occultism 116
Olive branches 61, 275
  oil as symbol 60-61
  tree as symbol 26, 47-56, 63-65, 75-76, 86, 282
Origins of Totalitarianism 168
Orthodox Jews 224-228, 288-293, 329

P

Partial hardening of Israel 8, 35, 233-234, 275, 301
Pascal, Blaise 117, 313
Passover, Festival of 4, 31, 42, 83, 189, 280, 286
Paul, the apostle 13, 27, 53, 60-61, 72, 78, 84, 174-175, 182, 266
  circumcision 108, 207
  conscience 113, 120, 240-241
  continuity of the Law 97-100, 132-135, 148, 186, 189, 196, 221-223, 304
  death's purpose 175, 312-314
  defining sanctification 3-4
  festivals 31, 114, 136, 189
  food laws 111, 322
  free will 116
  freedom from the Law 186, 189, 221-223, 244, 304
  generosity 116
  Israel 8, 92-93, 233-234, 275, 308, 320-321
  keeping Nazirite vow 112
  Noahic Covenant 317
  personifying Scriptures 68-70, 86
  sexual morality 124-127, 247
  the Sabbath 115, 122
Pella in Perea 33
Pentecost, Day of 36, 42, 62, 68, 74, 115
Peres, Shimon 225, 232
Pergamum 59, 220
Personification of Scriptures 69-70
Pesach 4. See Passover
Peter, the apostle 18, 20, 24, 31, 44, 68-69, 76, 86, 107, 174, 207, 260, 275, 327, 335
  confusion over circumcision 108
  morality 107, 125, 242, 262
  priesthood of all believers 18-21, 110, 191, 198, 215, 327
  revelation regarding food 110-111
  Scriptures 78
  similarity to Zechariah 52-53
Phillips, Jack, baker 249
Pilgrims, the 240, 243
Pilgrimages 113-114
Plagues, as curse 84, 103, 150, 164, 197

Egyptian 38, 41, 189
Playboy magazine 254, 257
Priesthood
    all believers 18, 20-21, 24, 60-61, 77, 109-110, 130, 145, 148, 191, 215-216, 303, 327
    Anglican 109-110
    Catholic 31, 109-110, 259
    Eastern Orthodox 109-110
    garments of 50, 109-110, 193
    High Priest 136, 152, 155, 164, 193-194, 214-216, 231, 307, 326
    of Levi 15, 21-23, 48-55, 60, 89, 109, 112, 122, 127, 133, 139-142, 152, 159, 212-216, 224, 297, 325-330, 337-338
    Melchizedek's 11, 19, 110, 198, 211-216, 303, 307, 327, 337-338
    Messiah's 18-19, 56, 214, 307, 328, 337-338
    Phinehas's 336
    Zadok's 15
Pogroms 161, 163
Polygamy 123
Popes, Roman Catholic
    Benedict XVI 291
    Gregory the Great 26
    John Paul II 100, 291
    Paul VI 224, 253, 291, 320
    Pius XII 33, 256
    Urban II 5
Pornography 257, 259
    Golden Age of 257
    Movie code 257
Prostitution, sacral 123, 246-247
    today 244
Protestants 31, 33, 117, 119, 224, 243, 250, 259, 286-287, 291

belief in God 286
colonial missionaries 341
'Conversionary' 339-342
executing heretics 117, 250-251
Fulfillment Theology 320
Replacement Theology 320
role in Hays Code 259
Supercessionism 320
under Revelation 13's first beast 223-224, 250-251
Provan, Iain 78

Q

Qur'an references 6

R

Rains, as testimony 182
    Israel's 281
Rape, heterosexual 123, 150, 157, 164, 193, 251, 253, 264
    homosexual 123, 264
Reformers' beliefs re baptism 117
    executing for heresy 117
Rehoboam, King of Israel 203
Religious Freedom Acts (RFRAs) 249
Remarriage 99, 121
Repetition, meaning of 59
Revelation, general 181-183
    special 7, 8, 81, 88, 107, 108, 111, 167, 176, 181-183, 212, 240, 267, 303
Roman Catholic Church [N.B. see *Slouching Towards Bethlehem* for radical improvements since Vatican II (1962-1965)]

apology for anti-Semitism
  101, 291-293
belief in God 286
bread and wine 31
church traditions 287
colonial missionaries 341
executing heretics 117, 250-251
Fulfillment Theology 320
Mary, mother of Jesus 33
pilgrimages 114
Replacement Theology 320
role in Hays Code 259
same-sex marriage 249-250
Supercessionism 320
the Sabbath 119
under Revelation 13's first beast 223-224, 250-251
Roman emperors
  Augustus 220, 223
  Constantine 42
  Diocletian 223
  Hadrian 176, 227
  Titus 57, 96, 133, 176, 300, 328
Rumkowski, Chaim 168
Russia 223
  pogroms 161
  Revolution 253

S

Sabbath-keeping
  as mandatory 121-122, 142, 225, 251-252
  as type 121-122
Sabbath years 267
Sackcloth 181, 183, 190
Samuel, the prophet 112, 153, 194, 305
  Books of 35
Sanctification, definition of 3-4.

See Holy.
re-sanctifying Jerusalem 296, 301
Santiago de Compostela 114
Sarah, wife of Abraham 66, 186
  symbolising New Covenant 186, 221-222
Sarid, Yossi 226
Satan, enemy of God 93, 133, 176-177, 180, 310
Scientific American, magazine 273
Secularism, definition of 239-240
  ascent of 238-239, 253-254, 306
  congruent values 244, 264
  heresy of 240, 243-245, 263
  hijacking the Revolution 253-258, 264
  Israel's 224-227, 234, 308
  redefining the value of life 244, 260-261, 264
  sexual mores of 244-246, 264
  theological success 261-264
  use of the Lord's name 244, 258-260, 264
Sedley, Rabbi David 329-330
Septuagint reference 136
'Serpent of old', metaphor for the Devil & Satan 310
Servetus, Michael 117
'Seven times', meaning of 149
Seventh Day Adventists 108
Sexual immorality, definition 122-125
  differing penalties for 251-252
Sheiman, Bruce 241
Shiloh 113, 138-139, 153-154, 210
"Signs of the times" 308
Silberman, Neil 199-200
Six Day War 10, 17, 228, 306
Smyrna 59

Sodom 37, 125, 283
  as type 29-30, 188-190, 195
Solomon, King 9, 54, 68, 74, 158, 203, 325
  Temple of 15, 21, 36, 58-59
Stalin, Joseph 94, 178-179, 220, 223
Stills, Stephen 252
Stuart, Douglas 72

T

Tabernacle, heavenly 20-21, 137, 323, 328
  David's 11, 140, 204, 206-207
  Moses' 57, 59-60, 68, 85, 113, 133-135, 137-139, 141, 194, 322-323, 337
Tabernacles, Feast of 115, 160
Tacitus, Cornelius 294
Tanakh 40, 83, 325
  meaning 36, 71
Temple, First 4, 9, 19, 21, 36, 54, 58-59, 135-141, 145-146, 193, 196, 201-202, 206, 330, 337
  Jesus as Temple 328
  Second 15-16, 21, 23-24, 49-50, 53, 55-57, 60-61, 63-64, 95, 112-113, 133-142, 145-146, 176-177, 187, 193-194, 232, 294, 304-305, 325, 328
  'spiritual house' 18-24, 55, 145, 191, 282, 303
  Third 14-17, 24, 34, 227
Temple Mount, the 1-3, 5-6, 10, 17, 216, 222, 227-230, 237, 300, 329
Tenney, Merrill C. 14, 27
Tertullian 26
The Libertine Police State, article 248

The Way, movie 114
Theft 124-125, 127, 193, 242, 244, 246, 264, 289, 318
Time, magazine 242, 257, 261, 287
'Times of the Gentiles' 8-9, 17, 34-35, 45, 93, 144-145, 172, 181, 190-191, 216, 221, 228, 234, 237, 265-266, 275, 301, 303
  metaphorical meaning of 25, 35, 45, 93, 181, 221, 307
Tithing 115-116, 160
Titus, Roman general and Emperor 57, 96, 133, 176, 300, 328
Tobacco 108, 111
Totalitarianism 168
Trans-substantiation, doctrine of 31
Trench, Archbishop R.C. 265
Treve, Sir Frederick 162, 271-272
Trim, D.J.B. 250-251
Twain, Mark 162, 270-271, 341
Twelve, significance of 43
Tyndale, William 136

U

Unleavened Bread, Feast of 115
Urim and Thummim 326

V

Vatican Council, the Second (1962-1965) 224, 291
Vengeance, definition 91, 97, 103
  'days of' 94-97, 305-306
  'for the covenant' 90-97, 103, 178-179, 305
  'sword of' 94, 178-179

W

Warren, Rick 252
Weigel, George 248
Wiesel, Elie 166, 169-170, 180
Westminster Confession of Faith, the 119, 121, 128
White House, the 208
Wilberforce, William 251, 318
Wilcock, Michael 29, 185, 219, 235
'Wilderness of the nations' 265
Witch-hunts 117
Woodberry, Robert 243, 339-342
Woodstock, the festival 256
Wright, N. T. 11, 29, 32, 185, 218, 235, 283

Y

Yad Vashem 101, 171, 274
Yom Kippur 4, 22, 136

Z

Zechariah, the Book of
    Chap 1 16, 49, 52-53
    Chap 2 16, 191
    Chap 3 47-52, 64
    Chap 4 47-50, 53-54, 58, 63-64, 76, 205
    Chap 6 18-19, 49, 55,
    Chap 7 52, 141, 233
    Chap 9 49, 208
    Chap 12 293-296, 299-302, 307
    Chap 14 114
Zechariah, the prophet 14, 16, 24, 47-65, 76, 86, 191
Zedekiah, King of Judah 204
Zerubbabel, the governor 49-50, 53-56, 63-64, 205
Zion, Mt 1, 3-6, 52, 156, 179, 209-211, 215, 297, 300
    literal meaning 208
    metaphorical meaning 208-209
Zionism 172, 224, 297-298
Zwingli 31

Other books by Graeme Carlé

Because of the Angels
(Unveiling 1 Corinthians 11:2-16)
This text has been largely lost to today's church because we have badly misunderstood some of Paul's Hebrew presuppositions regarding 'head', 'covering', the fall of Satan and spiritual warfare. Liberating for men and women of God as it restores much needed revelation on gender differences and relationships as well as the mystery of the Nazarite vow.

The Red Heifer's Ashes
(Mysteries of Ancient Israel)
Considered by Orthodox rabbis to be the greatest mystery of the Law of Moses, this is an astonishing revelation of Messiah. Every detail is gently unfolded as the reader today follows a supernatural path through the whole of the Old Testament, just as the two disciples did on the road to Emmaus.

Born of the Spirit
(A study guide for new believers)
This interactive Bible study is for all who want to develop their personal spirituality by checking the foundations of what Jude the Lord's youngest brother called 'the faith which was once for all delivered to the saints' (Jude 3). Avoiding all denominational allegiances, find out for yourself how God wants us to love, live and learn.

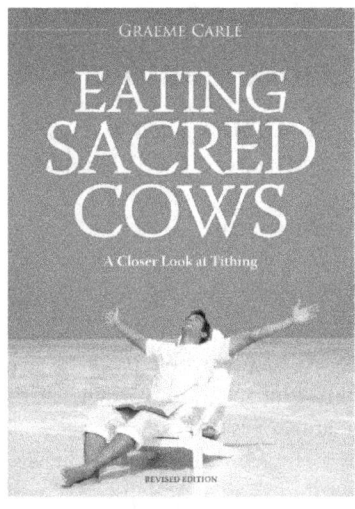

Eating Sacred Cows
A Closer Look at Tithing

Graeme Carlé

To tithe or not to tithe?
Tithing is one of the most misunderstood and abused aspects of modern day religion, and there are fine Christian leaders on both sides of the issue. Images of tele-evangelists and pastors living extravagant lifestyles can fuel resentment and mockery, but the defence is often that God's 'prosperity' ideal is being upheld (at least for the receiver of tithes).

But what of the givers?

Many Christians testify how God has blessed them for tithing, but many others are disappointed, often too ashamed to speak openly in case they are 'letting God down'. Sermons on tithing almost always quote Malachi's rebuke of ancient Israel, "You are cursed for you are robbing God! Bring the whole tithe into the storehouse…" (Malachi 3:8–9). But what exactly did Malachi mean? Doesn't God still want us to tithe? Well, not in the way we are usually taught today.

Citing Biblical texts about tithing that are rarely, if ever, referred to by those teaching tithing to fund the church, Graeme Carlé shows instead how God wants us to receive a revelation of His goodness as we take time off to enjoy annual holidays. He also wants us to be generous, giving freely to those in need rather than tying up our resources in unnecessary church assets. Find out for yourself how to stand firm in your freedom and enjoy being generous!

This newly revised version expands the original by 50%.

Available from
Emmaus Road Publishing
PO Box 38 823 Howick, Auckland 2014 New Zealand
www.emmausroad.org.nz

ISBN 978-0-9941058-1-3

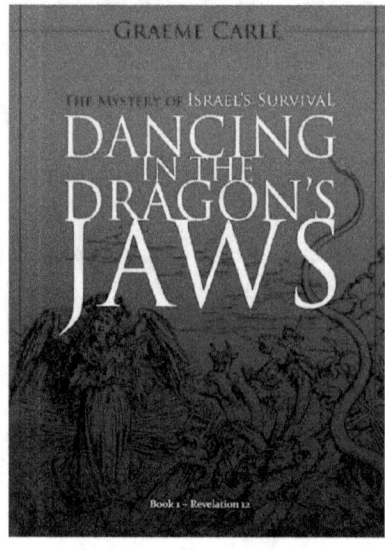

Book 1 in the Revelation series

Dancing in the Dragon's Jaws
The Mystery of Israel's Survival

Graeme Carlé

Why is the Book of Revelation so misunderstood?
　　Wasn't its whole point to give revelation? Well, in typically Jewish manner, yes and no.
　　The Book of Revelation was written as an apocalypse, a Jewish literary genre which also includes the extraordinary Books of Daniel and Zechariah. Profound truths were concealed from outsiders and opponents using elaborate symbolism, to be understood only by those properly taught – as Jesus explains in Matthew 13:10-13.

　　The apostle John's original 1st Century audience, having been led by Jewish Christians, would have readily understood his imagery from Jewish history. His plagues echo the ten plagues of Israel's exodus; his seven trumpets resonate of the Old Testament battle for Jericho.

　　Many think the keys to unlocking the Book of Revelation are lost. Not so. We still have Old Testament history and, for those who know where to look, full explanations of its symbols in the New Testament. What we need is the humility to learn from the 1st Century Jewish believers the mysteries of the woman, the Messiah, the dragon, the comings of Elijah, and 'the times of the Gentiles'. From these we can understand God's continuing purpose for Israel.

Available from
Emmaus Road Publishing
PO Box 38 823 Howick, Auckland 2014 New Zealand
www.emmausroad.org.nz

ISBN 978-09582746-5-4

Book 2 in the Revelation series

Slouching Towards Bethlehem
The Rise of the Antichrists

Graeme Carlé

The Lost Keys of Revelation?
It is often thought today that the keys to understanding the Book of Revelation have been lost and are irretrievable – but they're not.

They were just buried under centuries of rubble created by the Gentile church's foolish attempts to distance itself from its Jewish foundations. If, like any archaeologist, we dig carefully we can rediscover them.

In *Dancing in the Dragon's Jaws*, we found one key to understanding Revelation chapter 12 is the metaphorical "time, times and half a time" and we unlocked the last 4,000 years of Jewish history.

This book, *Slouching Towards Bethlehem*, unlocks Revelation chapter 13 and the last 2,000 years of the Christian era, with startling results. Not only can we now understand the forces shaping history and the deaths of some 270 million in 20th Century genocides but we can also project the future of Israel and the Middle East.

Available from
Emmaus Road Publishing
PO Box 38 823 Howick, Auckland 2014 New Zealand
www.emmausroad.org.nz

ISBN 978-0-9582746-8-5

Book 3 in the Revelation series

Gotta Serve Somebody
The Mystery of The Marks & 666

Graeme Carlé

Are you confused about 'The Mark of the Beast'?

You're not alone. The Mark and the number 666 have been controversial for centuries. Scholars and laymen alike have offered numerous interpretations, 'calculations' and wild guesses but most predictions have failed to materialize. Some say we just have to wait.

In this book, Graeme Carlé uses the keys recovered in the first two in his series (*Dancing in the Dragon's Jaws* and *Slouching Towards Bethlehem*) to unlock the symbols and 'times' of the most infamous and misunderstood mark in human history.

Instead of waiting for a world government or a global banking system that may never eventuate, Graeme believes and shows that The Mark is already here — and has been for the last 2,000 years! We've just not recognised it. It is actually the beast's counterpart of marks that God Himself placed on the forehead and hand of His people at the Exodus and in the wilderness, with a numbering system of names as described in the Book of Numbers.

We don't need a profound theological education or esoteric enlightenment but we do need a basic grasp of Jewish history and the Old Testament, as understood by 1st Century Jewish believers in Jesus of Nazareth.

Available from
Emmaus Road Publishing
PO Box 38 823 Howick, Auckland 2014 New Zealand
www.emmausroad.org.nz

ISBN 978-0-9582746-9-2

www.ingramcontent.com/pod-product-compliance
Lightning Source LLC
Chambersburg PA
CBHW070526010526
44118CB00012B/1069